John Freely was born in New York and joined the US Navy at the age of seventeen, serving with a commando unit in Burma and China during the last years of World War II. He has lived in New York, Boston, London, Athens and Istanbul and has written over forty travel books and guides, most of them about Greece and Turkey. He is author of *The Cyclades*, *The Ionian Islands* (both I.B.Tauris), *The Western Shores of Turkey*, *Strolling Through Athens*, *Strolling Through Venice* (all Tauris Parke Paperbacks) and the bestselling *Strolling Through Istanbul*.

D0901956

PRAISE FOR JOHN FREELY

The Cyclades: Discovering the Greek Islands of the Aegean

'A charming and informative companion for anyone exploring these enchanting islands.'
Andrew Steed, *Stanfords Maps and Travel Books*

The Western Shores of Turkey: Discovering the Aegean and Mediterranean Coasts

'. . . Enchanting guide . . . a work of genuine scholarship, lightly worn and charmingly conveyed. I fell in love with the book and stayed enamoured until the final page.'
Paul Bailey, *The Sunday Times*

'. . . the record of a journey undertaken by a man effortlessly able to convey in depth the meaning of what he sees.'
Marlena Frick, *Scotsman*, Edinburgh

Strolling Through Athens: Fourteen Unforgettable Walks Through Europe's Oldest City

'. . . magnificent walking guide to the city.'
Anthony Sattin, Book of the Week, *The Sunday Times*

Strolling Through Istanbul: A Guide to the City

'. . . a classic. The best travel guide to Istanbul'   *The Times*

Tauris Parke Paperbacks is an imprint of I.B.Tauris. It is dedicated to publishing books in accessible paperback editions for the serious general reader within a wide range of categories, including biography, history, travel and the ancient world. The list includes select, critically acclaimed works of top quality writing by distinguished authors that continue to challenge, to inform and to inspire. These are books that possess those subtle but intrinsic elements that mark them out as something exceptional.

The Colophon of Tauris Parke Paperbacks is a representation of the ancient Egyptian ibis, sacred to the god Thoth, who was himself often depicted in the form of this most elegant of birds. Thoth was credited in antiquity as the scribe of the ancient Egyptian gods and as the inventor of writing and was associated with many aspects of wisdom and learning.

CRETE

Discovering the 'Great Island'

John Freely

TAURIS PARKE
PAPERBACKS

Published in 2008 by Tauris Parke Paperbacks
an imprint of I.B.Tauris & Co Ltd
6 Salem Road, London W2 4BU
175 Fifth Avenue, New York NY 10010
www.ibtauris.com

First published by Weidenfeld & Nicolson in 1998
Copyright © John Freely 1998, 2008

Cover image: Chaniá seafront and White Mountains in the background
© Marco Simoni/Robert Harding

ISBN: 978 1 84511 692 7

A full CIP record for this book is available from the British Library
A full CIP record is available from the Library of Congress

Library of Congress Catalog Card Number: available

Printed and bound in India by Thomson Press India Ltd

FOR NIKOS STAVROULAKIS
AND JOHN CAMP

CONTENTS

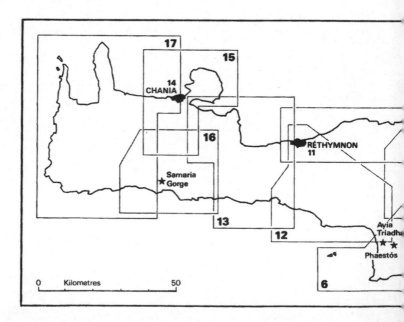

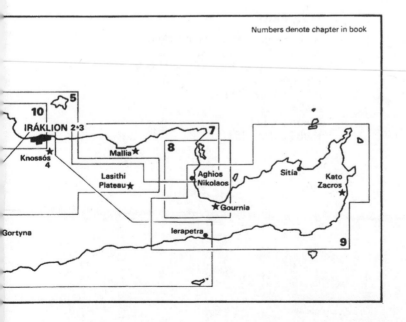

Numbers denote chapter in book

MAPS AND PLANS

MAPS

TOWN PLANS

SITE PLANS

1

THE GREAT ISLAND

Crete has been called the Great Island since the beginning of Greek history, for it looms lofty and horizon-spanning on all voyages through the eastern Mediterranean, where the Minoans developed the world's first maritime empire in the second millenium BC. I first saw Crete from the flying bridge of an American troopship one morning in October 1945, returning from China to the US after the end of World War II, catching a glimpse of the White Mountains as we passed through the Libyan Sea. As the Great Island disappeared from sight I thought that I would love to see it again one day, perhaps to live there for a while, but at the time my future was very uncertain. Thoughts of Crete were evoked again the following September, when I started my final year in high school, resuming the education I had interrupted two and a half years before, when I had enlisted in the US Navy at the age of seventeen. And what brought the Great Island to mind then was a passage in Book XIX of the *Odyssey*, in George Chapman's translation of 1614–15, where the disguised Odysseus describes to Penelope his own voyage home after a foreign war.

> In the middle of the sable sea there lies
> An isle called Crete, a ravisher of eyes,
> Fruitful, and mann'd with many an infinite store;
> Where ninety cities crown the famous shore,
> Mix'd with all-languag'd men. There Greeks survive,
> There the great-minded Eteocretans live,
> There the Dorensians never out of war,
> The Cydons there, and there the singular
> Pelasgian people. There doth 'Gnossus' stand . . .

1

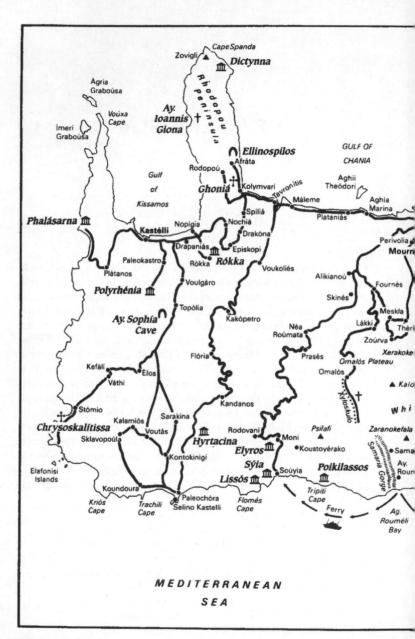

Western Crete

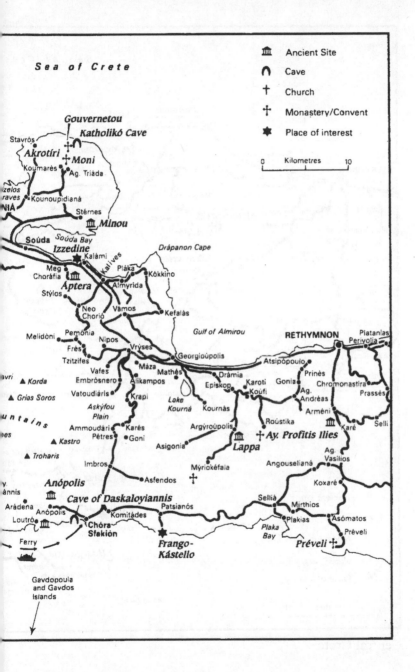

Central Crete

Legend:

🏛 Ancient Site

∩ Cave

✝ Monastery/Convent

† Church

✹ Place of interest

0   Kilometres   10

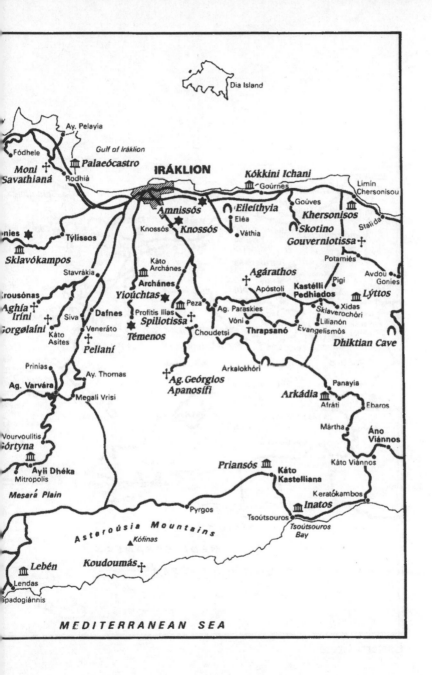

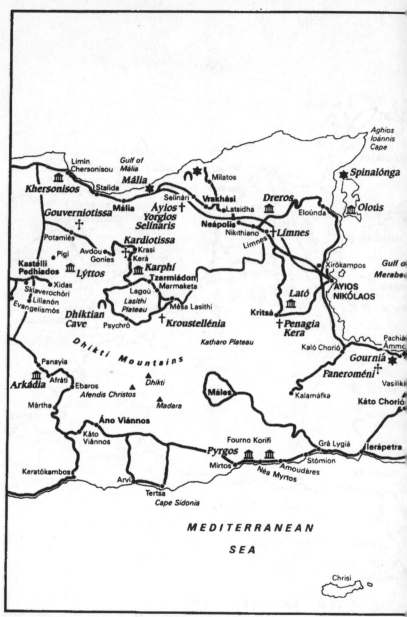

Eastern Crete

I did not see Crete again until January of 1961, when we passed the eastern tip of the island aboard a Russian cruise ship on a voyage from Istanbul to Alexandria via Athens. At the time I was accompanied by my wife Dolores and our three small children, travelling to Egypt on my first winter vacation at Robert College, the American school in Istanbul where I had begun teaching the previous September. This second sighting brought me no closer to visiting Crete than had my voyage aboard the troopship, for though we travelled through the Aegean every year during the two decades I taught in Istanbul and Athens, the Great Island somehow eluded us, hovering on the horizon of my mind as I imagined it had for Odysseus in his long wanderings through these same seas. But then finally in June of 1986, after Dolores and I had moved back to the US, the opportunity arose to spend the summer in Crete and to write a book about it. Though we could not afford to, we went at a moment's notice, drinking a toast to our good fortune above the clouds on our flight from Boston to Athens.

Most travellers to Crete land at Iráklion, the largest city and busiest port on the Great Island. But Dolores and I landed at Chaniá, and we used that town as the base for our explorations during the summer. We did so because our dear friend Nikos Stavroulakis had offered to let us use what he called his 'cottage' during our vacation: 'You can spend the summer in my cottage in Chaniá; it's on the old Turkish harbour at One Angel Street; I'll telephone Katina and ask her to tidy up the apartment on the top two floors.' The 'Cottage' at One Angel Street turned out to be a medieval Venetian tower (*pýrgos*), and our apartment was a lordly residence on the uppermost two floors, with a terrace overlooking all of Chaniá. After Katina had shown us round the apartment, Dolores and I went out on the terrace to take in the view, with the blue Aegean sparkling to our left and off to the right the White Mountains looming magnificently in the distance, still snow-crowned though it was mid-June. Then we sat down and had our first *oúzo* of the summer to celebrate our return to Greece, supremely happy to be embarking on our exploration of the Great Island.

We took our time settling into the Cottage, for we were exhausted after our long trip from Boston and from the arduous year that had preceded our return to Greece. We were also savouring the joys of Greek life again after an absence of five years and settling into its Mediterranean rhythms: a breakfast of goat cheese and olives on the terrace while we enjoyed a view of the Aegean and the White Mountains; a stroll at mid-morning through the labyrinthine alley-ways of Chaniá to shop in the covered market; lunch at a seaside

taverna after a swim; a nap in the afternoon when all of Greece stops
work to have a siesta; a twilight promenade with the townspeople
along the *paralía*, the quay that extends along both the old Turkish
and Venetian harbours; then to a café for an aperitif of *tsikoudiá*, the
lethal national drink of Crete, before supper at Michali's restaurant on
the quay beside the Venetian *arsenáli*, where we pick our food from the
steaming pots in the tiny kitchen. Later we move to the raffish
waterfront *ouzerí* of Yorgo Drakakis and listen to Cretan music until
the *óres mikrés*, the small hours; ending the evening with a nightcap on
our terrace under the stars, identifying the summer constellations and
watching the moon rise over the White Mountains and soar across the
sky, bathing the old town around us in its ashen light.

During our first week in the Cottage I began organizing my book on
Crete and planning the trips that we would take, the itineraries that
would lead travellers around the Great Island. During the morning I
read and took notes at a table in Nikos' study with its great Ottoman
hearth, his ghostly collection of whitened animal skulls arrayed on
ledges around the room, and after lunch I wrote in the walled garden
below, where Nikos kept his chickens and formerly tethered his goat
(he had once dreamed of keeping a camel there!) until, shortly before
we arrived, he had been forced to evict it because his neighbours
complained that it lowered the tone of their quarter, whose old
Venetian houses have been converted into pensions, cafés, disco-
theques and boutiques. In the midst of this modern commercialism
only One Angel Street has survived as a haven of old-fashioned
Ottoman serenity, where in the blissful quiet of siesta time I was lulled
by the processional shuttling sound of Katina's loom, which she
worked, seated in her widow's weeds like one of the Fates, sublimating
thus her grief for her departed husband Panos, whom she had lost just
the year before. Whenever I paused in my writing I rested my eyes on
the arcadian scene in the garden of the Cottage: the bamboo hedge
bordering the crumbling walls of the Venetian tower; the jungle of
orange, peach, olive and cypress trees; the thicket of rose bushes,
jasmine and ivy; the rococo Turkish wall-fountain with its reliefs of
cypresses eternally bending against an invisible breeze and the
haunting collection of old tombstones that made the courtyard look
like a dervish graveyard. The garden had in fact been an old
graveyard, for when Nikos purchased the Cottage and moved in (in
1956, when the tower was just a shell, its interior gutted during the
German air-raids on Chaniá in World War II) he found five Turkish
tombstones toppled there, marking the graves of former residents of

the tower in Ottoman times. (It was a felicitous Ottoman custom for Turks to be buried in their garden, their beloved *bahçe*, since this was the place where they were usually happiest when in life.) Nikos had also collected three other tombstones in his garden, two of them inscribed in Greek and the other in Hebrew, this last a relic of the former Jewish quarter of Chaniá, now vanished. Such were my surroundings when I began to write this book, the Greek, Turkish and Jewish tombstones my constant companions in this medieval Venetian garden, reminding me that Crete is quintessentially a palimpsest of history, like a much-used canvas that has been painted over time and time again, with each successive civilization layered upon those that came before, but with a continuity of human culture persisting through the ages. And so I began my book by writing an outline of the history of Crete, carrying it from remote antiquity to the present, always mindful of the Ariadne's thread that connects each cultural epoch with those that precede and follow it, interweaving them in time just as all things are interwoven in this ancient land. The immemorial sound of Katina's loom constantly reminded me of this.

Before one can begin to understand the history of Crete one must first study its geography, for this profoundly influenced the development of human culture on the Great Island. Crete is roughly equidistant from Europe, Asia and Africa, a stepping-stone between the three continents, with people always moving back and forth across the Aegean to the north and west and through the Libyan Sea to the south, producing a far greater cultural flux than in any of the lands around the Great Island. And it is indeed a great island, the fifth largest in the Mediterranean – after Sicily, Sardinia, Corsica, and Cyprus – with an area of 8350 square kilometres. It is an exceedingly long island, with a maximum length along its east-west axis of 257km; but it is very narrow for its size, varying from 61km at the centre to only 12km near Ierápetra. Crete is for the most part mountainous, with three principal ranges: to the west are the White Mountains, with a maximum altitude of 2452m; in the centre is Mount Ídha, known locally as Psilorítis, 2456m high; and to the east is Mount Dhíkti, at 2148m. East of Ídha there are some lower mountains, the best known of which is Ioúktas, the mythical grave of Zeus; and in the eastern end of the island are the mountains of Sitía, whose principal peak reaches a height of 1456m. These mountain ranges are split by many stupendous clefts, the most famous of which is the Samariá Gorge in the White Mountains, the largest natural canyon in Europe. The rugged Cretan mountains come right down to the sea along virtually the entire length of the south coast, but in the north and in the centre of the island they give way in many places to fertile plains. North of the White Mountains is the Cydonía Plain; north of Ídha the Plain of Mylopótamos; southwest of Ídha the Vale of Amári; south of Dhíkti the enormous Mésara Plain, the largest area of fertile land on Crete, which is cut off from the southern coast by the Asterousian Mountains; while the Ierápetra Plain lies between Dhíkti and the mountains of Sitía. Each of the three principal ranges has a high plateau ringed by gigantic mountain walls: Omalós in the White Mountains at an altitude of 1080m; Nídha Plain on Mount Ídha at 1400m; and on Mount Dhíkti the surpassingly beautiful Lasíthi Plain, at 866m. Besides these there is a fertile highland plain, Askífou, between the principal massif of the White Mountains and its eastern extremities. The Cretan mountains are also pitted with many caves, some of them enormous; a number of these caves have considerable importance in ancient Cretan religion and in mythology, the most famous being the Cave of Ídha, venerated in antiquity as the birthplace of Zeus, and the Dhiktaion Cave, where tradition holds that the god was cared for in his early childhood. And there is still another cave that some scholars in times past sought to associate with the fabled Labyrinth, where King Minos of Crete kept the monstrous Minotaur, and from which his daughter Ariadne led Theseus in his escape from the maze where he and the other Athenians had been imprisoned. Such is the island in which the first great European civilization began to develop.

The earliest human settlements on Crete appear to have been founded in the early Neolithic period, the New Stone Age, perhaps towards the end of the seventh millennium BC. Neolithic settlements have been discovered at more than half a dozen sites, most notably at Knossós, Mállia, Phaestós and Ayía Triádha, places that were to become important centres of civilization in later prehistoric times. These settlers eventually established the practices of agriculture and animal husbandry on the island, thus forming the basis for an agricultural economy based on the cultivation of cereals, olives, grape vines and the herding of animals, activities that have continued to be the mainstay of Cretan life up to the present day.

Around 2600 BC there was a great migration of people from western Anatolia to Crete, the Cyclades and the Greek mainland. These people brought with them the knowledge of how to create and work bronze, using it to make tools and weapons; thus began the Bronze Age on

Crete, bringing to an end the Neolithic way of life that had existed on the island for perhaps four millennia. But here, as in later cultural transitions on Crete, the older culture was not utterly swept away at once, but rather it was amalgamated over a period of time with the newer one. The new settlers on Crete seem to have arrived peacefully and to have absorbed the indigenous population without a struggle, together developing a civilization that Sir Arthur Evans named Minoan, after the semi-legendary ruler of Crete mentioned by Homer and other writers in antiquity. The ancient Neolithic sites at Knossós and Phaestós continued to be inhabited, but the principal settlements of this first era of Minoan civilization, known as the Prepalatial period (2600–2000 BC), developed on the Mésara Plain and at the eastern end of the island, the principal site being Káto Zákros. The settlements consisted of densely packed houses, probably like the villages one sees today on Crete, in which the farmers walked out to farm their lands in the surrounding area. During the Prepalatial period there were apparently no kings or local rulers, nor does there appear to have been any centralized authority on the island. The people seem to have been gathered into clans based on ancestral relations. The island appears to have been at peace during these first six centuries of the Minoan era, as evidenced by the absence of fortifications and by the scarcity of weapons surviving from this period. Agriculture developed and spread throughout the fertile areas of the island, and the Cretans for the first time became seafarers, trading their metalwares and agricultural produce with the people of the Cyclades, mainland Greece, western Anatolia, Syria, Egypt and Cyrenaica. The Minoans established a colony on the island of Cythera about 2300 BC, the beginning of what would become their great thalassocracy, or maritime empire, bringing the people of Crete into contact with a wide range of highly developed cultures, a very significant factor in the evolution of their own extraordinary civilization.

About 2000 BC a profound change took place in the structure of Minoan society, perhaps caused by some internal crisis or external threat. The institution of kingship emerged, along with an hierarchical aristocracy, a central government and a civil service, with Minoan society stratified into a class system in which the people on the lowest level worked as serfs and even as slaves. This brought about the construction, for the first time on Crete, of buildings grand enough to be called palaces, the largest of which were erected at Knossós, Phaestós and Mállia. These developments mark the beginning of what is called the Protopalatial period, which lasted from 2000–1700 BC.

The palaces at Knossós, Phaestós and Mállia, along with lesser royal residences elsewhere, formed the centre of sizeable towns, as the increased trade of the Minoans made the island far richer and more populous than it had ever been in the past, with Cretan ships carrying Minoan products as far abroad as Italy and Troy and returning with goods from all over the eastern Mediterranean. The Cretans undoubtedly had a formidable navy to protect their maritime empire, for throughout their history the great palace-towns of Minoan Crete were never fortified.

The Protopalatial period came to an end in about 1700 BC, when all of the Minoan palaces on Crete were destroyed, along with their surrounding towns. This was probably due to a catastrophic earthquake, which is known to have caused widespread disasters throughout the Mediterranean world at about that time, although some scholars have suggested that the destruction of the Minoan palaces occurred during an invasion by a foreign power. In any event, there was no break in the development of Minoan culture, which continued to progress without any apparent discontinuity from the level it had achieved around 1700 BC.

Shortly after the catastrophe new and grander palaces were built on the ruins of the older ones, the most magnificent being those at Knossós, Phaestós, Mállia and Káto Zákros. Thus began what archaeologists call the Neopalatial period, which lasted from 1700–1400 BC, the most brilliant era in Minoan history. These new imperial palaces were indeed majestic, particularly the great palace at Knossós, which must have been one of the wonders of the ancient world, as evidenced by the extensive ruins unearthed there by Sir Arthur Evans and his successors, and by the extraordinary frescoes that they discovered, depicting scenes of palace life. Aside from these new palaces, there were elegant villas built as summer residences by the Minoan lords, the best known of which is at Ayía Triádha, near Phaestós. As in the earlier Minoan period, there were large towns centred on the great palaces at Knossós, Phaestós, Mállia and Káto Zákros, with smaller settlements surrounding the royal villas at places like Ayía Triádha. Besides these communities, there were villages like Gourniá, which was a settlement inhabited by farmers, artisans, fishermen and mariners, whose more humble houses were probably much like those one sees today on Crete. During the Neopalatial period the Minoan thalassocracy reached its peak, and the prosperity of Crete was greater than it had ever been before or would be again up until quite recent years, supporting a population estimated to be about a million, twice as many as the number who inhabit the Great Island today.

Around 1450 BC almost all of the palaces and villas on Crete were destroyed, along with their surrounding towns and villages, most of them consumed by great conflagrations. This catastrophe is believed by some authorities to have been due to an extraordinarily severe volcanic eruption on the Cycladic isle of Thera, perhaps accompanied by an earthquake and colossal tidal waves. Other scholars think it was brought about by an invasion of Hellenes from the Pelopónnisos, people known in Homeric times as Achaeans and referred to by archaeologists as Mycenaeans. In any event, the Mycenaeans were definitely in control of Knossós by 1450 BC, while the other Minoan centres seem to have been deserted for some time after that. Shortly after 1400 BC another widespread catastrophe occurred on Crete, perhaps an earthquake or a war or a combination of both, resulting in the final destruction of the great palace at Knossós. All of the other surviving palaces and villas on Crete seem to have been destroyed at the same time, and none of them nor the royal residence at Knossós were ever again rebuilt, bringing to an end the imperial era in Minoan history.

The three centuries that followed the final destruction of the palace at Knossós, 1400–1100 BC, are referred to by archaeologists as the Postpalatial period. During this period Crete was dominated by the Mycenaeans and the commercial and political importance of the island greatly declined as the balance of power in the Aegean world shifted to the mainland of Greece. Nevertheless, elements of Minoan civilization survived on Crete, blending in with those of the dominant Hellenes. These included not only the Mycenaeans, but also the Dorians and other Greek-speaking peoples who migrated into the Aegean world during the last centuries of the Bronze Age. Knossós and many other former Minoan sites were reoccupied during this period by the Hellenes, while the Minoan people, thereafter known as the Eteocretans, seem to have founded new settlements in the eastern part of the island. Up until recent years, most authorities believed that Knossós and the other Mycenaean strongholds on Crete were suddenly and completely destroyed at the time of the Dorian invasions. But now most historians are of the opinion that the Dorian invasions were neither as sudden nor as destructive as had been believed previously, although the Eteocretans were probably reduced to the status of serfs under the Dorian kings and nobles.

The four centuries following the collapse of Mycenaean civilization, the period 1100–700 BC, are called the Dark Ages of the ancient Greek world; followed by the Archaic period, 700–490 BC; the Classical period, 490–323 BC; and the Hellenistic period, which on Crete lasted from 323–67 BC. During the early part of this millennium the Dorians consolidated their hold on Crete, developing there the same kind of Spartan communities that they had founded in the Pelopónnisos. The Dorian towns on Crete were so well regulated that their constitutions later became models for those of the city-states in mainland Greece, both in Attica and the Pelopónnisos, and during the Classical period they were often cited as ideal forms of government by philosophers, most notably Plato and Aristotle.

Throughout the Archaic, Classical and Hellenistic periods, Crete was a provincial backwater, retaining little of its former cultural, political and economic importance. During this time the city-states on Crete, estimated to be about fifty in number, were very frequently at odds with one another, and the island was often the scene of internal strife, with those who were dispossessed of their estates going off to fight as mercenaries in foreign lands or scouring the seas as corsairs. During the Hellenistic period Crete was a pawn in the struggles between the various powers that emerged in the eastern Mediterranean world after the death of Alexander the Great in 323 BC, controlled in turn by various of his successors and the dynasties they founded. In 69 BC the Cretans allied themselves with Mithridates, King of Pontus, in his second war against the Romans. The Romans retaliated by attacking Crete in force, with their final conquest of the island being achieved in 67 BC by Quintus Caecilius Metellus. Thereafter Crete, together with Cyrenaica, became a Roman province, with its capital at Górtyna. Górtyna was extensively rebuilt and expanded by the Romans, who also carried out many public works throughout the island, the impressive remains of some of them still visible today.

During the autumn of AD 61 the Apostle Paul landed briefly on the south coast of Crete while on his way to Rome. According to tradition, St Paul again visited Crete after he was released from prison in Rome in AD 64, and while there he commissioned Titus to complete his missionary work on the Great Island. Titus became the first Bishop of Górtyna, and the remains of a church dedicated to him still stand there today, the oldest relic of Christianity on Crete.

In AD 330 Constantine the Great transferred the capital of his Empire from Rome to Constantinople, beginning the Byzantine period in the history of the Mediterranean world. The Byzantine

Empire lasted for more than eleven centuries, though it was constantly beset on all sides by enemies, and during that time Crete and the other Greek islands were usually left undefended against foreign invaders and pirates, from whom they suffered grievously. The first period of Byzantine history in Crete ended in AD 824, when Górtyna was captured and sacked by a band of Saracen pirates from Spain led by a captain named Abou Hafiz Omar. The Saracens soon thereafter overran Crete, setting up their principal base at Iráklion, building there a stronghold called Rabdh-al-Khandah. Europeans would later refer to this fortress-town as Candia, a name that they eventually applied to all of Crete. The Saracens held Crete for 137 years despite repeated attempts by the Byzantines to recover the Great Island. Then in 961 Crete was finally recovered by the Byzantine general Nicephorus Phocas, the 'Pale Death of the Saracens', who two years later became Emperor of Byzantium, ruling as Nicephorus II. When Nicephorus II ascended the throne of Byzantium he set out to rehabilitate Crete, which had been devastated during the Saracen occupation. A number of noble Greek families, the *archóntes*, were sent from Constantinople to Crete in order to create the new aristocracy that the Emperor felt was necessary to re-establish the Byzantine presence on the Great Island. In addition, Christians from the eastern regions of the Byzantine Empire were resettled in Crete, including many Armenians. This was done to renew the Christian character of Crete, for many of the islanders had intermarried with the Arabs or converted to Islam, for convenience, during the period of Saracen rule.

The second period of Byzantine rule on Crete lasted from 961 until the beginning of the thirteenth century, when the Venetians finally gained full control of the Great Island in 1212. That same year the Venetians put down a fierce rebellion of the Cretans, the first of several that would occur during their rule for, despite savage repressions, the Cretans continued to resist their Venetian masters. The most serious rebellion took place in the early years of the sixteenth century, when the people of western Crete, under the leadership of George Kandanoleon, managed for a brief period to set up an independent state among the villages on the slopes of the White Mountains. But this insurrection was put down by the Venetians with their usual brutality: all of those who took part in it were killed, while other suspect Cretans were either exiled or reduced to the status of galley slaves.

The conquest of Constantinople by the Ottoman Turks in 1453 brought to an end the long history of the Byzantine Empire, and dashed all hopes that the Greeks might reconquer Crete from the Venetians. Even before the fall of Constantinople many Byzantine scholars fled the capital, most of them going to Venice but some finding refuge in Crete, so that the Great Island became the last outpost of Greek culture in the eastern Mediterranean. This Byzantine diaspora brought Crete into contact with the Italian Renaissance, so that, alone among the former lands of Hellas, the Great Island took part in this revival of European culture, a culture which had its first roots in Minoan civilization.

The Cretan renaissance ended when the island was captured by the Ottoman Turks, who finally took complete control when they captured Candia in mid-September 1669, after a memorable siege of more than twenty years. Thus began the Turkish occupation of Crete, which lasted for more than two centuries. The Great Island disappeared into another Dark Age, becoming a provincial backwater of the intellectually stagnant Ottoman Empire. But despite this cultural torpor the Cretans did not rest easy under Ottoman rule, particularly with the revival of Hellenic nationalism toward the end of the eighteenth century. During the period 1770–1897 at least ten serious Cretan revolts are recorded, all of which were put down by the Turks, invariably with barbaric reprisals against the Christian civilian population. The revolt in 1770 began in Sfakiá, the region on the southern slopes of the White Mountains that has always been the focal point of Cretan independence and resistance to foreign occupation. It was led by a wealthy landowner named Daskaloyiannis, and was part of a general uprising throughout Greece prompted by the expectation of military aid from Catherine the Great of Russia, who sent a fleet to the Aegean under the command of Alexi Orlof. But the Russian aid proved to be illusory, and after some initial gains the forces of Daskaloyiannis and the other Cretan rebels were crushed by the Turks. The War of Independence eventually led to European recognition of the Greek Kingdom in 1832, but Crete was not included within the boundaries of the new state. Thus the Cretans had to continue their struggle against the Turks, rising in revolt in 1833, 1841, 1858, 1866, 1868–9, 1878, 1889, and 1897; their goal being *énosis*, or union with the Greek nation. One of the leaders in the 1897 revolt was Eleftherios Venizelos, who would later become Prime Minister of Greece, emerging as the first international political figure from Hellas in modern times. Under the leadership of Venizelos, Crete was finally freed from Ottoman occupation in 1898, when all Turkish troops were removed from the island. Crete eventually

17

became part of the Greek nation on 14 December 1914, ending seven centuries of foreign domination.

Crete then receded into the provincial background of Greece, until the tides of history once again washed against its shores during World War II. After the German conquest of the Greek mainland was complete in late April 1941, the British and Commonwealth Forces that had been fighting in Greece were evacuated to Crete, landing in Soúda Bay under heavy aerial bombardment. On 20 May the Germans began a massive landing of paratroopers and airborne troops on the north coast of Crete, their main objective being the airfield at Máleme, west of Chaniá. These troops constituted the full force of the Seventh Parachute Division, which Hitler considered to be the flower of the German army. The German landings were valiantly opposed by the British and Commonwealth forces, who had themselves landed in Crete less than a month before, together with about a thousand Cretans who had been hastily organized into the semblance of a regiment of the Greek army. Aside from these regular forces, the Germans were opposed by the local people, including old men, women and boys, all of them fighting with customary Cretan heroism, though they were armed with only the most primitive of weapons. But within a week the Germans had captured the airport at Máleme and the issue was no longer in doubt. The surviving Allied troops were withdrawn to the south coast of Crete, from where they were evacuated to Egypt on the last four nights of May 1941. Thus the Battle of Crete ended with victory for the Germans, but the Seventh Parachute Division, the only one of its kind in the German army, suffered such heavy casualties that it was never again used as a unit in combat. What is more, the unexpectedly strong resistance to the German invasion of Crete disrupted Hitler's timetable for the invasion of Russia, which eventually began on 22 June 1941. The delay was to have significant consequences.

Hundreds of Allied soldiers, some of whom had escaped from German prisons, arrived at the south coast too late to be evacuated by the British fleet. Some of these later made their own way to Egypt in fishing boats or by other means, while others hid away up in the White Mountains or on Psilorítis, where they were sheltered by Cretan families who risked their own lives to do so. Some of the fugitives joined in with the growing Cretan resistance movement, which was coordinated by a number of British and Commonwealth intelligence officers who had been smuggled into Crete soon after the German victory. Throughout the four years of the German occupation (the

Italians were also in occupation, in the eastern part of the island) these intelligence officers and their Cretan accomplices remained in radio contact with Allied headquarters, providing valuable information on German troop movements and shipping. Even more important, this Intelligence Service was at the heart of the Cretan resistance movement; supplying the partisans with funds, weapons, ammunition, clothing and food. The most spectacular exploit of this resistance movement came on 26 April 1943, when two British officers and their Cretan accomplices captured Major General Heinrich Kreipe, commander of all German forces on Crete, after which he was taken in a submarine to Alexandria and later flown to London. This kidnapping and other acts of sabotage and resistance provoked the Germans into savage reprisals against the Cretans: they burned numerous villages and executed all of the inhabitants who had not fled to the mountains. But this barbarism only inflamed the Cretans, and during the last two years the extent and strength of the resistance movement continued to increase. By the beginning of 1945 the Cretan partisans together with a handful of Allied intelligence officers effectively controlled all of Crete except the town of Chaniá. (The Italian forces in the east of Crete had by then surrendered and had been evacuated from the island.) The Germans remained penned up inside Chaniá for five months, until they finally surrendered on 23 May 1945, almost exactly four years after their conquest of Crete. So the Cretans had prevailed once again, and seen one more invader depart from the shores of the Great Island.

A great deal of Cretan history and folklore is contained in the poetry and songs of the island, some of which have the status of national epics. The most renowned island poem is the *Erotókritos*, written by Vicenzos Kornaros of Sitia during the seventeenth-century Cretan Renaissance. The *Erotókritos*, a romance set in ancient times, was first published in Venice in 1713 after having achieved great popularity throughout Crete and elsewhere in Greek-speaking lands, often through recitations by professional bards called *rhymadóri*. Many Cretan folk songs are narratives of historical events, usually tales of Cretan resistance to tyranny during the years of Turkish occupation. Two of the best known of these are the *Song of Daskaloyiannis* and the *Song of Alidhakis*, epics that arose out of the Sfakiot rebellions of 1770 and 1777, respectively. The *Song of Daskaloyiannis* ends with lines of praise for the heroism of Daskaloyiannis and those who died with him in the cause of Cretan freedom, a recurring theme in the folk songs of the island.

Joy to the man who meets his death in battle
He who dies in battle is the winner, not the loser.
He wins a deathless name, a garland of honour.

Another category of Cretan folk songs are *ta rizítika tragoúdia*, 'songs from the roots', which are indigenous to the villages on the slopes of the White Mountains. The name comes from 'rízes', in this case meaning the roots or foothills of Lefká Óri, the White Mountains. Some of these songs are very ancient in their origins, going back to the Akrita cycles of the medieval Byzantine period. The songs of these cycles are named for Digenes Akrites, the legendary folk hero of the battles in the eastern marchlands of Anatolia between the Byzantines and the Moslem invaders, Arabs and Turks in turn, stirring epics of heroism and romance. Other *rizítika* songs are concerned with all aspects of life in the villages of the White Mountains in times past: the Cretan longing for freedom from foreign oppression; the gallantry and manliness of the *palikária*, the heroes who fought against the Turks; the sacred bonds of friendship, brotherhood, and family; the Cretan traditions of piety and hospitality; and *xeniteiá tragoúdia*, or songs of exile, a common theme in the nineteenth century, when so many Cretans were forced to flee from the island after unsuccessful revolts against the Turks.

Rizítika tragoúdia are of two general types: songs of '*távla*' and songs of '*stráta*'. The first type receives its name from the fact that these songs are sung around a *távla*, or dinner table, the centre of activities in a Cretan home. Thus the songs of *távla* have as their subject matter all of the celebratory events of Cretan life: weddings; baptisms; religious holidays; and the festivals of patron saints. A Greek celebrates his 'birthday' on the feast day of the saint for whom he is named, rather than on the actual day on which he was born, so that the whole country takes a holiday on St George's Day, Yorgo being the most common name in Greece. Songs of *távla* are heard most frequently at *paniyíria*, religious holidays that are really survivals of ancient Greek festivals such as the Dionysia. On such occasions all the Cretan sense of joy in life bursts forth unrestrained, as friends and family sing together around a table in their home or in a taverna, happy gatherings at which we have sometimes had the privilege of joining in the fun, serenaded with songs such as '*Kalopérasi*', 'The Good Life'.

Little by little the Lord sends the rain,
Then comes the quiet snow,

Cold in the mountains,
Snow on the hills.
And the man who has a well roofed house,
Fruit in his storerooms,
Oil in his jars,
Wine in his barrels,
Wood in his yard,
A girl to kiss as he sits by the fire,
He doesn't care what the north wind brings,
Rain or snow.

The second type of *rizítika tragoúdia* are songs of '*stráta*', the road. The songs of *stráta* are choral works that originated in the days of Turkish occupation, when the islanders formed caravans when going from one village to another so as to find safety in numbers, singing these songs as they moved along with their belongings loaded on donkeys and mules. The themes of the songs of *stráta* are as varied as those of the other *rizítika tragoúdia*, but one particularly lovely set are those of the wedding caravans, or *psíki*, which were formed when the groom and his family proceeded to the village of the bride, or vice versa, on the day or eve of the wedding. Such processions are now almost a thing of the past, but the songs of *stráta* that were once sung along the way are still sung at Cretan weddings. One witty old Cretan song still heard at wedding celebrations is '*Efhí Kóris*', 'The Girl's Prayer', which is usually sung by one of the bridesmaids, beginning with these wistful lines:

I beg you, Fate,
Send me a rich husband.
Let him have flocks and shepherds and cheesemakers,
A garden full of bees, with beekeepers,
Twenty yoke of oxen, grain both old and new.
But cotton plants, my Fate – not those.
I want to have soft hands.

The most characteristic and frequently heard Cretan songs are the famous *mantinádes*, which are really not songs at all but recited poems composed extemporaneously by Cretans in all walks of life for every conceivable situation. A *mantináda* consists of two rhyming lines each of fifteen syllables, but the art is as much in the originality of what is said as it is in the rhyme. The word originally comes from the Venetian *matináda*, a 'morning serenade', one sung in the small hours of the morning by a young man when courting his beloved. In Crete *mantinádes* are sung at all festive occasions, as well as in evenings at a taverna, but Cretans are liable to recite them to one another under any circumstance, even when passing on a village street. Virtually all Cretans are able to make up *mantinádes* on the spot, but certain *rhymadóri* are especially talented at composing these couplets, such as two ancients that I once heard in a taverna, the *mantinádes* of one old man eliciting those of the other, the rhymed couplets passing back and forth with plays-on-words and jest topping jest until they were both drowned out by the laughter and applause of their audience. But *mantinádes* can be sad as well as joyous, depending on the occasion, and sometimes the two emotions can be expressed in the same couplet. I heard such a *mantináda* at a wedding celebration in a mountain village, when her sister-in-law addressed these lines to *i nyphítsa*, the bride, whose father had died the previous year: 'If your father could see how happy you are today / He would ask permission from death to be at your side.'

The songs of Crete are invariably accompanied by the *lýra*, or lyre, though other instruments are used, including the *laoúto*, or lute, the *tambourás*, the *thiambóli*, the *mantoúra*, and the *áskavlos*; the first three of these are stringed instruments and the last three are flutes, with the latter, which is also called the *askomántoura*, being a double flute with a small animal's skin serving as a drone, so that it sounds like a crude form of bagpipe. But the *lýra* is the quintessential Cretan instrument, and it is played at all performances, in the home or in the taverna. Many Cretans make their own *lýra*, carrying it with them wherever they go, hanging it on a peg in their favourite taverna, so that when they come in of an evening they can just take it down from the wall and begin to play. The *lýra* has been played in Crete since remote antiquity, as evidenced by representations of the instrument being used to accompany a line of dancers in a Minoan figurine. The Cretan *lýra* is somewhat different in form than those played elsewhere in Greece, the Pontic *lýra* and that of the Dodecanese Islands. The Cretan *lýra* is a pear-shaped instrument with three strings, usually held upright on the left knee while the musician plays it in an underhand motion with a short arc-shaped bow, which in olden times would be strung along its length with tiny bells called *yerakokoúdouna*, to accentuate its rhythm.

Crete is renowned throughout Greece for the number and liveliness of its folk dances. The best known of the Cretan dances is the *pentozális*, which is believed to be the oldest of the steps done today on the island, based on the Pyrrhic dances of ancient Greece. The most spectacular of the Cretan dances are those in which one of the performers, using another as an anchor, makes acrobatic leaps into the air, clicking his feet together higher than his head; these have different names and variations in various parts of Crete, such as the *Kastrianós Pídikos* of Iráklion and the *órtses Anóyion* of Anóyia, with versions in other localities called the *angaliastós* and the *mikró-mikráki*. Another ancient step is the *Kritikí Soústa*, which is also a survival of the Pyrrhic war dances of antiquity, with the partners facing one another as if on the field of mock combat, each of them moving their arms up and down like the slowly flapping wings of an eagle in flight, simulating the movement of sword and shield held aloft as they swoop down upon one another in periodic shows of strength, though if one of the dancers is a woman then the motions become suggestive of those of great birds in courtship. Then there are dances of the *Kritikós Syrtós* type, with regional variations such as the *Chaniótikos Syrtós* of Chaniá, and the *Syranós Syrtós* of Iráklion. In these dances two or more performers are linked together and drawn along by their leader, who traces the circumference of a circle as he moves continually to his right, while the last person in the chain, the anchor man, remains close to a movable centre, rotating slowly with his left hand on his hip, palm outward, as the other dancers circle gracefully around him. In the *Syrtós* the leader holds with his left hand the right hand of the next dancer in line, or is so linked by a handkerchief, and the other dancers are similarly joined, the whole line moving sideways in a serpentine or spiralling manner, with the leader, who often waves a handkerchief in his free right hand, following in his movements the rhythm of the song, dancing alternately fast and slow, occasionally making prodigious leaps into the air or falling forwards on his knees and then springing upward with a miraculous rebound. The leader is often a woman. We saw such a dance late one night during our first week back in Chaniá, at the taverna of Yorgo Drakakis down on the old Venetian port, where I sat in a trance after having heard hours of Cretan music to the accompaniment of the *lýra*, then watched as a woman from the adjoining table led her companions in the harmonic circlings and graceful evolutions of a *Kritikós Syrtós*. I observed them as if in a dream, for we had drunk several bottles of the rough red local *krasí*, and appreciated how ancient is this beautiful ritual, for the *Kritikós Syrtós* is said to be the symbolic recreation of the Cretan myth in which Theseus and his companions are led out of the labyrinth by Ariadne.

And this in turn evoked these lines from the *Iliad*, where Hephaestus fashions a shield for Achilles:

> Next the god depicted a dancing floor like the one that Daedalus designed in the spacious town of 'Knossus' for Ariadne of the lovely locks. Young and marriageable maidens were dancing on it with their hands on one another's wrists, the girls in fine linen with lovely garlands on their heads, and the men in closely woven tunics showing the faint gleam of oil, and with daggers of gold hanging from their silver belts. Here they ran lightly round, circling as smoothly on their accomplished feet . . . and there they ran in line to meet each other. A large crowd stood around enjoying the delightful dance, with a minstrel among them singing divinely to the lyre. . . .

And so life passes on the Great Island, where past and present come together in the dance, songs and poetry of the Cretan people, as we came to know them during our stay in the Cottage at One Angel Street in Chaniá.

2

IRÁKLION

After I had finished writing the historical outline of my guide to Crete, I spent a few days planning the itineraries that would lead travellers around the island. I decided that the first of these itineraries should begin in Iráklion, the largest city in Crete and also the usual base for visiting Knossós, the most important Minoan site on the island. And so we packed an overnight bag and took a bus from Chaniá to Iráklion.

As we got underway in our modern airconditioned Pullman bus, we marvelled at how much public transport had improved since our first trip through Greece twenty-five years before with our three small children. We had travelled then in a broken-down old wreck over pot-holed dirt roads roughly carved out from the sides of precipitous mountains along the coast, with goats, chickens and crates of goods roped to the top of the bus. Extra passengers were crammed into aisle seats made from wooden slats, all of their possessions stuffed into the luggage racks along with the odd load of fish or sack of potatoes. The unshaven driver was assisted by a well-barbered master-of-ceremonies, who not only collected tickets but sang songs and told jokes and stories to keep us amused and also to distract our attention from the perils of the journey, as we sped around hairpin bends on sheer cliffs high above the sea, our chauffeur taking one hand off the steering wheel to cross himself repeatedly every time he passed a roadside chapel, his vision obscured by the many sacred icons, religious statuettes, rosary beads and good-luck charms that festooned his windscreen. As a warning to any other misfortunate road-users he continually blasted on his horn as he sped along on the wrong side of the road, the radio blaring a cacophony of Greek music at top volume.

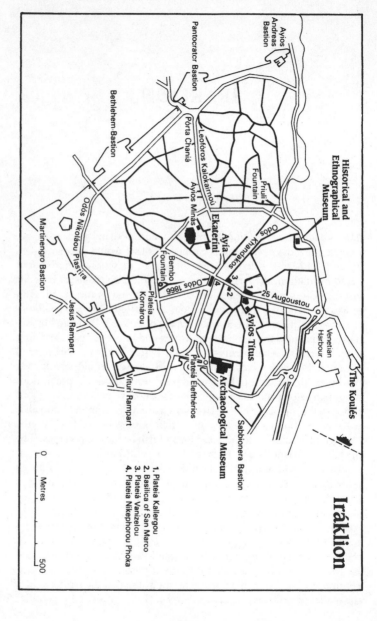

Iráklion

1. Plateia Kallergou
2. Basilica of San Marco
3. Plateiá Vanizelou
4. Plateiá Nikephorou Phoka

But on our journey from Chaniá to Iráklion in late June of 1986 all of that had changed, and we sped along the new coastal highway in comfort and safety with only the ear-piercing music on the radio to evoke the madness and high adventure of bygone bus journeys.

When we arrived in Iráklion we found a small hotel near one of the main squares, Plateía Venizélou. As soon as we had showered and changed, we walked over to the square, where we sat down for a drink at a sidewalk café beside the Morosini Fountain, the most famous landmark in Iráklion. This is the most pleasant place of all to sit and while away an hour or two on a hot summer afternoon, shaded by an awning and cooled by the spray from the Morosini Fountain, where the four heraldic lions of St Mark holding the upper basin are a reminder of the town's Venetian period.

Iráklion was known by its present name in antiquity, and Strabo, writing in the mid-first century BC, describes it as the port of Knossós. It continued to be known as Iráklion until Crete was captured by the Saracens in AD 824. Soon afterwards the Saracens fortified the part of town that had been known to the Byzantines as Castro, down by the old Venetian fort one sees today, and there they built a stronghold that they called Rabdh-al-Khandah, the Fortress with a Moat, later called Khándaks. The Turkish word for moat – *hendek* – is similar to the Arab word, and this is perpetuated in the Greek name for the ditch that still surrounds the old part of town, *to Khendéki*. (The street that leads northwest from Platéia Venizélou to the seafront, Odós Khandákos, follows the course of the medieval moat through that part of the town and bears its name.) The name for the moat became Candia in some European tongues, and eventually all of Crete came to be called by that name. This was corrupted to Candy in early seventeenth-century England, as Richard Zouche wrote in 1614 in *The Dove*, or *Passage from Cosmography*: 'Next Candy, Cradle of Reputed Jove/With nectar-dripping vines is over-spread.'

Virtually nothing now remains of either the Saracen or Byzantine periods in Iráklion, other than a few museum exhibits; the only antiquities one sees in the modern town are from the Venetian and Turkish eras. The Venetian period in the history of the Great Island began in 1204, when Venice purchased Crete from Count Boniface of Montferrat, one of the leaders of the Fourth Crusade, who had the previous year obtained it from the Byzantine Emperor Alexius IV. The first Venetian governor of Crete, Duke Tiepolo, was appointed in 1207. When the first colonists arrived from Venice he bestowed upon them grants of land in the fertile plains of the islands and also gave them mansions in Candia, which he made the capital. These estates and houses were taken from the native Cretans, who in 1212 rose up in revolt against the Venetians in an attempt to regain their property. This revolt, which took several years to put down, was the first of many insurrections by the Cretans against the rule of Venice, with many of the lower-class Venetians themselves joining the Greeks against the tyranny and oppression of their mother city.

Although the Venetians ruled harshly in Crete, the Great Island underwent a brilliant cultural renaissance during their occupation, a revival stimulated by scholars fleeing from the doomed city of Constantinople, which finally fell to the Turks in 1453. The town of Candia became a centre for the copying of ancient manuscripts that had been brought from Byzantium to Crete by these scholars, and at the monastery of St Catherine a school was founded to revive the study of ancient Greek culture. Most of the major figures in the Cretan renaissance of the sixteenth and seventeenth centuries studied at St Catherine's School in Candia, most notably Domenico Theoto-kopoulos, the painter who became famous in Spain as El Greco. Other renowned people who emerged from that school were Michael Damaskinos, the greatest of the many Cretan painters who adorned the churches of the Great Island, and some of those in Greece, with their frescoes and icons; Vicenzos Kornaros, author of the epic poem, *Erotókritos*: and the theologian Cyril Lucaris, who was six times Patriarch of Constantinople and once of Alexandria before he was executed by the Turks in 1638.

The Cretan renaissance came to an end with the final conquest of the Great Island by the Ottoman Empire. This occurred on 5 September 1669, when the Venetian defenders of Candia under Francesco Morosini surrendered to the Turkish forces led by Mehmet Köprülü, Grand Vezir of Sultan Mehmet IV. Although three Venetian forts on islets off the north coast of the island continued to hold out for some years afterwards, the conquest of Candia effectively began the Turkish occupation of Crete, which was to last until the end of the nineteenth century. The Ottoman occupation was different in many ways from that of Venice, but it weighed just as heavily on the Cretans, who rebelled even more frequently against the Turks than they had against the Venetians. One difference was that the cultural renaissance ended, with virtually all of the surviving scholars fleeing from Crete during the siege of Candia. Another difference was that the whole character of Cretan life changed because of mass conversion of the islanders to Islam. According to one estimate, by the beginning of the eighteenth century the Moslem population of Crete outnumbered the Christians by 200,000 to 60,000, and this without any substantial Turkish colonization of the island. The main reason for this mass apostasy was that Christians were subject to the *haratch*, the annual capitation tax imposed by the Ottoman government, while the Moslems were not; also 'turning Turk' freed one from many of the other oppressions of the foreign occupation. And so in this manner Crete disappeared into another Dark Age, which ended only when the Great Island once again became part of Greece in 1914. By that time the Moslem population of the island was in a distinct minority, for conversion of Greeks to Islam had virtually ceased during the nineteenth century, when the revolutionary atmosphere on Crete had given Cretans renewed pride in their Hellenism. Captain T. A. B. Spratt, in his *Travels and Researches in Crete*, published in 1865, writes that 'The Mahomedan population of Crete amounts now to about one-third of the whole, and may be thus reckoned at between sixty and seventy thousand. Many of them are descended from Christian parents, whose forefathers, under intimidation, or interest, changed their religion in preference to their location and personal prospects, but not their language. Thus Greek is the universal tongue of Crete still.' The several tens of thousands of Turks who remained in Crete after *énosis* were deported to Turkey in the population-exchange that followed the Graeco-Turkish War of 1919–22. In 1923 the name of the principal city on Crete was changed from Candia to Iráklion, its original name, which had been revived by Greeks during the rebirth of Hellenism in the nineteenth century. Iráklion was severely damaged by air-raids during the Battle of Crete in the last ten days of May 1941, and the city was occupied by the Germans up until the autumn of 1944, a time of great suffering and sadness for the townspeople. The war-damage to Iráklion has long been repaired, and since the end of World War II the city, now the fifth largest in Greece, has spread far beyond the ancient defence-walls that once bounded medieval Candia.

The Plateía Venizélou occupies the same site as the main square of the Venetian town of Candia, known as the Piazza delle Biade, the Square of the Cereals, because the grain market of the town was located here. The principal monument of the Venetian period remaining in Plateía Venizélou is the Morosini Fountain, which gives a very Italianate look to the square, as well as being the principal adornment of modern Iráklion. The fountain was created in 1638 under the direction of the Venetian governor at the time, Francesco Morosini, whose nephew of the same name surrendered Candia to the

Turks in 1669. Above the lower pool of the fountain there is an octofoil basin whose sides are decorated in relief with a frieze of marine deities and sea creatures from Greek mythology. At the centre of the pool there is a pedestal decorated on its upper half with the sculptured figures of four rampant lions, with water spouting from their mouths as well as from a pool above. The upper pool was once surmounted by a colossal statue of Poseidon, known to the Venetians as Nettuno. The figure of Poseidon was known in Candia as the Colossus, and the water source itself was called the Giant's Fountain. But the colossal statue of Poseidon vanished at some time during the Turkish occupation, never to be seen again, and so those who today sit in the cafés and restaurants around Morosini's Fountain are denied the monumental presence of the sea god.

There are a number of other monuments of Venetian Candia to be seen in downtown Iráklion, some of them situated on or near the Plateía Venizélou, a few of them so close that one can locate them without moving from a café table beside the Morosini Fountain.

The vaulted shops just opposite the fountain are all that remain of the Palazzo Ducale, the centre of the Venetian government in Candia. This was the seat of the Venetian governor, the Proveditore Generale, who presided there over a council of nobles, the Signoria. Beneath the Ducal Palace were the dungeons that served as the state prison, where rebels against the Venetian regime spent their last days before they were executed. Rebels were also executed in the square by the Turks during the Ottoman occupation, hung from the limbs of the giant platanos tree that until very recent years still shaded the cafés in the Plateía Venizélou. The Palazzo Ducale was still standing in Ottoman times, though it was no longer a centre of government. At that time it was known as Deli Marko Sarayi, the Palace of Crazy Marko, the word *Deli* in Turkish meaning Insane, in the sense of a sainted madman. That, apparently, was what the local Turks thought to be the character of the patron saint of Venice.

The northeastern corner of the Plateía Venizélou is dominated by the Basilica of San Marco, an impressive edifice distinguished by its five-bayed porch. The original church of San Marco was erected on this site in 1239, but this structure was destroyed by an earthquake in 1303. A second church of San Marco on the same site was destroyed by another earthquake in 1508, after which the present basilica was erected. The church of San Marco was the private place of worship of the Proveditore Generale, who attended services there in state with the members of the council of Signoria. The Venetian governors who died

30

during their term in Candia were always buried in the church of San Marco, laid to rest in ornate sarcophagi there. After the Turkish conquest in 1669 the church was converted into a mosque by Defterdar Ahmet Pasha, who was appointed as the Ottoman finance minister of Crete by the Grand Vezir Mehmet Köprülü, the conqueror of Candia. Ahmet Pasha demolished the belfry and erected a minaret, from which the first call to Islamic prayer was given from what had become Defterdar Camii, the Mosque of Defterdar. The mosque continued to function until 1915, when most of the Turks in its congregation left Crete after *énosis*. After the population exchange that began in 1923 the building reverted to the Greek government. In 1956 the Cretan Historical Society began restoration of the basilica as an exhibition area and five years later it opened as the Hall of Áyios Márkos. Today the basilica houses a permanent exhibition of reproductions of Byzantine frescoes dating from the thirteenth and fourteenth centuries; these are replicas of wall-paintings in Byzantine churches throughout Crete, most notably the Panayía Kéra, at Logári on the Plain of Kritsá, where the originals can still be seen.

The area just to the north of Plateía Venizélou is the Plateía Kalergón, and just north of that is a park named for El Greco. During the Venetian period the Plateía Kalergón was known as the Piazza dei Signori, because the various public buildings used by the governor and his council of nobles were located there: to the west was the Palazzo Ducale, the residence of the Duke of Crete; to the north the Palazzo del Capitan del Generale, the military governor; and to the east the Palazzo del Capitan Grande, the admiral of the Venetian fleet that defended Crete. During the Ottoman period the Turkish governor of Crete had his headquarters in the Palazzo del Capitan Generale, and at that time the entrance to the building was called the Pasha's Gate. These have all been replaced by later structures; one of these, a municipality building called the Aktárika, houses the renowned Vikelas Library, the largest collection of books in Greece outside of Athens.

The street that runs northeast from Plateías Venizélou and Kalergón to the port is Odós Martýron 25 Avgoústou. The street is named in memory of the Greeks who were killed there by the Turks on 25 August 1898, three months before the Ottoman forces were finally evacuated from Crete. During this massacre, in which seventeen English soldiers from the Allied Occupation Forces were also killed, a fire broke out and destroyed a large part of this quarter, so that most of the buildings one sees there today are of modern construction. This was one of the most important streets in Venetian Candia, the pompous religious processions passed along it on their way from the church of San Marco to the port. The street continued to be the main thoroughfare of Candia during the Ottoman period, and is now the most prestigious avenue in modern Iráklion, lined with banks, travel agencies, touristic shops and several hotels.

On the right side of Odós Martyron 25 Avgoústou as it leaves Plateía Kalergón there is a splendid Italianate building called the Loggia; this was originally erected in 1727–8 by Francesco Morosini the Elder, a decade or so before he built the fountain that still bears his name. The Loggia is thought to have been the work of Francesco Basilicata, the most renowned architect of his day in Candia, who designed the building in a variant of the Palladian style, using the Doric order on the ground floor and the Ionic on the second, surmounted by an elaborate frieze and sculptured emblems of the Serenissima, the Serene Republic of Venice, most notably the Lion of St Mark. The Loggia was the most magnificent of all the public buildings in Venetian Candia, the main gathering place for all the nobility of the town. The Duke of Crete reviewed processions from the upper balcony and all important public announcements were issued from there by his herald after a flourish of trumpets.

During the Turkish occupation the Loggia was the seat of the Defterdar, the Ottoman finance minister for Crete. After *énosis* efforts were made to restore the Loggia, but despite these it began to deteriorate and fall into ruins, the decay being aggravated during the German occupation of Iráklion in World War II. However, in recent years the municipality have completely and authentically re-constructed the Loggia in its original Palladian/Renaissance style, producing the splendid edifice one sees today. The Loggia is used for exhibitions and as a theatre and concert hall, adding a badly needed touch of elegance to the scene in Heraklion.

The large public building behind the Loggia is the Dimarcheíon, the city hall of Iráklion; this is a reconstruction of the Armeria, the Venetian armoury that stood on this site until late Ottoman times. Set into the northern wall of the Dimarcheíon there are the remains of a Venetian fountain, decorated with the figure of a woman, thought to be the personification of Crete. This fountain was made in 1602 for the Proveditore Generale Sagredo, and it was originally placed in the northwest corner of the Loggia. The Sagredo Fountain was dislodged from the Loggia at some time in the late Ottoman period, probably in an earthquake, and it was discovered in the foundations of a building nearby late in the last century. When the Armeria was being rebuilt the fountain was set into its façade, thus preserving a precious fragment of Venetian Candia. On the fountain an inscription in Latin informs one that 'This water runs due to Duke Sagredo'.

Behind the Loggia and the Dimarcheíon the church of Áyios Títos stands in the centre of a pleasant, tree-shaded courtyard, which we looked out upon from our balcony at the rear of the Xenodochíon Knossós. The original church on this site, dedicated to St Titus, was founded soon after Nicephorus Phocas recaptured Crete from the Saracens in the year 962. During the second Byzantine period this church served as the seat of the Orthodox Archbishop of Crete. After the Venetian conquest of the island their clergy took over Áyios Títos, which became the seat of the Roman Catholic Archbishop, although the Cretans were permitted to hold their own services there in the Orthodox rite as well. The church was destroyed or badly damaged at least three times during the Venetian occupation, the last occasion being in 1557, and after each disaster it was completely rebuilt. At the time of the Turkish conquest of Candia in 1669 the church was converted into a mosque by the Grand Vezir, Mehmet Köprülü, after which it was called Vezir Djami. The mosque was destroyed in an earthquake in 1856 and its reconstruction was not completed until 1872. The building served as a mosque for another half-century after that, until it was finally converted into a church after the expulsion of the Turkish minority from Crete in 1923. The minaret was then torn down and replaced by a belfry, and the church was rededicated to St Titus. The church of St Titus today is one of the most venerated sanctuaries on the island, though it is no longer the seat of the Archbishop of Crete. The church was the centre of a great celebration in May of 1966, when a reliquary containing the skull of St Titus was returned here from Venice after an absence of nearly three centuries.

The southern stretch of Odós 25 Avgoústou leads from Plateías Kalergón and Venizélou to Plateia Nikiphórou Phoká, the main traffic intersection in central Iráklion. The main street running due south past the intersection is Odós 1866, named after the Cretan revolution of that year. This takes one through the heart of the principal street market in town, the liveliest and most interesting quarter in all of Iráklion. Virtually everything that is used in Cretan daily life is laid out for sale along this and adjacent streets in the market, the merchants vying with one another in attracting and tempting the passersby with attractive displays. The most colourful are those on the marble tables of the butchers and fishmongers and the stalls of the fruitsellers.

Strolling hucksters hawk their wares above the din of the passing crowd in a wonderful atmosphere that is more reminiscent of carnival than shopping. After wandering through the market for a while one might want to stop and have lunch at one of the raffish little tavernas in among the shops, our own favourites being those that are half-hidden away down a side alley off Odós 1866. There you can just walk into the hole-in-the-wall that serves as the kitchen and point to the pots that smell best, and your meal, which originated just a few yards away in the market, will be served up to you at a table in the alleyway, whose narrowness does not permit the entrance of the sun even an hour past noon, the noise from the nearby market muted to the level of distant battle.

After passing through the market, Odós 1866 emerges into Plateía Kornárou, another busy intersection. Here one is inevitably drawn to the extremely pleasant sidewalk café on the far side of the roundabout, where exhausted shoppers from the market take their ease in the shade of a lovely old Turkish fountain-house with an overhanging roof, behind which there is an even older Venetian font, the Bembo Fountain, which together make this one of the most picturesque spots in all of Iráklion. The Turkish fountain-house is of the type called a *shadirvan*, where in Ottoman times water was distributed free to passersby from the grilled windows set into the façade of the octagonal structure. The *shadirvan* was probably built soon after the Turkish conquest of Candia in 1669, when the Venetian church that stood just behind it, San Salvador, was converted into a mosque, Valide Djami. (The name Valide was the title of the Sultan's mother, and so the mosque and the *shadirvan* must have been part of a pious foundation established by Turhan Hadice, mother of Mehmet IV, during whose reign Candia was conquered by the Turks.)

The Bembo Fountain is one of the most curious antiquities on Crete, a combination of Venetian and Roman art and architecture. It consists of a pair of piers flanking two columns, a colonnade of Venetian construction, flanking a headless Roman statue standing on a pediment decorated with carvings in low relief, with sculptured panels of the Graeco-Roman period decorating the façade, and what appears to be an ancient sarcophagus forming the basin of the fountain. The fountain was created in 1588 by the Proveditore Ioannis Bembo, who found the statue and the other ancient sculptures in Ierápetra and carted them here to adorn his foundation. The Bembo Fountain and the *shadirvan* appear in an illustration in Robert Pashley's *Travels in Crete*, published in 1837; in this print one can see the minaret of Valide

Djami in the background, with robed and turbaned figures standing around the two fountains, which are flanked by ramshackle Turkish structures that appear to be part of the bazaar, the ancestor of today's street market on Odos 1866. The two structures are described by Captain Spratt, who tells a curious tale about the Bembo Fountain, which the local Moslems considered to be a holy place, attaching talismans to the headless statue as he had noticed them doing to the tomb of a Turkish pasha outside the walls.

> The bust of a Roman statue, at a fountain within the town . . . is similarly decorated and paid reverence to by some Turkish devotees every Friday (the Mussulman's sabbath), besides having a lamp with oil or incense set before it also. This is the only instance of image-worship which I have ever observed amongst the Mohamedans; and I was informed that it was due to a belief among the superstitious that it was the petrified remnant of the body of a sainted Ethiopian Mussulman who was killed in the war, and whose head and lower members were cut off by the Christians, but who was destined to rise to life when the Ghiaour are to be exterminated from the island.

The avenue that passes through Plateía Kornárou is part of a ring road that circles inner Iráklion, the oldest part of the town. Walking east from the traffic intersection, one passes Plateía Arkadíou and then Plateía Feréou, after which one comes to the square in which stands the huge church of Áyios Minás, the cathedral of Iráklion and the seat of the Orthodox Archbishop of Crete. Construction of the cathedral began in 1862, but work was halted by the revolution of 1866 and the edifice was not completed until 1895. The church is designed in a pseudo-Renaissance style; in plan it is a Greek cross, 42m long and 30m wide, with a dome supported on a high drum over the centre of the nave, and with two belfries 32m in height. The cathedral, one of the largest and most splendid in Greece, can accommodate a congregation of some 8000, surpassing even the Metropolitan church in Athens. The iconostasis, which was not completed until 1930, was designed by Anastasios Orlandos. The principal adornments of the church are six icons by the renowned Cretan painter Michael Damaskinos, one of them bearing the date 1591. The side chapel to the right is dedicated to Áyios Títos and the one to the left to Ayíi Dhéka, the Holy Ten. The latter were the ten saints who were martyred in Górtyna during the persecution of the Christians by the Emperor Decius (AD 249–51). These martyrs are the exemplars of Cretan faith and heroism in the early days of Christianity on the Great Island.

On the northwest side of the square, to the left of the entrance to the cathedral, there is a smaller and older church also dedicated to Áyios Minás. This was probably founded in the late medieval period and was originally named for Ayía Panayía Pantanassa, Our Lady of Candlemas, but later it was dedicated to Áyios Minás as well. In 1735 the church became the seat of the Archbishop of Crete, and it served as the Metropolitan church until the opening of the present cathedral in 1895. In 1821, at the beginning of the Greek War of Independence, the church was the scene of a massacre, when the Turks murdered Archbishop Gerasimos Pardhalis along with four other Cretan bishops. A much larger massacre was averted in 1826, when the Christian townspeople took refuge in the church to escape from the fury of a Turkish mob who were threatening to kill them. Pious tradition holds that they were saved by the intervention of Áyios Minás, one of several miraculous deliverances attributed to the saint during the days of Ottoman occupation.

At the northeast corner of the square there stands the venerable church of Ayía Ekateríni, St Catherine, dating from early in the Venetian period. The church originally served as the *metóchion*, or monastic seat, of the Monastery of St Catherine on Mount Sinai, which had representatives here as well as in Alexandria and Constantinople. After the fall of Constantinople to the Turks in 1453, the monastic school of St Catherine in Candia became for a time the most renowned institution of higher learning in the Greek-speaking world, and some of the leading figures of the Cretan renaissance studied there. The school was closed when the Turks conquered Candia in 1669, whereupon the church was converted into a mosque, Aya Katerina Djamisi. St Catherine's now serves as a museum to exhibit Cretan icons, removed there from remote churches all over the island, an appropriate use for the place where El Greco is reputed to have studied before he left Crete.

After leaving St Catherine's, turn right and walk straight ahead on Odós Ayíi Dhéka, the short street that leads out from the northeast corner of the square. Then at the first main intersection turn right onto Leofóros (Avenue) Kalokairinoú, the main east-west street in Iráklion, known in Venetian times as Strata Larga, the Large Street. Then at the next corner bear right onto Odós Ídis, which in two short blocks brings one back to Plateía Nikiphórou Phoká. From there one might go back along Odós 25 Avgoústou and continue north past Plateías Venizélou and Kalergón and on to the seafront; there one emerges at the western end of the old Venetian port, one of the most picturesque sights in all of Crete.

The medieval Venetian port of Iráklion is almost completely landlocked, enclosed on the seaward side by an enormous breakwater that is anchored at the Koulés, the great fortress that guards the narrow entrance to the harbour. (The name Koulés comes from the Turkish word *kule*, or tower, usually the main bastion of a fortress.) The Koulés stands on a rocky islet that was probably joined to the mainland by a mole in the medieval period, and it was fortified in turn by the Byzantines, Saracens and Venetians. The first Venetian fortress on the islet was built in 1303, but this was destroyed by an earthquake early in the sixteenth century. The present mighty fortress was built in 1523–40 as a defence against the growing maritime threat of the Ottoman Empire, which reached its peak during the reign of Sultan Süleyman the Magnificent, 1520–66. The first major Turkish assault on Crete occurred in 1538, when the coasts of the Great Island were raided by the Ottoman pirate-admiral Hayrettin Pasha, better known in the West as Barbarossa, who commanded a fleet of some two hundred warships on a commission from Sultan Süleyman to conquer and plunder all over the Aegean. Many of the Aegean islands surrendered to Barbarossa on that campaign, but although Réthymnon was sacked the Venetian fortresses at Candia and elsewhere on Crete were strong enough to resist capture by the Turks.

The Ottoman invasion of Crete began in the summer of 1645, during the reign of Sultan Ibrahim the Mad, when a Turkish fleet under the command of Yusuf Pasha laid siege to Chaniá, which surrendered two months later. Réthymnon fell to the Ottomans in 1646, and in the spring of 1648 the Turks attacked Candia, beginning a memorable siege that would last for more than two decades. The last stage in this siege began in 1666, during the reign of Mehmet IV, son and successor of Sultan Ibrahim, with the Ottoman forces led by the Grand Vezir Mehmet Köprülü. At that time the fortress at Candia was defended by a force of less than 10,000, including Venetians, Greeks and other European soldiers, commanded by Francesco Morosini. There are no reliable records on the number of the Turkish forces then besieging Candia, but it is evident that they greatly outnumbered the defenders. Köprülü pressed the siege with terrific intensity for the next twenty-eight months, during which time there was great loss of life on both sides, and the town of Candia was reduced to rubble. (According to one estimate, the Turks suffered 118,754 casualties during the siege, and the defenders 30,985.) By the beginning of the year 1669 the situation in Candia had grown so desperate that the Pope appealed to the Christian rulers of Europe, asking them to save Crete from being conquered by the infidel Turks. King Louis XIV responded by sending a force of 8,000 French soldiers under the command of the Duc de Navailles; these troops were transported to Crete by a fleet of fifty French warships commanded by the Duc de Beaufort. The French force arrived at Candia on 19 June 1669, to find the defenders virtually without resources. Eight days later the Duc de Beaufort was killed while leading a sally outside the walls of Candia, after which the Duc de Navailles soon lost heart and sailed back to France with his troops, accompanied by most of the surviving European allies. That left Morosini's forces hopelessly outnumbered, and so on 5 September 1669 he sent word to the Ottoman Grand Vezir that he wanted to surrender. Köprülü and Morosini agreed to the terms of the surrender, and within twelve days the Venetians abandoned the Koules and the other fortifications of Candia and the Turks took over the town, beginning the Ottoman occupation of Crete. During the Turkish period the old Venetian defence-works were allowed to fall into disrepair, and the Koulés was used as a prison, principally for Cretan rebels against the Ottoman regime. Within recent years the Koulés has been splendidly restored, and now during the summer months it is used as an outdoor theatre for dramatic and musical productions, many of them connected with Cretan history and folk culture.

A wonderful time to stroll out to the Koulés is late in the afternoon, an hour or so before sunset, when the old Venetian port quarter comes to life after the siesta. At that hour the fishermen and mariners of Iráklion are usually working on their boats tied up along the inner side of the breakwater, their nets spread out along the quay to dry and be mended, some of them preparing to go out for a night's fishing on the Aegean. As one approaches the entrance to the Koulés, one sees above the castle doorway a large relief representing the Lion of St Mark framed in the doorway of a classical temple, symbol of the Serene Republic of Venice; the inscription bears the date 1523, the year when the Venetians began construction of the fortress. After entering the Koulés one can wander through some of the twenty-six chambers of the fortress, including a huge vaulted hall and a labyrinth of rooms used by the garrison, some as storerooms for provisions and ammunition. One can also wander out onto the battlements, from where the Venetian cannons looked down on the narrow entrance to the port. The sculptured figures of three lions still stand there as symbolic sentinels of Venice. Across the harbour, on the eastern side of the inner port, one can see the great arched portal of one of the Venetian *arsenáli*, the arsenals that once lined the waterfront of Candia, each of them berthing one of the great Venetian galleons that were once the terror of the eastern Mediterranean. Some of the arsenals still survive as warehouses along the waterfront, although all but one of their great portals have been demolished in recent years.

One very interesting way to spend a morning or afternoon in Iráklion is to walk the circuit of the medieval defence-walls of Venetian Candia. A good place to begin is at the foot of the breakwater on the old Venetian port, walking westward from there along the shore to the point where the land-walls meet the sea, a pleasant stroll of about one and a quarter kilometres along Leofóros Venizélou.

About 250m west of the breakwater along the shore road one passes the Xenía Hotel, and on the seafront just beyond that is the Glass House, the most famous of all the tavernas in Iráklion. No visit to Iráklion is complete without spending at least one evening at the Glass House, for it features the best Cretan music, singing and dancing of any taverna on the island, in an extremely pleasant environment.

Behind the Xenía Hotel, on Odós Kalokairinoú, is the Historical and Ethnographical Museum of Crete. This an extremely interesting museum, and one should not miss visiting it while in Iráklion, perhaps after visiting the more famous Archaeological Museum, which will be passed towards the end of the present stroll.

After passing the Xenía Hotel and the Glass House, the shore road curves around a deep bay called Dermatás, which some still call by its old Turkish name, Kumkapi, the Sand Gate. This was an ancient postern in the Venetian sea-walls that extended from the mole of the Koulés to the north-western end of the land-walls, giving access from Candia to Dermatás Bay. In the year 1666 Kumkapi and Dermatás Bay were the scene of furious fighting between the Turks and a relief party of French troops under the command of the Duke de la Feuillade, most of whom were drowned when their ships were sunk by the Ottoman artillery.

The street that leads due south from Kumkapi is called Odós Delimárkou. A short stroll along this street brings one to the vicinity of an interesting monument of Venetian Candia, the Priuli Fountain, known locally as the Fountain of Deli Marko. The façade of the fountain is in the form of a classical Greek temple with a colonnade of four columns, and with a pair of niches flanking a central panel. A Latin inscription on the panel records that the fountain was built in

1666 by the Proveditore Generale Antonio Priuli, who thus brought precious water to Candia after the Morosini aqueduct was cut by the Turks during their siege of the town. The neighbourhood in which the Priuli Fountain stands was up until late Ottoman times the Jewish quarter of Candia, a fact noted by Pashley during his visit to the town in 1834.

Just before one comes to the northwestern end of the land-walls, the shore highway veers off to the left and becomes Odós Makaríou, the beginning of the ring road that goes around the inner town just inside the fortifications. Here one can walk past the seaward extremity of the land-walls to Odós Efódou, the street that runs outside the fortifications along that stretch. In doing so one passes the site of the ancient Gate of Áyios Andréas, which was just seaward of the defence-tower that anchored the land-walls to the sea at their northwestern end, a great bastion named for the same saint. This portal was known in Ottoman times as Yürüsh Kapisi, the Gate of the Assault, because the Turkish forces made one of their major offences against the walls of Candia at this point during the final days of the siege late in the summer of 1669.

One now begins walking the circuit of the old Venetian walls of Candia, a distance of about 4km. The original Byzantine defence-walls enclosed a much smaller area, extending from the present Plateía Nikephórou Phoká to the sea in two arcs, one of which is still defined by Odós Khandákos. After the fall of Constantinople to the Turks in 1453, the Venetians realized the need to construct a new line of defence-walls to protect Candia, for by then the town had grown beyond its Byzantine limits, and so the new line of fortifications was laid out to protect the outer suburbs as well, the area known as the Borghi. Construction of the new defence-walls began in 1462 under the supervision of Michele Sammicheli, a Venetian who was the leading military engineer of his day. The building of these great walls, in places 80 metres thick, continued for more than a century, and their strength is evidenced by the fact that it took the Turks more than twenty years to penetrate them when they began their siege of Candia in 1648. Moreover, these mighty walls were guarded along their periphery by a circlet of seven powerful bastions of the type called *mezzoluna* (half moon), facing outwards toward the enemy like the blades of scimitars; and outside the walls and bastions there was a huge moat, some 50m wide. Although this has been filled in along much of its length, one can still see the deep ditch in many places, particularly at the north-western end of the circuit, where Odós Efódou heads inland from the sea. There were also five great gates in the defence-walls, beginning with the Gate of Áyios Andréas at the north-western end; two of these are still standing today, continuing as main entrances to the inner city. When one passes through their great arched portals one realizes that Iráklion is still a walled town.

The first bastion that one passes on strolling around the walls is that of Áyios Andréas. In Ottoman times the seaward end of this bastion was called Yali Köshk, the Shore Kiosk, after a Turkish seaside mansion that stood there, probably the pleasure-dome of some pasha.

Walking along the walls, either inside the periphery along Odós Makaríou, or outside on Odós Efódou, the next semi-lunar shaped fortress one comes to is the Bastion of the Pantocrator, known colloquially as the Panígra, and just beyond that one comes to the first of the two surviving Venetian gates, known both as the Pórta Panígra and the Pórta Chaniá, since the road from Chaniá entered Candia at this point. The roadway entering the inner city here passes through a splendid arched portal, dated by its sculptured reliefs to c. 1565, with its handsome façade revetted in stone continuing along the inside of the street to the left, giving the neighbourhood a grand and Venetian appearance. Pashley entered Candia at this point after having travelled from Chaniá, and his description gives one some idea of the scene at that time, in the spring of 1834:

> . . . we reached the gate of 'Megalo-Kastron', and the usual adjunct of a large Mohammedan town, an extensive burial ground. On entering within the walls of the city, I saw I was once more in Turkey: and the bazaars, although filled with fewer articles outside of eastern luxury, are still so exclusively Turkish in their character as to recall those of Smyrna and Constantinople.

Continuing along, one comes next to the Rampart of Bethlehem and the site of the Venetian gateway of the same name, now vanished. But the entrance to the city through the walls here is still called the Bethlehem Gate, though the Venetian portal itself has long vanished. The entrance is also called the Gate of Áyios Andréas, after a church of that saint that stands inside the walls just to the right as one enters the city.

Now comes the southernmost sector of the defence-walls, where one is advised to proceed inside the circuit along Odós Nikoláou Plastira. Down this street one finds on the right the entrance to a roadway leading to the top of the Martinengro Bastion, the southern-most of the mezzolunar fortresses that ring the walls of Venetian

Candia. This is the last resting place of Nikos Kazantzakis (1883–1957), the great Cretan writer, whose grave is marked by a large wooden cross and a simple slab of marble standing on a stone platform. On the slab is an inscription quoting these lines from the writings of Kazantzakis, an appropriate epitaph for this independent spirit: 'I hope for nothing. I fear nothing. I am free.'

Before leaving the Martinengro Bastion, one might pause for a moment to look out over the area to the south, an outer quarter of the city that was once part of the vast Turkish cemetery that lay outside the walls of Candia to the southwest, a sight described by both Pashley and Spratt. Spratt writes:

> To the south of the city lies a large Turkish cemetery, which unlike Turkish graveyards in general, is without a single cypress tree; it is, in consequence, a mere forest of tombstones, of interest only in containing many that fell in the great siege, and for the ancient fragments that may be found in it.

Returning to Odós Nikoláou Plastíra, one next passes the Rampart of Jesus, just beyond which is the Pórta Gésu, the Gate of Jesus, the second of the two surviving Venetian gateways of Candia. This is also called Kenoúryia Pórta, the New Gate, since iᵗ was the last of the main gates to be built in the Venetian walls of Candia, completed in 1587. The great arched portal of the gateway, adorned with sculptured reliefs that evoke memories of Venetian Candia, still hovers over the roadway where it enters the city.

The next fortress along the walls is the Vituri Rampart, which formed the south-western angle of the fortifications, today part of a public park. The ring road here changes its name to Odós Pediádos, turns north as it passes the park and then opens into Plateía Eleftherías, Liberty Square. This is the largest and most attractive square in Iráklion, giving an almost ceremonial aspect to the western entrance to the inner city, the periphery of the green lined with cinemas, outdoor cafés, a luxury hotel, the Prefecture of Iráklion and the Archaeological Museum, whose entrance is on the right side of the street that leads out of the square to the north, Odós Xanthoudídou. In and around the square there are a number of honorific monuments that add to its ceremonious character; in the green there are statues of Nikos Kazantzakis and of the Unknown Soldier; just outside the walls, on the left side of the roadway that leaves the inner city from the southeast side of the square, there is a statue of the great Cretan statesman Eleftherios Venizelos; and a short way along on the right side of that avenue there is a statue honouring the Emperor Nicephorus Phocas and another commemorating the Battle of Crete. The latter two monuments span a thousand years of Cretan history.

The Venizelos statue stands close to the site of the medieval gate of Áyios Yeórgios, St George, also called the Gate of the Lazaretto. The latter name stemmed from the fact that the gate led to the Lazaretto, where all of those who wished to enter Candia were quarantined for a period of time, as a precaution against the plague. During late Ottoman times the Lazaretto had become filled to overflowing with swarms of lepers, unfortunate wretches who lived in a village outside St George's Gate because there was nowhere else for them to go. (A leper colony was finally founded in 1903 on the islet of Spinalónga, near the town of Áyios Nikólaos.)

From the Plateía Eleftherías, Odós Doúkos leads off to the northeast along the last stretch of the Venetian walls, which end with the Sabbionera Bastion. The walls once extended from that bastion to the sea, ending on the eastern side of the Venetian port. However, these fortifications have long since been demolished, destroyed by the British forces in 1898 during the Allied occupation of Crete. Thus on reaching the Sabbionera Bastion one has finished the long walk around the walls of Venetian Candia, completing this exploration of the medieval city. Captain Spratt completed his own tour of the Venetian walls at this point, the grandeur of the ruins leading him to write nostalgically of 'Candia . . . the best fortified and finest city of its time in the Levant'.

3

⊟⊟⊟

THE MUSEUMS OF IRÁKLION

ARCHAEOLOGICAL MUSEUM

All visitors interested in the ancient culture of Crete are inevitably drawn to the Archaeological Museum in Iráklion, which has, among other exhibits, the world's greatest collection of antiquities from the Minoan era. Ideally, one should try to visit this museum both before and after seeing the archaeological site at Knossós, for this repetition will deepen one's understanding of Minoan culture, a good preparation for seeing the other Minoan sites on the island. The Archaeological Museum also has exhibits from all of the post-Minoan epochs in Cretan antiquity, up through the Classical, Hellenistic, and Roman periods. After seeing all of these exhibits, one might then go across to the other side of Iráklion to see the Historical and Ethnographical Museum, which has exhibits from the Byzantine, Venetian and Ottoman periods in Cretan history, as well as some that bring the story of the Great Island up to modern times. In this way one can acquire a feeling for the whole vast scope of Cretan culture, from its prehistoric beginnings up to the present day. What follows is a brief summary of this great procession of Cretan culture, as one sees it in strolling through these two museums in Iráklion.

The (numbered) exhibits in the Archaeological Museum of Iráklion are arranged chronologically, so that one can see how Cretan culture developed throughout antiquity. But before proceeding through these exhibits in sequence, one might first go to Room XIII, which is just to the left of the entry, for on display there is a huge cut-away model of the central area of the great Minoan palace at Knossós, where many of

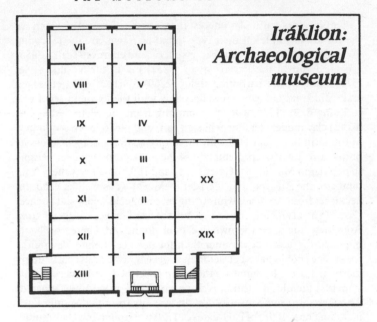

Iráklion:
Archaeological
museum

the objects in the museum were discovered. After having examined this, one can then go back to the entrance lobby and walk into Gallery I, where the exhibition begins. (The time-spans given for the various periods in Minoan culture are approximate, and are still a matter of discussion among scholars on the subject.)

Gallery I has exhibits from the Neolithic era (c. 6500–2600 BC) and the Prepalatial period (2600–2000 BC). These objects were found at Knossós and a number of other Minoan sites, of which the most interesting for the very earliest eras is the Cave of Eileithyia. Eileithyia, a daughter of Zeus and Hera, was the goddess of childbirth, a role which she shared with Artemis, and which both of them inherited from the very ancient fertility goddess who was worshipped in the eastern Mediterranean world and in Anatolia in the Neolithic period and the Bronze Age. Among the objects exhibited in Case 1 in this gallery is a primitive figurine (no. 2716) representing this fertility goddess, with more developed examples on display in other galleries. Elsewhere in the room there are ivory statuettes of a male figure, the most elaborate (287) shown seated on a stool or throne; these stylized figurines are identical with the Cycladic *idoles*, funerary deities found in Bronze Age graves on the Aegean isles north of Crete.

45

Other objects of particular interest in this first gallery, all of which are the earliest examples of their type found on Crete, are the following examples of pottery, stonework, jewellery, and engraved seals: (7485) a conical cup in the Pýrgos style; (5231) jug in the Vasilikí style; (5775) vase in the barbotine style; (2260) fourteen-sided engraved seal; (2719) lid of a stone jewellery box with the figure in relief of a reclining dog; (1201) a lovely stone jug from the islet of Móchlos; (4743) clay model of a four-wheeled cart; and (4676) a terracotta vase in the form of a giant bull with three tiny acrobats draped across its horns, a very early representation of the bull-sports that later became so popular in Minoan art. Cases 16, 17 and 18A contain jewellery from tombs of the Mésara, and the islet of Móchlos, as well as beautiful necklaces from Archánes with strung pieces in gold, ivory and faience. Case 18A also contains some bronze and silver daggers from Archánes, the oldest-known weapons found on Crete, probably intended for adornment rather than for defence. Before leaving the room, one should have a closer look at the engraved seals, particularly those in Case 11. Some of these are inscribed with hieroglyphic symbols, the oldest form of writing on Crete, as yet undeciphered. There are also some inscribed cylinder-seals from the Middle East, including one (1098) of later date (c. 1750 BC) from King Hammurabi of Babylon, evidence of the trade that took place between the Minoans and their neighbours in very early times.

Gallery II is devoted to the Protopalatial period (2000–1700 BC), principally from Knossós, Mállia and a number of mountaintop sanctuaries, mostly from Týlissos and Mount Ioúktas. These peak-sanctuaries are among the oldest shrines in Greece. In historic times they were generally shrines of Zeus, who inherited the attributes of more ancient Cretan deities, and the sites are still sacred today, usually as chapels of Áyios Profítis Ilías, the Prophet Elijah. The festival times of these peak-sanctuaries were the days of winter and summer solstice, when huge fires were lighted on the mountaintops, with worshippers throwing into the flames various votive offerings. Some of the most interesting exhibits in this room are of men and women worshipping at these shrines, particularly the figurine (405) of a male devotee with a dagger thrust into a scabbard at his waist, and several of women naked to the waist with their arms crossed over their breasts in reverential attitudes. Other fascinating objects from these shrines are representations of various parts of the human body, obviously used with prayers for the healing of illness; these are identical in character to the *ex-votos* found in shrines of the healing god Asclepius in the

Classical period, and one finds similar votive objects today in the glittering aluminium plaques hanging by the scores in churches all over Greece. An interesting exhibit from a shrine in the palace at Knossós is in Case 24, along with objects from these peak-sanctuaries; this (2582) is a representation of a tri-columnar shrine with three doves perched on the capitals, said to depict the epiphany of the goddess worshipped at the temple. Another very interesting exhibit is in Case 25: a group of faience plaques with detailed representations of house façades, which when assembled in a box together make up a picture of a Minoan town. Cases 26, 27 and 29 contain vases from Knossós and Mállia, of which the most exceptional are two (4390, 7691) in the Kamáres style.

Gallery III has more exhibits from the Protopalatial period, all of them from the palace of Phaestós, including superb examples of pottery, worked-stone, modelled-clay and engraved seals. Case 30 contains some of the earliest known examples of pottery in the Kamáres style; these receive their name from the place where they were found, the Kamáres Cave on Mount Ídha. Cases 31 to 39 contain numerous examples of pottery in the Kamáres style from Phaestós, with two outstanding examples being a krater (10578), adorned with sculptured flowers in high relief, and a fruit bowl (10580) with a serrated rim. Case 33 also has a unique cylindrical sculpture (18199) showing two dolphins diving at the bottom of the sea; while Case 36 has a rhyton (a ritual drinking vessel) with a figure in relief of a *kri-kri*, the long-horned wild goat of Crete. This is one of the earliest representations of the *kri-kri*, which up until very recent years ran wild on the mountains of Crete, but which can now be found only in game sanctuaries on islets off the north coast of the island.

The most extraordinary exhibit in Gallery III is the famous Phaestós Disc. Both faces of this clay disc are covered with hieroglyphics arranged in spiral zones, with the groups of symbols separated from one another by vertical lines. A total of 45 different signs have been distinguished on the disc, a few of them identical with hieroglyphics found on other objects in the Protopalatial period, and it is believed that each group of signs represents a word. Some of these groups of symbols are repeated in the disc, which has led some scholars to suggest that it records a religious hymn, the repetitions being the refrain of the song. But this and other interpretations are still uncertain, and the Phaestós Disc remains one of the unsolved mysteries of Minoan culture.

Gallery IV is the first of several rooms with exhibits from the

Neopalatial period (1700–1400 BC), all of them from the golden age of Minoan civilization, and the exhibits in this and other galleries devoted to the Neopalatial period give one a glimpse into the brilliant culture that flourished then on the Great Island. During this period a new type of pottery replaced the older Kamáres ware, the decoration consisting of floral and marine motifs. In Case 45 one sees examples of this style in the famous 'Lily Vases' of Knossós, with other examples of floral motifs in Case 46. In Case 49 there is a superb jug whose surface is completely covered with a depiction of grass leaves. Also in Case 49 there is a rhyton with a vivid decoration in motifs, with the principal figure being that of an *argonauta nautilus*. This is patterned on the chambered seashell which gave its name to the Argonauts who sailed with Jason in search of the Golden Fleece, the creature being a small cephaloid of which the female has a parchment-thin shell and webbed arms resembling sails. Case 46 also has an interesting example (8931) of the vessels that were used at Knossós in the strange cult of the sacred serpent; this is a clay vase in the form of a honeycomb around which a snake is coiled, apparently about to strike. It is believed that these vessels were used to house the sacred snakes, which sipped milk from a cup attached to the vase. Other decorative themes are used in a cup (8407) exhibited in Case 49, adorned with 'sacred knots' and the *labyrs*, the double axe, the symbol of the god-king in the Minoan world. Scholars believe that *labyrs* is the root from which came the word *labýrinthos*, and thus the Labyrinth of Cretan mythology is really the royal palace of Knossós, the House of the Double Axe. Case 50 has two of the most famous exhibits in the museum, a pair of multi-coloured faience figures (63, 65) called the 'Snake Goddesses'. Each of them is dressed in a long skirt and with bare breasts emerging from her bodice; one of them has a serpent draped over her shoulders and hanging down along her sides, wearing a huge conical tiara; the other is crowned with a tiara on which crouches a tiny panther, while in her outstretched hands she holds wriggling snakes. These figures undoubtedly represent priestesses involved in rituals associated with the cult of the sacred serpent, a chthonic, or earthborn deity that is one of the most ancient forms of worship in the Greek world, found also in the very earliest prehistoric period in Athens. Another very famous exhibit, this one found in the 'Little Palace' at Knossós, is seen in Case 51 (1368), a rhyton in the form of the steatite head of a bull with golden horns, its eyes fashioned out of crystal, its eyelashes of jasper and its white muzzle out of nacreous mother-of pearl. The bull is another very prominent figure in Minoan art, representing the male procreative deity, a symbol also used in Anatolia from the Neolithic period down through the Bronze Age. Yet another famous exhibit is shown in Case 56: the 'Bull-Leaper' from Knossós, the ivory figurine of a youth shown as if in mid-air after somersaulting over the horns of a bull, a scene depicted in a Minoan fresco exhibited elsewhere in the museum. Case 57 contains one of the most interesting exhibits in the museum, the famous 'Draughts Board' from the palace at Knossós; this is a multicoloured board made of ivory, rock crystal, blue glass paste and gold and silver leaf. It is accompanied by four ivory objects that were undoubtedly the pieces in this royal game, perhaps a predecessor of chess. Other interesting exhibits in this gallery are: (69, in Case 55) a faience plaque decorated in relief with the figure of a *kri-kri* suckling its kid; (8362) a terracotta mace head in the form of a leaping leopard; (270) a 'Greek Cross', which was actually a stellar symbol for the Minoans; (636) the golden sheathing of a sword handle decorated in relief with the figure of an acrobat, perhaps a bull-leaper; and (2630) the inside of a cup with hieroglyphic script written in cuttlefish ink. This writing is an example of Linear A, a new script that came into use on Crete at the beginning of the Neopalatial period, c. 1700 BC. Archaeologists use the word 'linear' to differentiate this script from the earlier hieroglyphic ideograms used by the Minoans, because it was no longer a series of 'pictures', but instead consisted of lines inscribed in abstract groups. The Linear A script of Crete has never been deciphered, nor is it known what language it records, though a number of scholars have suggested that it is based on one of the pre-Hellenic tongues of western Anatolia, the Asian sub-continent from whence in c. 2600 BC came the people who developed Minoan civilization on the Great Island.

Gallery V is devoted to the last half-century of the Neopalatial period, 1450–1400 BC, with exhibits mostly from Knossós. All of the other Minoan palaces had already been destroyed by this time, and only Knossós remained, apparently occupied by Mycenaean rulers. Thus in the exhibits here one sees a strong Mycenaean influence in the Minoan art. The style of pottery decoration remained the same as it was earlier in the Neopalatial period, with floral and marine motifs predominating, as in the vases exhibited here in Cases 60, 63, 63A, 64, 66, 67 and 68. It is interesting to note that among the vases exhibited in this display those in Case 60 date from c. 1450 BC, the time when the first of the two catastrophes of that century destroyed all of the Minoan palaces on Crete except Knossós, while those in Cases 64 and 66 date to c. 1400 BC, and thus must have been made just before Knossós itself was destroyed in the second catastrophe. During the last half-century of the Minoan epoch a new mode of decoration is seen in the pottery from Knossós, the so-called Palace style. Here the familiar floral and marine motifs are executed in a different mode, reflecting Achaean influence, as in (8832) a three-handled amphora with stylized flowers in the form of spiral-pairs; (7757) a *pithos* (large urn) decorated with double axes, rosettes and papyrus plants; and the 'Ephyraean' *kylikes*, or goblets (21154, 21155, 21156) with spiral and floral decorations. Also exhibited are examples of some of the superb carved stonework of the period, most notably fragments of a sculptured frieze from Knossós. The carved stone vases and other objects in Case 62 were imports from Egypt, with the lid of an alabaster jewellery box decorated with the cartouche of the Pharaoh Khian the first of the Hyksos kings who ruled from Thebes in the period 1720–1570 BC, invaluable evidence in connecting the chronologies of ancient Egypt and Crete. Case 68 has exhibits of metalworking at Knossós during this last half-century of the Minoan era, including objects in gold, silver and bronze. The most interesting of these is a bronze figurine from Katsambá, which was a port serving Knossós; this shows a male figure wearing a curious tall conical cap, a headdress very similar to those shown in Hittite reliefs of the same period. Case 69 is of especial interest since it contains examples of both Linear A and Linear B scripts, with the latter appearing for the first time in Crete at Knossós c. 1450 BC. Linear B is now known to be a modification of Linear A used for palace inventories; it is written in a language that has been deciphered as Mycenaean Greek, the earliest-known form of the Hellenic tongue, evidence that the Achaeans were in control of Knossós at that time.

Gallery VI has exhibits from the last half-century of the Neopalatial period at Knossós, as well as other objects from the period 1400–1300 BC, the first century of the Postpalatial period, with the latter objects found at the burial grounds at Knossós, Archánes and Phaestós. Crete was dominated by the Mycenaeans during the whole of the Postpalatial period (1400–1100 BC), as evidenced by strong Achaean influence on Minoan art during those three centuries. Case 71 has three terracotta models of extraordinary interest, found in a *tholos* tomb near Phaestós. One of these (15072) represents a banquet scene, with models of doves and 'horns of consecration' attached; the latter, known as *bucrania*, are stylized models of the horns of the bull, symbols of the male deity both in ancient Crete and Anatolia. The second model (15074) appears to be of a shrine with a façade of two columns; inside are four figures, apparently representing a funerary rite. The third model (15073) is the most interesting of all, showing four women doing a circular dance with their hands around one another's shoulders, exactly as in the folk dances one sees today on Crete, an extraordinarily evocative scene that links ancient Minoan culture with present life on the Great Island.

Dramatic evidence of the presence of the Mycenaeans on Crete is provided by the number of weapons exhibited in Gallery VI, including gold-nailed swords, a boar's-tooth helmet, and a bronze helmet with cheek-protectors, all of which Homer mentions in describing the siege of Troy in the *Iliad*. Other evocative reminders of the Mycenaean presence on Crete are the exhibits of gold jewellery, reminiscent of the treasure of King Priam discovered by Schliemann at Troy, pieces of quite barbaric beauty, most notably the Isopata Ring (424), representing the epiphany of a goddess and a griffin in flight before her. Other interesting objects in the room are: (8345) a figurine representing the *kourothropos*, a goddess holding a divine infant, the Minoan forerunner of the Madonna and Christchild; (366) an ivory plaque representing a *kri-kri*; (Case 75A) objects from the sacrifice of a horse found in a warrior's tomb at Archanes; and (Case 82) an alabaster amphora from Egypt with the cartouche of the Pharaoh Tuthmosis III, who reigned from 1504–1450 BC, another important piece of evidence linking the chronologies of ancient Crete and Egypt.

Gallery VII has objects from mansions and caves in central Crete dating from the Neopalatial period. Some of these mansions were luxurious royal villas, most notably that at Ayía Triádha, while others are smaller structures called megarons, edifices centred on a great hall of the same type that Schliemann discovered at Troy, the Palace of Priam. Within the room there are drawings of two types of megaron that have been excavated at Týlissos, as well as a photograph of the Psykhró Cave, above the Lasíthi Plain; this and other caverns were popular shrines during the Neopalatial period, as evidenced by the rich funerary offerings found within them.

Most of the pottery exhibited in Gallery VII is similar to that found in the royal palaces of the same period, but there are three unique steatite vases from Ayía Triádha that are unlike any of those pieces. The first of these (184, in Case 94) is a vase in the shape of an ostrich egg. This is called the 'Harvesters' Rhyton', because it depicts a procession of farmers carrying sickles and with winnowing forks over their shoulders; four of the figures are seen to be singing and one of them is carrying a musical instrument, as if they are in procession at a religious festival, perhaps a harvest feast. The second of these vases (498, in Case 96) is a vessel in the shape of an icecream cone with four zones of decoration: the upper and the two lower zones showing boxing and wrestling matches, while the fourth zone depicts a scene of bull-sports, with athletes somersaulting over the horns of charging bulls. The third steatite vase from Ayía Triádha is known both as the 'Cup of the Chieftain' and the 'Cup of the Report'; the main scene shows two men, one holding a sceptre and the second holding a sword and standing at attention as if reporting to his chieftain. Another interesting steatite object in this gallery is the seated figure of a sphinx (384), very similar to some Hittite sculptures of the same period. Among the exhibits from the cave sanctuaries there are some superb bronze figurines of both humans and animals, the first type representing worshippers and the second their offerings, probably presented in lieu of the real sacrificial animals of an earlier time. The most interesting of the figurines representing humans is the statuette of a male worshipper (1831, in Case 89), showing him standing to attention with his right hand raised in salute, a marvellous realism evident in the posture of his supple body. Among the animal figurines the most interesting are two (822, 823 in Case 102) bronze miniatures depicting the *kri-kri*, who in both pieces is shown in a very naturalistic attitude of repose. Also of interest in other display cases are swords, daggers and three huge tripod cauldrons, similar to those found in late Bronze Age sites from eastern Anatolia through the Mediterranean world up into central Europe. Case 101 displays some gorgeous gold jewellery, with the star exhibit being (559) a pendant with two bees storing a drop of honey in a honeycomb, a brilliant work of great technical ingenuity. Also on display in this case is a beautiful gold necklace (138), and jewels in the form of a lion (123) and a duck (124). Outside the cases there are carved stone *bucrania* and double axes of gold.

Gallery VIII has exhibits from the Neopalatial period found in the palace at Káto Zákros, in eastern Crete. One exhibit of particular interest here is in Case 109, a jug with a vivid design of swimming argonauts; this is identical to a vase now in the Museum of Marseilles that was discovered in Egypt in the last century before archaeological excavations began on Crete. Other exhibits of interest in this gallery are the following: (13985, in Case 107) an amphora decorated with a very live-looking octopus, so different from the symmetrical geometric renditions of this creature in classical Greek times; (2085, in Case 110) a rhyton decorated with starfishes and tritons, marine snails with a stout spiral shell, metamorphosized in Greek mythology into the form of mermen, the sons of Poseidon and Amphitrite; (2734, in Case 118) one of several so-called 'communion cups', because they resemble Christian chalices, in this case a stone vase with a quatrefoil lip; (2721, in Case 109) an exceptionally lovely rhyton of rock crystal, with a collar and handle made of crystal beads; (2764, in Case 111) a rhyton in green stone from Káto Zákros decorated with a scene showing wild goats at a peak-sanctuary (the discolouration of the stone was caused by the fire that destroyed the palace c. 1450 BC); (2720) a beautiful stone amphora with elaborate handles in the shape of question marks; (311, in Case 117) a rhyton in the shape of an argonaut; (323, in Case 117) an ivory butterfly, whose surface has also been discoloured by the fire that destroyed the palace. There is a very interesting exhibit in Case 108, a cup containing olives that was found in Káto Zákros just as it is displayed here. When this was first unearthed the olives were as fresh as if they had just been taken from the tree, but since then they have shriveled up in the air from which they were protected for some 3500 years.

Gallery IX has exhibits from Neopalatial sites in eastern Crete. Two objects of some unusual interest here are in Case 125 (2861, 3378): cylindrical vessels with rosette-shaped mouths, believed to have been used to collect the blood of sacrificial bulls for use in funerary rites. Other interesting exhibits are: (5459, in Case 122) a pithos decorated with double axes and the heads of bulls; (5407) a vessel in the shape of a wicker basket, modelled on a tote-bag that is still used today by Cretan women when they go to market; (5413, in Case 122) a rhyton in the form of an ox; (9832, in Case 123) the figurine of a woman devotee shown naked to the waist, with a long plaited skirt hanging from her hips, her right hand held across her breasts in a reverential attitude, one of a number of statuettes of male and female worshippers found at a peak-sanctuary at Piskokéfalo; (9823, in Case 123) the head of one of these statuettes, showing the elaborate hairstyle and headdress of a Minoan woman of the period; (142, 143, in Case 124) ivory figurines representing babies, one of whom is represented sitting up as if in a cradle. Besides these, the most striking exhibits in this gallery are in Cases 124 and 128; there one sees a display of inscribed seals and seal impressions of the period, all of them of remarkable ingenuity and showing an exceptionally high degree of craftsmanship and technical skill.

Gallery X has exhibits of the Postpalatial period, 1400–1100 BC, when Crete was under the domination of the Mycenaeans, as is most evident in the pottery of the period. The most interesting objects here are terracotta figurines representing the Minoan fertility goddess, shown in several cases, the most notable of which are: (9305) the 'Poppy Goddess', a female figure with closed eyes and hands raised as if in prayer, three poppies protruding from her headress, believed to be a representation of the goddess who brought sleep and death; (9306) a goddess with a crown of doves, symbolizing her epiphany; (3864) another goddess of the same type but with a curious bird-like face; (18505, in Case 138) a woman riding sidesaddle on a horse; and (14360, 1850, in Case 138) children's *larnakes* (terracotta sarcophagi). The most fascinating exhibit in this room is a terracotta group (3903, in Case 132) representing three women performing a dance, with a fourth woman in the centre playing a lyre, a hauntingly evocative scene.

Gallery XI has exhibits of the Subminoan (1100–1000 BC) and the Proto- and Early Geometrical periods (1000 BC), with the latter eras named for the geometrical style of pottery which evolved at that time. The Subminoan exhibits are in Cases 148 and 154, while the objects from the Proto- and Early Geometric periods are in the remaining cases. The Subminoan period represents the last century of Bronze Age culture on Crete, with Minoan refugees fleeing from the coastal areas during the great migration of the Doric Greeks to the island. These refugees perpetuated some of the earlier forms of Minoan art, most notably the figurines of the goddess with her arms raised in prayer; one interesting example of this (11043, in Case 148) is the Goddess of Karphí, who wears the horns of consecration as a headdress. The most distinctive exhibit in this gallery is (11046, in Case 148) a rhyton in the shape of a chariot drawn by three oxen. The exhibits from the Proto- and Early Geometric periods comprise pottery, miniature sculpture, and metalwork in miniature, including jewellery and votive offerings, some of them from a cave-sanctuary of Eileithyia, showing that this ancient fertility goddess was still worshipped in post-Minoan times. Some of these caverns are still sacred places today, many of them devoted to the Spilliótissa, Our Lady of the Cave – another example of the continuity of culture on the Great Island.

Most of the exhibits in Gallery XII are from what is called the Mature Geometrical period (800–725 BC) and the Orientalizing period (725–650 BC), eras named for the style of pottery decoration prevalent during those times. The Mature Geometric period is represented in Cases 159, 165, 166 and 167; while objects of the Orientalizing period are displayed in Cases 162, 163, 164 and 168. Besides these, the exhibits in Cases 160, 161, 161A and 161B contain objects from the shrine of Hermes Dendrites at Sými, ranging in date from the Minoan era to the Hellenistic period. Prominent among the pottery of the Mature Geometric period are the funerary urns from the burial ground at Fortétsa, the medieval Venetian fortress in Réthymnon. The Orientalizing period is so named because of the strong Eastern influence on Greek art in that era, and the exhibits here include pottery, miniature sculpture and metalwork, including jewellery. Perhaps the most vivid painting exhibited here that shows this Oriental influence is on a jug (7961, in Case 163), where two young lovers, perhaps Theseus and Ariadne, are shown greeting one another. The most striking piece of pottery exhibited in this gallery is a terracotta vase (14809, in Case 162) in the form of a truncated tree with a flock of birds flapping on its branches, a very animated scene. An extraordinary example of post-Minoan sculpture exhibited here is a bronze group found in the Idhaean Cave, representing a galley with oarsmen and a man and woman as passengers, perhaps a scene from the myth of Theseus and Ariadne. Another miniature sculpture of interest is (8104, in Case 8104) shows a musician playing a lyre. There is also a collection of jewellery of the period from a treasure found in Tekes (the Turkish word for a dervish monastery), of which an outstanding piece is a pendant in the shape of a golden half-moon with satellite crescent moons of gold centred on pieces of rock-crystal.

Gallery XIII is devoted to Minoan sarcophagi from the same burial grounds as the objects displayed in Galleries VI–X, all of them dating from the Neopalatial and Postpalatial periods. These sarcophagi are all made of clay, modelled on the wooden caskets used in the Protopalatial period, all of which have rotted away. In earlier times it was the common practice to bury the dead in large urns called *pithoi* (singular, *pithos*) or in terracotta *larnakes*. Virtually all of these terracotta sarcophagi have painted decorations in the same style as the pottery of the two periods, using the same floral and marine motifs, such as the flowers in 7396 and 9341; the octopuses in 7624 and 9499; the fish in 11163; with a different theme in 9499, where the figures of horned animals are shown, one of them suckling its young.

One now goes upstairs to Gallery XIV, the first of three rooms devoted to an exhibition of Minoan wall paintings, one of the most extraordinary collections of ancient art in the world. These frescoes once decorated the walls of the palaces and great houses of Crete, the oldest of them dating to c. 1600 BC, with scenes of the brilliant culture that flourished there in the golden age of Minoan civilization, which seems to have been distinguished by its joy in life. Most of the frescoes are from the great palace at Knossós, with the second largest group coming from the royal villa at Ayía Triádha, as well as some from the megarons at Amnisós, Nírou Kháni and Týlissos, as well as houses on the islet of Pseíra. Virtually all of the Knossós frescoes are from the Neopalatial period, with a group of wall paintings from Ayía Triádha dating from the early Postpalatial period and thus contemporary with those of the Mycenaean palaces of mainland Greece.

After entering Gallery XIV, one might first walk over to look at the exhibit in the centre of the Room, Case 171, for on display there is one of the most interesting exhibits in the museum, the Ayía Triádha Sarcophagus, dated c. 1400 BC. This is made of stone, the only such sarcophagus ever to have been found on Crete; it is covered inside and out with plaster that has been painted in fresco with scenes from the funeral of a royal personage, perhaps a Mycenaean prince. These scenes in their various details are a rich mine of information about funerary practices in ancient Crete, with the most fascinating episode being the sacrifice of a bull. Considering the date of the sarcophagus it is interesting to look for Mycenaean influences, both in the art and the customs depicted.

One might now return to the north-west corner of the room, opposite the stairway, where the exhibit of Minoan wall paintings begins. (In Case 172, near the west end of the room, there are fragmentary frescoes from Knossós.) The description that follows will proceed from there, left to right along the western side of the north wall up to the second door, then along the entire south wall from left to right, then finally along the eastern stretch of the north wall. The first fifteen of the numbered frescoes in this room are from Knossós, 16–17 are from Amnisós, and 18–24 are from Ayía Triádha. The first painting in the exhibition is (1): a fragment of a fresco representing the leg of a bull, from the upper Hall of the Double Axes in the palace at Knossós. One then goes on from there to look at the numbered paintings that follow in order. (2–5): four large pieces of the Fresco of the Procession, of which the best-preserved figure is that of the Cup-Bearer (5), a young man carrying a large conical rhyton; this is part of a vast scene estimated to have comprised some 350 figures, which in c. 1450 BC was painted on the walls of the Corridor of the Processions in the palace at Knossós. (6): the Griffin Fresco, from the Throne Room at Knossós, blackened by the flames that destroyed the palace c. 1400 BC. (7) Figure-of-Eight Shields, modelled on shields covered with sewn animal skins, part of the painted decoration on the walls of the royal apartments at Knossós. (8): the Lily Prince, a young man wearing a necklace of lilies and a flamboyant headdress of lilies and peacock feathers, thought to represent the priest-king of Knossós. (9): the Head of a Bull in low relief, c. 1600 BC; this was originally part of a scene showing the capture of a wild bull, and decorated the stoa at the north entrance to the palace at Knossós. (10) the Ladies in Blue, showing women of the royal court, a largely restored scene that once adorned the big anteroom of the Throne Room in the eastern wing of the palace at Knossós. (11): Fresco of Dolphins, c. 1600 BC, from the Queen's Megaron at Knossós. (12–13): Multicoloured Spirals, once painted on horizontal wooden beams set into the walls of the palace. (14): Fresco of Partridges, a frieze in the 'Caravanserai', a small structure east of the palace. (15): The Bull-Leapers, the most dramatic of all the frescoes in the museum, showing a young man somersaulting over the back of a charging bull, while a pair of young women assist from in front and behind; this was found in a room at the eastern wing of the palace at Knossós. (16–17): Frescoes of the Lilies, c. 1600 BC, from a villa at Amnisós. (18): Fresco of a Kneeling Woman, from the villa at Ayía Triádha; this and the frescoes immediately following, (19): A Woman at a Shrine, and (20): A Wild Cat, were all in the same room, and are blackened by the fire that destroyed the villa c. 1450 BC. Also from the villa at Ayía Triádha are the remaining two fragments at the easternmost end of the north wall in Gallery XIV, these are (21): Procession of Men and Women, and (22): Procession of Women, in which a deer is led to a shrine to be sacrificed. Case 24, at the eastern end of the room, has a painted pavement from the villa decorated with dolphins, octopuses and fish.

The exhibition of Minoan wall paintings continues in Gallery XV. In the description that follows the numbered frescoes begin on the side wall to the left. The four frescoes here date from the sixteenth century BC, and decorated chambers on the second floor of the west wing of the palace at Knossós. (1): A Sacred Grove, in which a group of men and women watch a religious ceremony. (2): A Tripartite Shrine, perhaps the one in the west wing of the palace at Knossós. (3–4): The Libation Fresco, in which the most prominent figure is the lady known as 'La Parisienne', a name given to her when she was first discovered in 1903. The remaining exhibits in the room are Minoan reliefs, while Case 173, in the centre, has fragmentary frescoes from Knossós and Týlissos. The most interesting object here is a representation (69) of the mythical labyrinth, a motif found at a much later date on the Greek coins of Knossós.

The exhibition of Minoan frescoes continues in Gallery XVI, beginning with the second panel to the left; this is (1): the Fresco of the Saffron-Gatherers. This fragmentary fresco, which is inaccurately reproduced in the panel to the left of this, (2), shows a blue monkey gathering saffron flowers and offering them to a female figure, a priestess or a goddess. This painting was originally found in the northwest part of the palace at Knossós, as were the following frescoes. (3): The 'Captain of the Blacks', a fragment of a group in which a running white warrior leads a group of blacks, perhaps mercenaries from Nubia. (4) The Dancer, from the Queen's Megaron at Knossós. (5) A Tricolumnar Shrine, in which the figure of the *labyrs* is shown on the columns. (6–8) Three fragmentary frescoes in which olive trees appear. (9–11): Three fragmentary paintings from the 'House of Frescoes' at Knossós, perhaps depicting the royal gardens, with (9) showing a bluebird among flowers, and (10–11) depicting monkeys searching for eggs in a floral setting. (12–13) two painted reliefs from houses on Pseíra. (14) Fresco of the Sacred Knot, from the megaron at Nírou Kháni. Finally, in the centre of the room Case 174 has several fragments of frescoes from Knossós, including the poorly preserved 'Palanquin Fresco', in which a priest is carried in a chair in some rite, and a fragment (34) showing a young woman about to leap over the horns of a bull.

The remaining four galleries of the museum, XVII–XX, are presently closed to the public due to lack of funds, and those who wish to see them should make enquiries at the museum offices. Gallery XVII contains the Giamelakis Collection, an extremely interesting exhibition of Minoan art; Gallery XVIII is devoted to Minoan art from the Archaic period to the late Roman era (7C BC–4C AD); Gallery XIX has exhibits from the Archaic period (650–500 BC); and Gallery XX has a collection of Graeco-Roman sculpture, ranging in date from the fifth century BC to the fourth century AD.

HISTORICAL AND ETHNOGRAPHICAL MUSEUM

One might now cross to the other side of Iráklion to visit the Historical and Ethnographical Museum, which brings the story of Crete from ancient times up to the modern era.

The collections of the Historical and Ethnographical Museum follow chronologically after those of the Archaeological Museum, with objects from the early Christian era, the two Byzantine periods, the Venetian and Ottoman periods, and some exhibits bringing the history of Crete up to modern times. The museum is housed in one of the few remaining Neoclassical mansions of Iráklion, built by the Krasakis family in 1835. During the last Cretan revolution against Ottoman rule, in 1897–8, a crowd of Christians took refuge here when pursued by a Turkish mob, who set the building on fire to drive them out, killing many Greeks in the process. The building was reconstructed in 1903 and at that time redecorated in the Neoclassical style; it was finally converted into a museum in 1952 by the Society of Cretan Historical Studies.

Across the street from the museum is a medieval monument that has survived from Venetian Candia. This is the Vrísi Idomenéa, the Fountain of Idomenaeus, which is mentioned by Kazantzakis in his novel *Freedom or Death*. The façade of the fountain has a pair of columns framing an arch surrounding the niche of the basin, a very attractive piece of sculpture that once adorned this part of Candia as well as supplying water to the neighbourhood, whereas now it is an almost forgotten relic of the Venetian past.

In the garden of the museum there are some reminders of Crete's martial past: four Venetian cannons and a pyramid of Venetian cannonballs standing side by side with unexploded bombs dropped on Iráklion by the Germans in May 1941. On entering, one sees the following objects displayed in the lobby of the museum, from left to right: a *firman*, or imperial directive, of Sultan Mahmut II (1808–39) appointing Callinichos as Archbishop and renewing the rights and privileges of the Cretan church under Ottoman rule; *baltas*, or battle axes, of the seven Turkish pashas who were killed during the Ottoman siege of Candia in 1648–69 (the suburb east of the walls where they died is still called the Quarter of the Seven Axes); breastplates, swords, and stirrups of the Venetian soldiers who defended Candia in that siege; a sword and rear-admiral's uniform worn by Prince George of Greece when he was High Commissioner of Crete.

The exhibit of the historical collection really begins on the ground floor, which is approached by going down the stairs at the end of the corridor. Room 1 is devoted to early Christian and Byzantine sculptures, principally architectural members and reliefs. Some of these are from the church of Áyios Títos in Górtyna, erected in the sixth century, an edifice that was the cathedral of Crete during the first Byzantine period. Room 2 has sculptures of the Venetian period.

Above the entrance to the room there is a Lion of St Mark from the fortress of Áyios Demétrios, which stood outside the walls of Candia just to the east of the town; this bears a Latin inscription proclaiming 'I protect the Kingdom of Crete'. Within the room there are a number of interesting tombstones and reliefs with medieval Venetian armorial bearings, as well as a fragment of the sculptured frieze that once adorned the Loggia in Candia, with representations of armaments of the period. On one wall of the room there has been re-erected a pretty Venetian street-fountain of the cascade type, dated c. 1600. There is also a sculptured panel from the gate of Áyios Yeórgios, with a relief representing St George. Room 2A has sculptures from the Venetian period, including a number of reliefs from churches in medieval Candia. Room 3 is devoted to inscriptions from the Venetian period, with a very interesting panel bearing the names of the Latin kings who ruled in Constantinople during the period 1204–61, after the Crusader capture of the Byzantine capital. Room 4 has sculptures dating from the Ottoman occupation, including a marvellous collection of tombstones inscribed with the names of high-ranking Turkish officials, the stones topped with representations of the turbans of the deceased, the different styles of headdress designating their rank and station. The room at the end of the corridor is designed as a small chapel in which are exhibited frescoes of the thirteenth and fourteenth centuries, taken from a Byzantine church near Kastélli-Pedhiádha, destroyed during World War II. The collection continues on the first floor of the museum in Room 5, which has more exhibits from the Byzantine era, as well as work done in the Byzantine tradition during the Venetian occupation. The post-Byzantine paintings of the Venetian era constitute one the great artistic heritages of Crete, and some of the finest icons of that period, which once hung in churches all over the Great Island, have now been brought to the museum for safekeeping; these include several from the monastery of the Panayía Gouverniótissa, near the village of Potamiés in Pedhiádha, dating from the sixteenth and seventeenth centuries. Room 7 has mementoes of Cretan revolutionary heroes and a flag of the Cretan state that existed during the first decade after the end of the Ottoman occupation and before *énosis* with the Greek nation. In the corridor there is the prow of a Venetian galley sunk during the Ottoman siege of Candia in 1669, as well as more prints and photos of Cretan heroes.

The second floor of the museum is devoted principally to the folklore collection of the museum. Room 11 has textiles, embroideries, folk costumes, jewellery and handicrafts, all of it Cretan work dating from the seventeenth to the nineteenth century. Room 8 has Cretan documents, books and maps dating from the tenth to the nineteenth century. Room 9 is devoted to the great Cretan writer Nikos Kazantzakis, with collections of his works and memorabilia of his life. Another room is devoted to Manoli Tsouderos, the Cretan who was Prime Minister of Greece at the time of the German invasion in 1941. This room also contains memorabilia of Eleftherios Venizelos, the great Cretan statesman. Room 10 is designed as the reconstructed interior of a Cretan house of the last century, a wonderful recreation of the gracious way in which ordinary islanders managed to live even in the very difficult years of the Ottoman occupation. In another part of the second floor there are exhibits concerned with the Battle of Crete in May 1941 and of the four years of German occupation that followed, including some harrowing photographs of the hell that the islanders endured during that period, fighting against the invaders with typical Cretan heroism despite the hopeless odds they faced. The most moving exhibit here is a photograph taken by a German soldier in the village of Perivólia, on the lower slopes of the White Mountains above Chaniá, a portrait of Manoli Katsanevas and his son just before they were executed by a firing squad, the expressions in their eyes a haunting evocation of what Crete has gone through in its long and heroic struggle for liberty.

4

KNOSSÓS

The high point of any trip to Crete is a visit to Knossós, where one sees the remains of the great palace discovered by Sir Arthur Evans and his associates during the early years of this century, an excavation that continues up to the present day. This is a cultural pilgrimage to the centre of ancient Minoan civilization, of which Homer wrote in Book XIX of the *Iliad*: '. . . there is Knossós, the great city, the place where Minos was king for nine-year periods, and conversed with great Zeus.'

According to tradition, these conversations were held so that Minos could obtain from Zeus, his divine father, the laws by which he governed his Cretan kingdom. Since Minos ruled at Knossós, that city would seem to have continued as the capital of Crete throughout the Postpalatial period. His two younger brothers, also sons of Zeus, were Rhadamanthys, who ruled over Phaestós, and Sarpedon, king of Mállia. Sarpedon contested for power with his eldest brother, but Minos emerged triumphant. After his defeat Sarpedon was forced to flee to Lycia, in south-western Anatolia, whose forces he led against the Achaeans during the Trojan War. Minos achieved his victory over Sarpedon through the intercession of Poseidon, to whom he after-wards prayed to send him a bull so that he could sacrifice it as an offering of thanksgiving to the sea god. When Poseidon answered his prayer, Minos so admired the bull from the sea that he decided to keep it for his own and sacrificed a lesser beast instead. Poseidon discovered what Minos had done, and as punishment he caused the king's wife, Pasiphae, to fall in love with the bull that he had sent from the sea. Pasiphae mated with the beast, and their offspring was a monster called the Minotaur, with a man's body and the head of a bull. King

Minos was so horrified by this that he had Daedalus, the greatest inventor in the ancient world, construct at Knossós a maze called the Labyrinth, in which the monstrous Minotaur was confined. At this point the mythology of Crete and Attica become intertwined in the person of Theseus, son of King Aegeus of Athens. Androgeos, a son of King Minos, had been murdered in Attica because of the jealousy he aroused in winning all of the contests at the Panathenaic Games. Because of this Minos made war against Athens and her ally Megara to take revenge. After Megara fell to the Cretans the Athenians were forced to sue for peace. Among the terms of the peace treaty was the provision that every nine years the Athenians would have to send to Crete a tribute of seven youths and seven maidens, whom King Minos would put into the Labyrinth to be devoured by the Minotaur. Theseus, son of King Aegeus, volunteered to be one of the sacrificial youths, for he intended to slay the Minotaur and free Athens from this frightful tribute. When Theseus led the other Athenian youths and maidens ashore on Crete he was observed by Ariadne, a daughter of Minos, who immediately fell in love with him. When the Athenians were put into the Labyrinth, Ariadne gave Theseus one end of a length of thread, and she held the spool while he and his companions were led into the maze. Theseus succeeded in killing the Minotaur and was able to follow the thread to lead his companions out of the Labyrinth to rejoin Ariadne, whereupon they all set sail for Attica. They stopped en route on the island of Naxos, where Theseus abandoned Ariadne while she slept, after which the Athenians continued their homeward journey. The still-sleeping Ariadne was discovered on Naxos by Dionysos, who was joined to her in a sacred marriage by the gods. Ariadne's bridal wreath was then set up amongst the stars, where it still illuminates the night sky as the constellation Corona Borealis. As Hesiod describes the happy ending of this myth in his Theogony: 'And golden-haired Dionysos took for his buxom wife brown-haired Ariadne, the daughter of Minos, and the son of Kronos made her deathless and unaging for him.'

According to Homer, the Cretan contingent that fought alongside the other Greek allies in the Trojan War was led by Idomeneus, a grandson of King Minos. Some idea of the importance of Crete at this time can be gained from the Homeric Catalogue of Ships that took part in the siege of Troy, in which Agamemnon commanded 100 vessels; Idomeneus and Diomedes, 80 each; Menelaus, 60; Achilles, 50; Ajax the Less, 40; Ajax, son of Telamon, and Odysseus, 12 each. The Cretan warriors who fought under the command of Idomeneus came from a number of towns in the central part of Crete, most notably Knossós, Phaestós and Górtyna. Idomeneus stood in a different relationship to Agamemnon than did most of the other leaders, in that he sailed to Troy as a voluntary ally of the Achaean king rather than as a vassal owing him feudal service. Idomeneus had long been a friend of Menelaus, Agamemnon treated him with great respect, and the Cretan king won renown as a warrior and wise counsellor during the siege of Troy. But, like other Greek leaders after the siege of Troy, Idomeneus found trouble when he returned home. According to one version of the myth, his wife Meda had committed adultery with a noble called Leucus, who then murdered her and made himself king of the realm that had formerly been ruled by Idomeneus. When Idomeneus returned to Crete he was unable to re-establish his rule and was driven from the island by Leucus, after which he went off into exile in southern Italy, where he died. Thus ended the dynasty of Minos, and although shrouded in myth, the epic story of Idomeneus is undoubtedly a folk memory of the collapse of the last Bronze Age kingdom on Crete, which fell at the time of the great Dorian invasions, c. 1100 BC.

Knossós is just 5km to the south-southwest of Heraklion, approached by the road that leaves Plateía Eleftherías along Leofóros Dimokratía. Romantics might be tempted to walk there from the town as Nikos Kazantzakis did on his own pilgrimage, of which he wrote in *Report to Greco*. But in recent years the area between Heraklion and Knossós has become very built-up and industrialized so that the walk is not a very pleasant one. It would be advisable to go by bus or taxi. Buses for Knossós depart frequently from the waterfront at the eastern end of the inner town, setting one down at the main gate of the archaeological site.

When we first entered the archaeological site at Knossós we thought we were well prepared for what we would see, for we had read several books about the great Minoan palace and about the excavations carried out there by Sir Arthur Evans, including his imaginative reconstruction of the palace buildings (he called it a 'reconstitution'), as well as his preservation of the surviving frescoes and their replacement by reproductions. Nevertheless, we were still overwhelmed by the extent and complexity of the site, as indeed was Evans himself when he began excavations in 1900, for the palace of Knossós is truly a labyrinth and one on a colossal scale, with an area of about 4.3 acres, the centre of a city that he estimated to have had a population of perhaps 80,000 people in the golden age of Minoan civilization. Most of the palace was built on several levels, the number of floors varying with the slope of the hill on which it stood, terracing down along the sides, sometimes reaching a height of four or even five floors. As Evans began to dig deeper he had to rebuild the upper floors as he went along, using the evidence of what he had found there in the way of structural members and guided by his evolving conception of the architectural plan and layout of the vast complex of rooms, corridors, stairways and courtyards. All of this slowly began to become clear to us as we walked around the site with a detailed archaeological map, remembering the model of the palace we had seen in the Iráklion Museum.

One approaches the site of the palace by a path that leads along the right side of what was once its West Court, whose ancient retaining wall is visible straight ahead. Just beside this path is one of the Minoan ramps that led to the western entrance to the palace, with a second ramp cutting diagonally across the West Court to the northwest corner of the complex and the so-called Theatrical Area. To the left of the path there are three large circular pits known in Greek as *koulourás*; these may have originally been intended as storage areas for grain, but when unearthed by Evans they were found to be full of potsherds and other debris. The pits have now been cleared and at their bottoms one can now see the remains of houses dating from before the foundation of what is called the Old Palace, structures dating from the period 2050–1900 BC. One now comes to the monumental façade of the New Palace, which still shows marks of blackening from the fire that destroyed Knossós c. 1400 BC, its flames fanned by a wind from the south. In front of this façade there are stone slabs that were part of the foundations of the Old Palace, an edifice destroyed around 1700 BC, with the New Palace afterwards erected on the same site, adding to the complexity of this vast labyrinth. To the left of the path here, between the slabs and the west façade, there is an altar base that probably marks the site of an older entrance to the palace. And on the right just before the end of the path are the West Entrance and Porch, the ceremonial entryway to the New Palace, where the king of Knossós or his representatives probably received guests and important visitors. Within the site of the west porch one can see the base of an enormous column and the outline of the two rooms that formed the vestibule here.

Here one turns right into the Corridor of the Processions, which led around the southwest corner of the palace. This was decorated with frescoes depicting the great processions that once passed along this

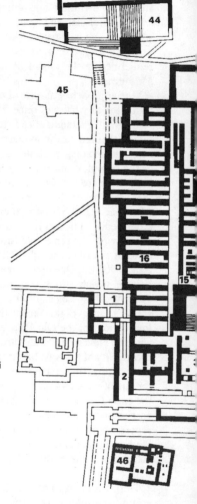

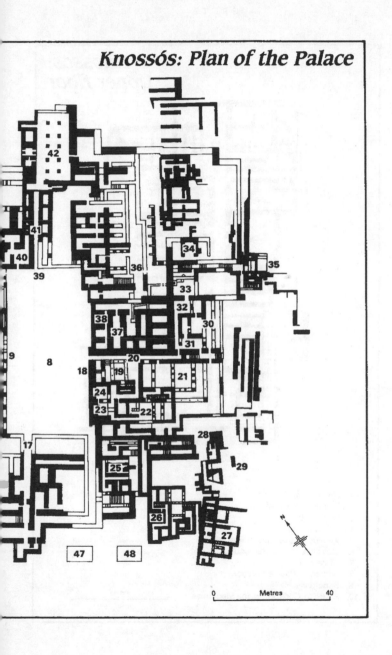

Knossós: Plan of the Palace

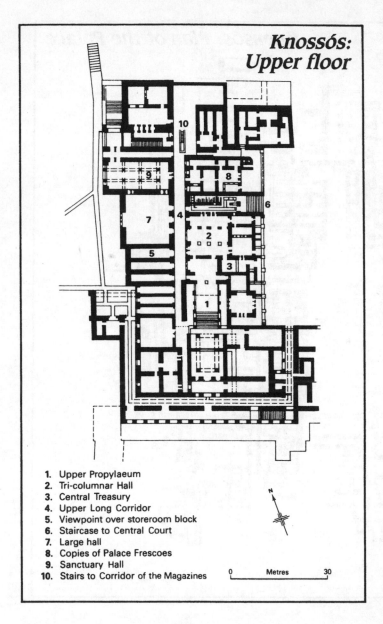

Knossós:
Upper floor

1. Upper Propylaeum
2. Tri-columnar Hall
3. Central Treasury
4. Upper Long Corridor
5. Viewpoint over storeroom block
6. Staircase to Central Court
7. Large hall
8. Copies of Palace Frescoes
9. Sanctuary Hall
10. Stairs to Corridor of the Magazines

N

0   Metres   30

corridor on their way from the West Entrance to the royal apartments, fragments of which paintings are now preserved in the Iráklion Museum. At the south-west corner of the complex this corridor turned left to pass somewhat less than halfway around the south side of the palace before turning left again to enter the Central Court. On the right wall of the last part of the corridor there is a reproduction of the Fresco of the Lily Prince in the same spot where the original was found, a painting that adorned the place where the great processions entered the centre of the inner palace, perhaps with the priest-king of Knossós leading the way as he is shown here in the fresco. On the top of the outer precinct wall at this point one sees a large restored model of the 'horns of consecration', comparable in size to the broken original found by Evans in the Theatral Area.

Halfway along the southern stretch of the Corridor of the Processions one sees on the left the South Propylaeum, the monumental entryway to the upper part of the palace on the western side of the Central Court, the area that Evans called the Piano Nobile. Passing through this entryway, one ascends a broad staircase that brings one to the Piano Nobile, where part of the upper section of the South Propylaeum has been restored. One is now on the fifth floor of the palace at this level, a good vantage point from which to look around and orient oneself, as we did, with the aid of a detailed plan of the archaeological site. Standing beside the restored upper part of the Propylaeum and looking north along the Piano Nobile, one can identify the following chambers on this uppermost level of the palace: just to the right is a small area identified as a Treasury; straight ahead is a Tricolumnar Shrine; just to the left a long corridor leads to the northern end of this floor; to the left of the corridor the first large area is the Great Hall, identified by the two column bases on its long axis; beyond that is the Sanctuary Hall, with six column bases marking the site of its colonnade; to the right of this there is an enclosed chamber that Evans reconstructed over the Throne Room complex, decorating it with reproductions of some of the frescoes now in the Iráklion Museum; beyond this, above the north-west corner of the Central Court, there is a loggia from which one has a good view over the inner palace below; and at the end of the corridor there is a stairway that leads down to the ground level. Before descending this stairway one might look down into the Corridor of Magazines, so named because of the series of long and narrow storage rooms that open off from its western side; one can still see within these chambers some of the huge *pithoi* that were used to store wine and olive oil.

One now descends to the Central Court, a large open area 58m long and 27m wide, around which the rooms of the inner palace cluster on all sides. This area coincides with the top of the hill on which the original settlement of Knossós was made at the end of the seventh millenium BC. The peak of the hill was levelled off when the first palace was built on this site c. 2000 BC, with the earlier settlements simply covered over by the builders at that time, to be unearthed nearly four millennia later by Evans.

One might now explore the West Wing of the palace, where most of the ceremonial chambers were located, with the domestic quarters across the way in the East Wing. The most historic part of the West Wing is the section that opens onto the Central Court near its northeastern side, just to the right of the broad staircase that once led up to the Stepped Portico on that side, for this contains the chamber identified by Schliemann as the Throne Room. One approaches this section through a polythronon with four doors that leads into the anteroom of the Throne Room, a chamber with a wooden throne at the centre of its north wall between gypsum benches. The throne in the anteroom is a wooden replica placed there by Evans on the evidence of a mass of carbonized wood he found at the spot when he excavated the chamber. The porphyry basin in the centre of the anteroom was found nearby, and it was placed in its present position because Evans thought that it originally stood there, perhaps filled with holy water for lustrations. Looking into the Throne Room from the inner doorway of the anteroom, one sees the famous 'Throne of Minos' in the centre of the north wall, flanked by gypsum benches that continue around the side walls. This perfectly preserved carved throne, which stands exactly where it was found, is also made of gypsum, but it is obviously a replica of a wooden prototype, perhaps an earlier throne that was destroyed in a fire. The walls of the throne room are decorated with replicas of the original frescoes representing confronted pairs of wingless griffins, based on fragments of the original paintings now in the Iráklion Museum. Opposite the throne on the south side of the room at a lower level approached by six steps is a 'Lustral Basin', which Evans in his notebook called 'Ariadne's Bath'. The Throne Room with its furnishings and frescoes dates to the period when the Mycenaeans dominated Knossós, and it is believed that it served as a sanctuary in some religious rite, in which a priestess rather than a king sat on the throne as the divine presence. West of the Throne Room is a suite of small rooms called the Inner Sanctuary, which may also have been used in this rite.

After seeing the Throne Room, one might explore some of the other rooms in the West Wing of the Palace, now looking at those south of the great stairway to the Stepped Portico. There one comes first to the Tripartite Sanctuary, from which one passes to the Lobby of the Stone Seat. To the right of this lobby are the Temple Repositories and the Room of the Tall Pithos, while the two rooms with central pillars beyond the lobby on its inner side are the Pillar Crypts. The rooms were used to store the most precious treasures of the palace and its shrines, and it was in the eastern repository that the two snake goddesses now in the Iráklion Museum were found, while in the Tripartite Sanctuary there was found a box with the first-known examples of the Linear B script.

One might now cross the Central Court to its eastern side, in the centre of which is the Great Staircase. This brings one down at the first landing to the Hall of the Royal Guard, and from there one descends to the Hall of the Colonnade, beyond which is the Hall of the Double Axes. It is believed that the Hall of the Double Axes is where the King of Knossós held court, for there is evidence that the royal throne once stood here, which means that this would have been the destination of the great procession depicted in some of the frescoes now in the Iráklion Museum. Penetrating deeper into the labyrinth on the south side of the East Wing one comes to the Queen's Megaron, which is decorated with a reproduction of the Dolphin Fresco now in the museum. The rooms just to the west of this contain the Queen's Boudoir and the Queen's Bath and Toilet, which was equipped with the flush-toilet whose remnants are displayed nearby, as well as a corridor known as the Court of the Distaff.

One can now go on to explore other quarters of the labyrinthine palace. One interesting room in the South-east Wing is the small enclosed Shrine of the Double Axes, apparently built after the destruction of the palaces c. 1400 BC, when Mycenaean kings were ruling in Knossós. North of the Grand Staircase in the East Wing one finds the following chambers: the Magazine with the Medallion Pithoi; the Corridor with the Bays; deep in behind these are the Treasury; the Eastern Portico; the Potter's Workshops; the Court of the Stone Spout; the Giant Pithoi; the Schoolroom, with its benches apparently for students, although some scholars say that this chamber was used by artisans; and the East Bastion. Evans suggested that the flat ground between here and the river below was the site of an arena where spectators sat to watch the bull-sports depicted in the frescoes now in the Iráklion Museum. At the northeast corner of the Central

Court is the Corridor of the Draughts Board, so called because the royal game-board now in the Heraklion Museum was found here. Here one can see the exposed drainpipes of the Old Palace beneath a metal grille. From the top of the stairs by the Corridor of the Draughts Board one can see a series of chambers which may have been palace workshops, and beyond these to the right was the Pottery Storehouse, while at the far right hand corner of the complex on that side is the North-east House. The section north of the Central Court contains storage magazines on the right side; to the left are the Stirrup Jars Room; and the North-west Portico; in the centre is a long and narrow ramp that leads to the Northern Entrance and the Great Pillared Hall, whose Propylaeum is on its western side. Off to the north-western side of the palace is the Theatral Area, so called because it has a paved courtyard at the foot of shallow steps or terraces, as well as a raised rectangle which might have been the base of a royal box. These arrangements have led to the suggestion that it was used for public ceremonies or displays, although one theory holds that it was a court of law; in any event, its situation makes it seem certain that the Theatral Area was also used as a place to receive distinguished guests, for it was the terminus of the royal road that led to the palace from the two seaports of Knossós on the north coast; these were Katsambá, near present-day Iráklion, and Amnisós, some distance to the east. The paved way that led off to the west from the Theatral Area has been called the 'First Road in Europe'. The road is remarkably well paved and drained, and for 130m it is lined on both sides with the remains of houses, workshops, and other structures, more evidence of the 'modernness' of Minoan civilization. One of the structures halfway along this road from the Theatral Area and on the right side was identified by Evans as the Armoury, for a large number of arrowheads was found there, along with an inventory of weapons. Across the way on the left side of the road was the 'House of Frescoes', which was decorated with the 'Bluebird Fresco' and the frescoes showing monkeys searching for eggs in a flower-garden, paintings now in the Iráklion Museum.

Those with time to spare might now want to explore the environs of the palace. However, a number of the interesting sites are locked up and permission to visit them can only be obtained by enquiring at the Archaeological Museum in Heraklion a day in advance.

One might begin by visiting the Little Palace; this is about 250m northwest of the main palace complex, and can be reached either by walking along the paved way from the Theatral Area or going back

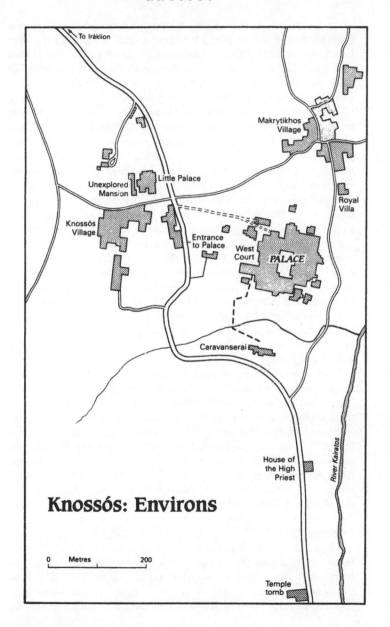

Knossós: Environs

0   Metres   200

along the main road from Knossós to Iráklion, leaving the road by a flight of steps to the left over a bank and a small bridge over the river Kairatos. The Little Palace is the largest of the villas and town houses that were built in the environs of the great palace of Knossós, all of them presumably used by royalty, aristocrats and wealthy business-men. Since the Little Palace was partially cut into the surrounding rock, its walls on that side have been preserved to a greater height than in the main palace itself in most cases. One and one-half flights of the main stairs are still standing, covered by a shed for protection, but the principal rooms have fallen away due to the slope of the ground, and what one sees today has largely been reconstructed. These main rooms are quite large, with the remains of the piers and columns of its colonnade still evident. The Little Palace consists of the main room, which was a double chamber, and a third room, the Hall of the Peristyle. Beyond the north half-room to its west is a lavatory, and to the east there is a small porch which was probably a verandah, with a view out over the valley. A smaller shed covers the eastern front of the north half-room; this is called the Fetish Shrine, and is thought to have been originally a bath that was converted into a sanctuary after the destruction of Knossós in 1400 BC. At the south end there are a number of pillared basements; in one of these at the southwest corner several cult objects were found that had fallen in from a sanctuary or treasury, including the famous bull's head rhyton now in the Iráklion Museum.

Two more of these Minoan mansions are still being excavated behind the Little Palace. The one on the south was called by Evans the 'Unexplored Mansion.' In the middle of the Unexplored Mansion there are the remains of a fine hall; this seems to have been destroyed c. 1400 BC, and then afterwards to have sheltered newcomers who quite literally moved in and made themselves at home among the ruins. In excavating the Little Palace, archaeologists had to remove accumu-lated material from as late as the 3C AD, representing seventeen centuries of occupation after the mansion was destroyed at the end of the Minoan period. Among the discoveries made by archaeologists during this excavation was the remains of a Roman house dated to the first century AD.

Three other sides of interest are to be found south of the palace; these can be approached by going back along the Iráklion-Knossós road, which turns to the left to go around beyond the south side of the complex, then turning left to go south again. About 100m after crossing a bridge over the Kairatos one takes a path leading left to a structure known as the Caravanserai, which is about 100m south of the palace. The Caravanserai is so called because Evans believed that it served as an inn to house travellers who came to Knossós from elsewhere in Crete or abroad. The main room of the Caravanserai, designed as a porch, was adorned with the Fresco of the Partridge now in the Iráklion Museum. In the room west of this a footpath leads to a Spring Chamber with a basin equipped with a bench or ledge around it; votive offerings found here indicate that this spot may have been used as a shrine for a time after c. 1100 BC.

Continuing along the road southward for another 250m brings one to the remains of what is called the House of the High Priest, and 200m farther south beyond that one finds the so-called Temple Tomb, an impressive burial place of the Neopalatial period.

One can now return past the Caravanserai and Spring-House to look at the remains of the Minoan aqueduct below the southwestern corner of the palace. Continuing towards the palace beyond that, one sees the remains of the Stepped Portico that formed the south-western extremity of the palace, and also the remnants of the South House above that.

One might now wander over to the area outside the south-eastern corner of the palace, where one can identify the remains of five great houses that stood there in Minoan times. These are: the House of the Sacrificial Oxen; the House of the Fallen Blocks; the House of the Chancel Screen; the South-east House; and the House of the Monolithic Pillars.

One might now take the path that leads around the eastern side of the palace towards the village of Makrytíkhos. About 150m beyond the northeast corner of the palace one finds the so-called Royal Villa, the last of the great Minoan mansions to be visited on this tour. Like the Little Palace, the Royal Villa was partly cut out of the surrounding rock. The situation of this villa, believed to have been in three storeys, must have been very pleasant, with gardens that stretched down to the stream below, perhaps planted with some of the flowers that one sees in several of the frescoes now exhibited in the Heráklion Museum.

When we had completed our tour of the archaeological site, we retired to a shady spot and had a picnic of bread, goat cheese, tomatoes and olives, washed down with a bottle of red Cretan wine. After we finished eating we opened a second bottle of wine and sipped that while we gazed at the ruins, talking about the history of Knossós in later times, for the consuming interest in Minoan culture has obscured the fact that this city existed for more than two thousand years after the final destruction of the great palace. During historical times Knossós continued to be one of the most important cities on Crete, vying for supremacy with Lýttos and Górtyna, with the latter city achieving dominance during the Roman period. During Graeco-Roman times Knossós minted coins with a representation of the maze that had by then been long established in Greek mythology as the Labyrinth. Then, after the conquest of Crete by the Saracens in AD 824, Knossós and the other cities of Crete were utterly destroyed, disappearing from sight until they were unearthed by archaeologists in the past century. Now all of the accumulated debris of more than three millennia have been cleared away by Sir Arthur Evans and his successors, and the splendid remains of the great palace of Knossós have been exposed to view, evoking visions of what this fabulous labyrinth was like in the golden age of Minoan civilization.

5

EXCURSIONS FROM IRÁKLION

Iráklion's central location makes it the ideal base from which to explore all of central Crete. The present chapter describes some of the places that can be visited on a day-trip from Iráklion, sometimes in just a few hours, in other cases taking the whole of the day. Other more distant sites that can be seen in day-long trips from Iráklion are described in the following chapters. A number of travel agencies in Iráklion offer excursions to all of these places in airconditioned buses, with tours of the important sites accompanied by English-speaking guides.

The most popular excursions from Iráklion are to the beaches east of the city. There are excellent beaches all along the coast from Iráklion to Mállia, but the closest to the city is at Amnisós, just 8km away, with buses leaving every half-hour in summer from the station on the waterfront. There are tavernas on the beach at Amnisós where one can have lunch, a very pleasant way to spend an afternoon after touring the archaeological site at Knossós or visiting the museum in Iráklion.

During Minoan times Amnisós was the principal port for Knossós, and archaeological excavations there have unearthed a villa and a shrine with a circular altar. (The archaeological site is signposted.) The villa at Amnisós was decorated with the Frescoes of the Lilies, now exhibited at the Archaeological Museum in Iráklion; these paintings, dated c. 1600 BC, are among the earliest frescoes discovered on Crete. Amnisós is mentioned by Homer in Book XIX of the *Odyssey* as one of the places where Odysseus stopped on his way home after the siege of Troy. As this visit by Odysseus is described in the superb translation by Richmond Lattimore:

He stopped at 'Amnisós', where there is a cave of Eileithyia
in difficult harbours, and barely had he escaped from the stormwind.
He went up to the town and asked for Idomeneus,
for he said he was his hereditary friend, and respected;
but it was now the tenth or the eleventh day since Idomeneus
had gone away with his curved ships for Ilion.

The Cave of Eileithyia, which is known locally as Neraidaspílios, or the Cavern of the Nymphs, is only about 2km from Amnisós, approached by the side road that leads inland to Elía and Váthia. This is one of the most ancient and important shrines in Crete, dating back to the Neolithic period, and votive offerings found within the cave indicate that it was dedicated to Eileithyia, the goddess of childbirth, who was worshipped there from at least 3000 BC through Graeco-Roman times and into the Christian era. Eileithyia, daughter of Zeus and Hera, was the protectress of women in childbirth, an attribute of the ancient fertility goddess. Eileithyia is renowned in Greek mythology for having assisted Leto when she gave birth to Apollo on the isle of Delos, the divine midwife having been summoned there by her mother Hera.

There are also places to swim along the coast west of Iráklion, the nearest being the suburban resort of Amoudára, where there are several luxury hotels. But one can find better and more secluded beaches farther west around the Bay of Linoperámata, which has some of the most beautiful coastal scenery in all of Crete. The Linoperámata coast has not yet been developed for tourism, so one must go there by taxi, asking the driver to return at some preappointed time.

The most picturesque site along this coast is Palaeócastro, the Old Castle, named for the ruined fortress that one sees brooding above the sea below the mountain village of Rodhiá. (The full name of the castle is Palaeócestro Rodhiás, to distinguish it from all the other old fortresses that one sees along the coasts of Crete.) Palaeócastro Rodhiás was originally built in 1206 by the Genoese adventurer Enrico Pescatore, Count of Malta, one of fourteen strongholds he erected on Crete at that time in an attempt to gain control of the island after Constantinople fell to the Latins in 1204. The fortress was captured by the Venetians in 1206, when the forces of the Serenissima defeated Count Pescatore and drove him from the island. The Venetians rebuilt the fortress during the last quarter of the sixteenth century, part of their preparations to defend the island against the Turks at that time. The Venetians finally abandoned the fortress during the last years of the Ottoman siege of Candia, 1648–69, whereupon the Turks occupied it. The fortress of Palaeócastro Rohdiás had little strategic importance during the Ottoman occupation and ultimately it was abandoned, falling into the ruined state one sees today. Though ruined, it is still a splendid and romantic sight, with a large sculptured Lion of St Mark still visible on its ramparts along with the coats-of-arms of several of its Venetian commanders. J. D. S. Pendlebury, in his magisterial work, *The Archaeology of Crete*, identifies Palaeócastro Rodhiás as the ancient Minoan site of Kyttaion.

A somewhat lengthier excursion from Iráklion takes one along the coast past Palaeócastro Rodhiás and then inland to the village of Fódhele, a distance of 28km. This gives one an opportunity to see more of the beautiful coast west of Iráklion, with good beaches at Ayía Pelayía and Kólpos Fódhele. The beach at Kólpos Fódhele was where the Turkish forces under the Grand Vezir Mehmet Köprülü landed in 1668, at the beginning of the last year of the siege of Candia, and soon afterwards a great battle took place there between the Ottoman and Venetian navies, with the latter emerging victorious.

The goal of this excursion is the pretty village of Fódhele, which in recent years has become famous as the birthplace of El Greco (1545–1614). There is some uncertainty as to the town in which El Greco was born, with some scholars holding that he was from Iráklion, for he studied there at St Catherine's School. But most authorities now agree that he was probably born in Fódhele. The great artist, who was known in Europe as El Greco, the Greek, signed his paintings as Domeníko Theotokopoulos, Cretan, and a variant form of his family name still survives in Fódhele. El Greco is now honoured in Fódhele with a monument erected in 1934 by the students and faculty of the University of Valladolid; the memorial is made from stone quarried in Toledo and includes a fine bust of the artist and an inscription honouring him in both Greek and Spanish.

From Fódhele one can make a further excursion out to the convent of Savathianá, a hike of about an hour. For those with time to spare the excursion is well worth the time and effort, for the scenery en route and the setting of the convent are superb.

A much longer excursion takes one to the Idhaean Cave on Psilorítis, one of the legendary birthplaces of Zeus. Starting out on the highway westward from Iráklion, at 10km from the town the route turns left onto the road for Týlissos, Goniés and Anóyia, bringing one into a fertile valley with vineyards and olive groves. The first stop on this excursion is at Týlissos, 13km from Iráklion. The village of

Týlissos stands on the ruins of the ancient Greek town of the same name, which in turn was built on the site of Minoan Týlissos. The site was excavated in 1902–13 by the Greek archaeologist J. Khatzidakis, who unearthed the remains of three Minoan villas, as well as numerous other antiquities, now on exhibit in the Iráklion Archaeological Museum. The Minoan villas now visible at Týlissos, principally the three villas, date mostly from the period 1600–1450 BC.

The excursion continues westward through the pleasant countryside of Malevísi, the province just to the west of Iráklion, with the great massif of Psilorítis looming magnificently to the south, dominating the landscape. Seven km beyond Týlissos one sees to the left of the road a Minoan site known as Sklavókampos, the Camp of the Slavs, taking its name from the long and narrow valley here. This name perpetuates a resettlement of Slavs here by the Emperor Nicephorus Phocas (963–69), one of a number of such place names on Crete. The Minoan site at Sklavókampos was discovered in 1930 when the road to Anóyia was being built, and just prior to World War II it was excavated by Spyridon Marinatos. Marinatos identified the ruins at Sklavókampos as those of a palace of the late Minoan period, dated c. 1500 BC. Twenty rooms of the palace have been identified, and there are indications that it stood in the centre of a Minoan settlement, all of which was destroyed by an intense fire in the Late Minoan period and never again rebuilt.

Five km farther along, the road passes the village of Goniés, and then 10km farther along it comes to Anóyia. Anóyia is one of the most renowned villages on Crete, preserving a heritage of folklore and folkways unsurpassed by any other community on the Great Island. During World War II Anóyia was a centre of the Cretan resistance movement, and in retaliation the Germans burned it to the ground and executed all of the villagers who had not fled to the mountains. Anóyia was completely rebuilt after the war by the surviving villagers, and it is now flourishing once again, its cottage industry of weaving revived and its people profiting from the many tourists who come to the village to see its old-fashioned Cretan way of life. One old edifice that survived the German destruction in World War II is the village church, dedicated to St John the Baptist, which has some notable frescoes.

A road leading southward from Anóyia leads up to the Nídha plateau, a beautiful highland pasture ringed round with the peaks and ridges of Psilorítis. After a drive of some 20km the road comes to an end at the tourist pavilion, from whence one can walk up to the Idhaean Cave in about twenty minutes. The entrance to the cave, which is high above the western rim of the Nídha plateau at an altitude of 1450 metres, was discovered by a shepherd in 1884, and has since been excavated by archaeologists. The cave has been identified by some scholars as the mythical birthplace of Zeus, son of Kronos and Rhea, the ancient fertility goddess. According to mythology, Rhea was terrified that Kronos would devour her newly born son as he had their previous children, so she delivered him in the bowels of this great cavern, the young warriors known as the *Kuretes* dancing around them and shouting out as they beat their shields together like cymbals, thus drowning out the crying of the infant god so that he would not be destroyed by his father. Afterwards Rhea presented Kronos with a stone wrapped in swaddling clothes, which he swallowed believing that it was her baby, a strategem that spared Zeus from being devoured by his father.

Above the mouth of the cave, which is 9 metres high and 27 metres wide, there is a Roman inscription identifying this as a sanctuary of Idhaean Zeus. On the south side of the cave mouth there is a large rock fashioned into an altar, and below this are the foundations of a house used by the custodian of the sanctuary in Roman times. Within the cave a labyrinthian passage leads to the main cavern, which measures 35 by 40 metres on the ground level and has a maximum height of 60 metres. This cathedral-like space was the *cella* of the cave-sanctuary, while a recently discovered grotto beyond it was apparently used as an inner sanctuary for initiation rites in a secret cult of Idhaean Zeus. Excavations in the cave have unearthed objects dating back to the ninth century BC, and the findings indicate that it was used as a sanctuary of Idhaean Zeus up until the imperial Roman era, a full thousand years during which it was one of the most important places of worship on the Great Island. The most interesting objects found in the cave are votive objects in the form of bronze shields, one of which is on exhibit in the Iráklion Museum. These were meant to symbolize the clashing shields of the *Kuretes*, a ceremony which would have been re-enacted here in rites celebrating the birth of the god who came to rule over the Greek pantheon.

One can also use Anóyia as a base for climbing Psilorítis, in which case one should consult the Greek Mountaineering Club in Iráklion for information.

Another and more popular base for climbing Psilorítis is Kamáres, a village 56km from Iráklion at the southern foot of Mount Ídha. This is also the best base for visiting the famous Cave of Kamáres, a three-hour hike from the village. (A guide is essential.) The cave is below the double peak of Sélla tou Digení, the Saddle of Digenes, which is at an altitude of 1524 metres. Excavations of the cave in 1896 unearthed polychrome Minoan pottery dated c. 2000 BC, a style that subsequently came to be known as Kamáres ware; these vessels were apparently votive offerings from the rulers of Phaestós to the goddess Eileíthyia, who was worshipped in a cave-sanctuary there. The excavations also indicated that the cave was inhabited in Neolithic times.

A popular excursion south from Iráklion is to Archánes, 13km by road from the city. This is actually a pair of villages, Káto (Lower) and Epáno (Upper), with the latter more simply called Archánes. Káto Archánes is first mentioned in a Venetian document of 1271, along with a nearby community of Asómatos, of which there now survives only a church with frescoes, dated by an inscription to 1315. The church of Ayía Triádha in Archánes also has frescoes dating to the early fourteenth century, while the church of the Panayía has a number of Byzantine icons.

The village of Archánes stands on the site of ancient Archana, and a number of Minoan remains have been found in its vicinity. The first systematic investigation of these antiquities began in 1964 under the direction of Ioannis and Efi Sakallarakis, who in the immediate vicinity of Archánes unearthed the remains of a Minoan palace from c. 1600 BC, now believed to have been a summer residence of the kings of Knossós. On the nearby hill of Phourní, at a place called Anemóspilia, or 'Caves of the Winds,' they discovered a complex of Minoan structures and tombs ranging in date from 2500–1250 BC. The most fascinating of these structures, a temple dating to c. 1700 BC, contained human skeletons in circumstances suggesting that the deceased were sacrificial victims in some Minoan rite, the first evidence of human sacrifice ever found on Crete.

One can continue this excursion to the site of Vathýpetro, a site some 5km beyond Archánes, where Spyridon Marinatos has discovered a Minoan villa of the sixteenth century BC. The ruins are in a superb site with an extensive panorama of the countryside to the south and west, as well as of Mount Ioúktas, the legendary burial place of Zeus.

The best approach to Mount Ioúktas is a turn-off from the Archánes-Vathýpetro road, which in 3km brings one to a dirt road leading to the peak. The peak when seen from certain points looks like the head of a recumbent old man, which is undoubtedly the origin of the legend that Zeus lies buried here. The legendary burial place of Zeus is variously located in one or another of two caves on the peak, and those wishing to see the grottos should engage a guide, otherwise one can simply enjoy the superb view from the peak, which is the most distinctive landmark in the countryside south of Iráklion. There is a modern Greek chapel on the peak dedicated to the Metamorphoses, the Transfiguration of Christ, and a *paniyíri* is held here every year on 6 August, a festival that attracts people from all over the surrounding region. This is undoubtedly the survival of an ancient festival of Zeus, and the chapel itself stands on the site of a Minoan peak-sanctuary, of which some archaeological evidence has been found.

Another excursion south of Iráklion is to the village of Profitís Ilías, better known by its former name of Kanlí Kastélli, which is 19km south of the city. This village dates back to the early Venetian period, when it was called the Burgo, its inhabitants being the *villani*, the serfs who cultivated the estates of the nobility in Candia. It was also used as a refuge by the people of Candia in times of siege, for its situation made it a natural fortress. The former Turkish name of the village, Kanlí Kastélli, means Bloody Castle, stemming from the Turkish siege of 1647, when there was great loss of life on both sides. Kanlí Kastélli was also besieged by the Turks in the revolution of 1897, when a local force of 100 men and 200 women, with only 40 rifles between them, held out for five hours against a Turkish army of 4000.

South-east of the village there is a rocky promontory 507 metres high known by its old Venetian name of Rocca, which was known in Byzantine times as Témenos, a name that is still applied to the surrounding district. Témenos was a fortress built by Niphorus Phocas after his capture of Khándaks from the Saracens in 961, two years before he came to the throne as Nicephorus II. Nicephorus originally attempted to resettle the entire population of Khándaks in Témenos because of its more easily defended position. But after a few years the townspeople moved back to Khándaks and fortified the port there, after which Témenos was inhabited only by a Byzantine garrison. The fortress was later taken over by the Venetians, who renamed it Rocca, the Rock, but by 1575 it was abandoned and in ruins. The defence-walls of the fortress are still standing to some extent, along with the ruins of five churches, some of them dating from the time of Nicephorus Phocas. Archaeological excavations have revealed that the acropolis rock was inhabited as early as the period known as Early Minoan II, c. 2400–2100 BC, with other finds dating from early in the first millennium BC. The acropolis is believed to be the site of ancient Lýkastos, one of the Cretan cities that sent contingents to fight in Agamemnon's army at the siege of Troy.

Another and somewhat longer excursion into the countryside south of Iráklion brings one to the monastery of the Spiliótissa, which is 21km from the city by road, and then to the Monastery of Áyios Yórgios Apanossífis, which is 31km distant. The Spiliótissa, Our Lady of the Cave, is one of a number of churches and monasteries in Greece founded on the site of cave-sanctuaries of the ancient fertility goddess, who on Crete is usually identified with Eileithyia. The Monastery of the Spiliótissa celebrates its *paniyíri* on 15 August, the great festival of the Blessed Virgin, which attracts people from all over the surrounding area. The Monastery of Apanossífis celebrates two *paniyíria*, the first on 23 April, the feast-day of St George, and the second on 3 November. The Apanossífis was founded c. 1600 and became one of the richest and most influential monasteries on Crete, serving as an intellectual centre for the education of monks throughout the island. During the 1821 revolution the Turks attacked the monastery and killed 18 monks there, but the surviving monks made Apanossífis a centre of resistance and several assemblies of the leading members of the Cretan independence movement took place there. This led the Turks to destroy Apanossífis during the revolution of 1856 and seize all of its valuables, but the monastery was later rebuilt and still has a rich collection of liturgical vessels, vestments and other treasures.

Two more monasteries can be seen on a longer excursion of about 47km by road to the southwest of Iráklion; these are Vrondísi and Valsamónero, both of which are at the southern foot of Psilorítis along the central part of its southern slope. The monasteries are approached via Ayía Varvára, a village on the road from Iráklion to Phaestós, and on the drive westward from there one has in view to the north the beautiful Roufá Forest on the slopes of Psilorítis.

The Vrondísi monastery, which is near Zarós, stands in a magnificent location on the southern slopes of Psilorítis. The monastery was founded c. 1400, with one aisle of its church, the oldest, dedicated to Áyios Antónios, and the other, a more recent addition, dedicated to the Apostle Thomas. There are still some fragmentary frescoes of the early fifteenth century in the oldest part of the church, along with some fine woodcarvings of that period. At the entrance to the monastery there is an ornate fountain with sculptures in relief depicting Biblical scenes, a work dating to the fifteenth century. The Vrondísi monastery was renowned during the Venetian period as a cultural centre, its community of monks active in teaching, writing works of literature and theology, copying manuscripts and painting icons. There was also a famous school of painting here in Venetian times, and tradition holds that El Greco studied at the monastery under the tutelage of Michael Damaskinos. The monastery served as a place of refuge during the revolution of 1866, and when the Turks attacked it they burned the church and ten monastic cells, killing four of the monks. Most of the books and manuscripts in the library had already been destroyed in the manufacture of cartridges for the rebels.

The monastery of Valsamónero, which is near the village of Vorízia, is now abandoned, with only its church still surviving. The northern aisle of the church is dedicated to the Virgin Mary, the southern one to St John the Baptist, and the transverse rear aisle to Áyios Phanoúrios, to whom the monastery itself was dedicated. Apparently the oldest part of the church is the north aisle, which appears to date to the early Venetian period, with inscriptions bearing the dates 1332 and 1404. An inscription in the southern aisle bears the date 1400–28, while the transverse aisle is dated 1400, with another inscription in the latter recording that the frescoes there were done in 1431 by the Cretan painter Constantine Ricos. These frescoes have survived, along with those in the northern and southern aisles and in the narthex, with the painting there also by Ricos. It is sometimes said that some of the frescoes are by Michael Damaskinos and El Greco, but there is no evidence for these attributions. Nevertheless, the surviving frescoes in the Valsamónero monastery constitute one of the finest heritages of the Cretan renaissance, all of them restored by the painter Kanakis in a recent reconstruction of the church. The church also possesses two notable icons, one of them depicting Christ and the other Áyios Phanoúrios – the latter being the work of the Cretan painter Angelos and dated 1600. Another icon by Angelos is now preserved in the Vrondísi monastery, which has always had close links with the monastery of Valsamónero.

A pleasant excursion to the south of Iráklion brings one to the large village of Áyios Mýron, the capital of Malevísi province, a distance of 18km from the city by road. The district around Áyios Mýron is famous for its sultana raisins and for its sweet Malevísi wine. The present name of the village appears in Venetian records as early as 1281. In antiquity it was known as Ravkos, an important city that at times was an ally of Górtyna against Knossós and Lýkastos, though it was destroyed by the Gortynaeans in 166 BC. Early in the Byzantine era Ravkos was renamed for Áyios Mýron, the miracle-working saint who was born here and later became one of the first bishops of

Knossós, dying a martyr's death during the persecution of Christians by the Emperor Decius (249–51 BC). The most spectacular miracle attributed to Áyios Mýron was his slaying of a dragon, in Greek *drákos*, who had been devouring his parishioners. After the saint killed the dragon he threw a stone at it, whereupon an avalanche was unleashed that buried the monster. This miracle occurred outside the church of Christós Sotíras, which is still standing near the village, and nearby there is a huge rock called Drákos that is said to rumble and foam in late autumn if a hard winter is coming, in which case the old people say that 'The Dragon is roaring'.

One can continue this excursion by driving 5km farther along to the village of Káto Asítes, from where one can climb up to the monastery of Áyios Yórgios Gorgolaíni, one of the most beautiful on Crete. The monastery is shaded by two venerable trees, a plane and a cypress, said to be the two tallest of their kind on Crete, and in its courtyard there is an old fountain in which water has been flowing since Venetian times. There are also two monuments in the courtyard, one of them a Venetian lion with an inscription recording the date 1617, and the other a memorial to the Cretan hero Mastrakhas, who was killed here in a battle against the Turks in 1866, one of several nineteenth-century revolts in which the monastery played an important part.

One can then drive a short distance to the north of Káto Asítes to see the pretty hamlet of Sárchos. In the vicinity of Sárchos there is a large cave that served as a refuge for the people of the surrounding region during the revolution of 1866. There they endured a long siege by the Turks without surrendering.

After seeing Sárchos and its cave one can drive on a short way farther to Kroussónas, a mountain village renowned for its weaving. Then from Kroussónas one can climb up to the convent of Ayía Eiréne, one of the most prominent landmarks in Malevísi, perched on the eastern slope of Psilorítis at an altitude of 700 metres.

An excursion to the south-east of Iráklion takes one to Kastélli-Pedhiádos, 35km from the city. En route, at 18km from Iráklion, the road goes through Pezá, a local agricultural centre famous for its *rozaká* grapes. Then at Ayiés Paraskiés the route turns east and afterwards south as far as Vóni. The church of Ayía Marína in Vóni is a shrine famous for its miraculous cures, and on the *paniyíri* of the saint, which is celebrated on 17 July, pilgrims flock here from all over Greece. The route then goes on to Thrapsanó, a village noted for its ceramic ware. Continuing on, the road passes Evangelismós and Sklaverokhóri, the Village of the Slavs. Sklaverokhóri is another village whose name perpetuates a resettlement of Slavs in this region by the Emperor Nicephorus Phocas II, although these people may actually have been Armenians who had been in earlier times moved from eastern Anatolia to the Balkans by the Byzantines. Sklaverokhóri is mentioned in Venetian records as early as 1279, and in the local church, dedicated to the Presentation of the Virgin, there is an inscription dated 1481. The church is adorned with well preserved frescoes of the fifteenth and sixteenth centuries. One of these paintings depicts St Francis of Assisi, a clear indicator of western European influence on the art of the Cretan renaissance.

The route finally brings one to Kastélli-Pedhiádhos. This is the principal town of the picturesque region known as the Pedhiádha, with the first name of the community stemming from the fact that it was built on the site of a medieval castle. The eponymous castle, now vanished, was probably one of the fourteen fortresses built in 1206 by Count Enrico Pescatore. During the revolution of 1867 the Turkish general Omer Pasha had his headquarters here.

There are several further excursions that one can take from Kastélli-Pedhiádhos. The most interesting of these leads one 3km eastward along the main road to Xidhás, a village at the northwestern foot of Mount Dhíkti. There are two Byzantine churches in Xidhás, Áyios Nikólaos and Áyios Yórgios, the latter adorned with notable frescoes. Above the village, on the hill known as Argaíon, are the ruins of Lýttos, which was one of the most important cities in Crete from the Archaic period until the end of antiquity. Polybius writes that Lýttos was the most ancient city in Crete, which should be interpreted to mean that it was the oldest of the Dorian colonies founded on the Great Island. However, the origins of Lýttos are far older than the Lacedaemonian migration to Crete, for there are numerous references to it in Greek mythology and in the earliest Greek literature. According to one myth, when Rhea became pregnant with Zeus she was sent to Lýttos by her parents, Ouranos and Geia, who hoped that in this remote place she could give birth to her child safe from Kronos. Lýttos is also mentioned by Homer, listed in the *Iliad* as one of the Cretan cities that sent troops to fight in Agamemnon's army at the siege of Troy. According to tradition, Lycurgos the Law-giver lived in Lýttos when he was studying the constitutions of the Cretan city-states, which were a model of their kind in ancient Greece. During historic times Lýttos often dominated the whole of eastern Crete as far as the Gulf of Merabéllo, its principal rivals being Knossós and Górtyna. In 220 BC Knossós and Górtyna entered into an alliance and conquered Lýttos, destroying the city and dispersing its surviving populace. But the Lyttians eventually returned to the site and rebuilt their city, though Lýttos never again achieved its former dominance. A second excursion from Kastélli-Pedhiádhos brings one 2km north to the village of Pigí, formerly known as Bitzarianó. The present name of the village means 'spring', stemming from an ancient water-source that is now enclosed within the old church of Áyios Pandeleímon. The site of Áyios Pandeleímon was occupied from antiquity up through the medieval Byzantine period. The first church was erected over the sacred spring in the tenth century, and included architectural members from older edifices in its structure. The present church of Áyios Pandeleímon has some interesting icons and frescoes, with the latter said to be the oldest extant Christian wall paintings in Crete.

Another short excursion from Kastélli-Pedhiádhos brings one south for 2km to Lilianón. The village church in Lilianón is a two-aisled basilica dating to c. AD 1200, although the Ionic capitals that support its pointed arches undoubtedly were taken from some more ancient structure in the vicinity.

When returning from Kastélli-Pedhiádhos to Iráklion one might take the road leading westward via Apóstoli to Ayiés Paraskiés; in that case one can make a very short detour to the village of Sabás to visit the Monastery of Agárathos. This is one of the oldest monasteries in Crete, mentioned in manuscripts dated 1532 and 1559, the latter in the British Museum. According to tradition, the monastery takes its name from the fact that its sacred icon, depicting the Assumption of the Blessed Virgin, was originally found under an agarathia plant, and later the monastery and its church were built on the site. The Monastery of Agárathos was a great centre of learning during the Venetian period, with its most distinguished alumnus being the Patriarch Cyril Lucaris. The monastery was a centre of resistance during the Ottoman invasion of Crete and in 1646 its abbot, Athanasios Christophorus, organized an armed band of Cretans and killed a large number of Turks, whom he beheaded, fashioning their skulls into a triumphal arch for the Venetian general.

One particularly pleasant and interesting excursion from Iráklion is to Lasíthi, the surpassingly lovely plateau on Mount Dhíkti, known in travel brochures as the Valley of the Windmills. A number of other sites can also be seen on this excursion, which is usually climaxed by a visit to the Dikthían Cave, one of the mythical birthplaces of Zeus.

This excursion leads eastward from Iráklion along the new coastal highway as far as a turnoff at the 22km mark, where a signpost directs one on a road to the right for Lasíthi. This leads one southward into the Langádha valley through olive groves and carob trees, passing the ruins of a Roman aqueduct which once carried water from springs in Lýttos to its port of Limín Khersonísou. After passing on the right the road to Kastélli-Pedhiádhos, the road turns south-east and runs along the right bank of the Aposelémis river, through colonnades of oleanders, planes and orange trees. At the approaches to the village of Potamiés, 33km from Iráklion, one sees on the left the abandoned monastery of the Panayía Gouverniótissa, standing in a grove of olive trees, cypresses and locust trees. The Gouverniótissa is one of the oldest monasteries on Crete, founded by an unknown Byzantine emperor soon after the reconquest of the Great Island by Nicephorus Phocas in 961, at which time the twin villages of Apáno and Káto Potamiés were built. The walls of the monastic church are covered with frescoes of the fourteenth century, but some of these were damaged when the monastery was used to house Italian prisoners-of-war toward the end of World War II. The church was also adorned with icons dating from the sixteenth and seventeenth centuries, but these have now been removed and are on exhibit in the Historical Museum in Iráklion. Copies of the frescoes are also exhibited in the Basilica of San Marco in Iráklion.

Within the village of Potamiés one can also see the Byzantine church of Christos. This dates from the early Venetian period and is decorated with frescoes of the fourteenth to fifteenth century.

Continuing, one comes next to the village of Avdhoú, 38km from Iráklion. Avdhoú is first mentioned in Venetian records of 1583, and it has four churches of the fourteenth to fifteenth century, all of them adorned with frescoes of that period; these are dedicated, respectively, to the Annunciation, Áyios Antónios, Áyios Yórgios, which is in the cemetery, and Áyios Constantínos, which is one kilometre to the south-west of the village. The latter church bears an inscription recording that its frescoes were done in 1445 by the brothers Manuel and John Fokas, who may also have done the frescoes in Áyios Yórgios. Some of the frescoes from Áyios Antónios are now on exhibit in the Basilica of Áyios Márkos in Iráklion. There are also two caverns in the vicinity of Avdhoú; one of these is the Cave of Ayía Fotiní, and the other is the Cave of Phaneroméni, in which Spyridon Marinatos has discovered objects dating to the Archaic period.

After passing the village of Goniés, 40km from Iráklion, the road begins winding uphill towards the Lasíthi *plátanos*. Six kilometres farther along it passes the village of Krási, where a gigantic plane tree, said to be the oldest and largest tree on Crete, casts its immense shade over a fountain with a gushing spring, making this a very pleasant place to pause before setting out on the final stage of the ascent to the Lasíthi plateau.

Three kilometres farther along, the road approaches the village of Kerá. Before entering the village one should drive down to visit the monastery of the Panayía Kerá, also known as the Kardiótissa, Our Lady of the Heart. The Kardiótissa is believed to date from the early Venetian period, and frescoes of the fourteenth century have recently been uncovered on its walls. The church was renowned for a miracle-working icon of the Virgin, which was thrice taken away to Constantinople and returned to Kerá of its own accord. According to local legend, the icon was then chained to the column that still stands in the church courtyard. Nevertheless, the icon was taken away to Rome in 1498, and it remains there to this day in the church of San Alphonso, venerated by Roman Catholics all over the world as Our Lady of Perpetual Help. The monastery of the Kardiótissa at Kerá still celebrates the *paniyíri* of the Virgin on 8 September, a local festival that goes back to Venetian days.

After passing through Kerá, the road continues to wind uphill toward the Lasíthi plateau. Just beyond Kerá one can see a spire-like peak jutting up to the east of the road; this is Karphí, which in Greek means the 'Nail', with its summit some 1150 metres above sea level. Arthur Evans discovered an ancient site on the peak of Karphí in 1896, and John Pendlebury excavated there just before World War II, unearthing a sanctuary and tombs dating to the post-Minoan era. Pendlebury's findings indicate that after the collapse of Minoan civilization the inhabitants of the inland cities fled to mountaintop eyries like Karphí, where they could better defend themselves against the invaders who seem to have overrun Crete at that time.

The road continues to climb until it reaches the pass at Séli Ambélou, at an altitude of 900 metres, where a line of windmills stands on the northern edge of the plateau. One might pause here at the roadside tavern to enjoy the magnificent view, for on a clear day one can see out over the northern coast of Crete and across the Aegean as far as the volcanic isle of Santoríni, the southernmost of the Cyclades. After passing Séli Ambélou, the road emerges onto the northern side of the Lasíthi plateau, one of the loveliest sights in all of Crete, particularly when the myriads of windmills are working on a breezy day, their spinning white sails animating the chequerboard of

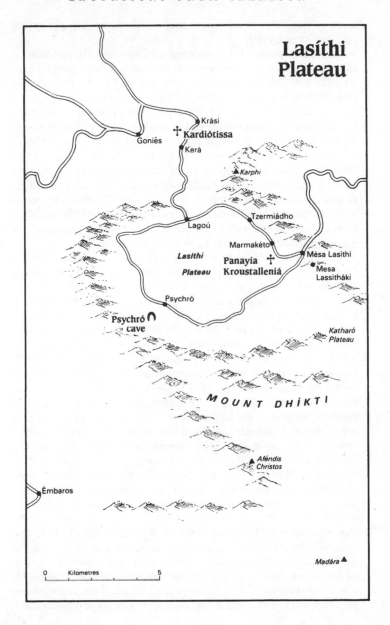

Lasíthi Plateau

Krási
† Kardiótissa
Goniés
Kerá

▲ Karphi

Tzermiádho
Lagoú

Marmakéto
Lasíthi   Panayía †   Mésa Lasithi
Plateau   Kroustalleniá   Mesa
Lassitháki

Psychró

Psychró ∩
cave

Katharó
Plateau

MOUNT DHÍKTI

Aféndis
▲ Christos

Émbaros

Madára ▲

0   Kilometres   5

green and amber farmland ringed round with the turquoise mountain wall of Mount Dhíkti.

The Lasíthi plateau is an enormous basin set into Mount Dhíkti at an average elevation of 866 metres, measuring 12km along its east-west axis and 6km from north to south. The plateau is surrounded by some of the highest peaks of Mount Dhíkti, whose rugged crags give it the appearance of an ancient and long-extinct volcano, with Seléna (1559m) to the north; on the west Louloudháki (1163m); to the south-west Sarakinó (1588m); to the south Toúmba Moútsounas (1538m), Aféndis Christós (2141m), and Madára (2148m), the highest Dhikthian peak. These peaks and their connecting ridges create a great mountain barrier between Lasíthi and the lowlands beneath the plateau, with only nine entrances: Ampélos and Tsoúli Mníma to the west, to the south Klóros and Aléxana; to the east Alóidha, Toú Patéra, and Ta Seliá; and to the north Giofíryia and Asfendámi, the pass by which the road from Kerá enters the plain.

Excavations made in 1936 by John Pendlebury indicate that the Lasíthi plain was densely populated in antiquity, with the earliest remains dating to the end of the Neolithic period, c. 5000 BC. The oldest inhabited site is the Cave of Trápeza on the Kastélo hill at the northern side of the plateau, where the earliest Neolithic tombs were discovered, of particularly great interest because they are miniature replicas of the houses of that period, the earliest dwellings on Crete. The site appears to have been used continuously up to the Middle Minoan I period, c. 1950–1850 BC, by which time the houses there had been converted into tombs and the cave itself set apart as a hallowed shrine, soon to be surpassed in importance by the great cave at Psychró, revered as the birthplace of Zeus. Lasíthi appears to have been inhabited continuously from the end of the Neolithic period onward, with the cave-dwellers emerging from the Trápeza and Psychró caverns to establish a new settlement on the plateau itself in the Middle Minoan II period (1750–1550 BC). This site has been identified at Papoura, north-west of Lagoú, the second village that the present excursion passes on its way around the plateau. The settlement at Papoura continued in existence throughout the remainder of the Minoan era and on through the Dark Ages that followed; then it actually increased in population so that during the Archaic period, 650–490 BC, it is believed to have been the fourth-largest city on Crete, identified by one authority as Eranos. The people who dwelt there are believed to have been the ancestors of the present population of Lasíthi, whose roots probably go back to Minoan days, comparable in antiquity with those of the Sfakians, those who dwell on the White Mountains.

During the Venetian period Lasíthi was a centre for revolutionary activity against Venetian rule, with a number of rebellions starting there. The Venetians put down these revolts savagely, and in 1263 they executed all of the rebels and destroyed the villages of Lasíthi, cutting down the orchards there and issuing an edict forbidding anyone to farm or graze their flocks on the plateau under pain of dismemberment or death. This cruel and insane policy was enforced for two hundred years, until in 1463 a shortage of grain forced the Venetians to allow the cultivation of Lasíthi once again, and by the second half of the sixteenth century new villages had arisen on the plateau, among them Tzermiádho. Lasíthi once again became a revolutionary centre in the nineteenth century, this time against Ottoman rule, with Turkish armies ravaging the plateau in 1823 and again in 1866. The people of Lasíthi suffered once again during World War II, when the Germans destroyed numerous villages on Crete and executed many in reprisals against the resistance movement. But since then the damage of the war has been restored and the Lasíthi plateau is once again flourishing, one of the loveliest regions in all of Greece. It is estimated that there were once 10,000 windmills in operation on the plateau, but many of these have now been replaced by gasoline pumps to power the flow of water through the irrigation canals. Nevertheless, enough of these towers still remain with their sails spinning in the wind to maintain the picturesque and distinctive spectacle that gave the Lasíthi plateau its romantic name, The Valley of the Windmills.

After passing Lagoú, the ring road around Lasíthi comes to Tzermiadho, the largest village on the plateau, first mentioned in Venetian records of 1583. East of the village is the Cave of Trápeza, the site where Evans and Pendlebury found evidence of human habitation dating back to the Neolithic period, the first settlement on the Lasíthi plateau.

A short way farther along the road comes to the little village of Marmakéto, where some of the local houses and farm buildings have been converted into an ethnological museum, an extremely interesting evocation of life on the Lasíthi plateau in times past. The main house in the museum was the birthplace of Manolis Kazanis (1793–1846), a hero of the Cretan resistance against the Turks who also fought in the defence of Mesolónghi from 1822 to 1826.

The road now comes to a junction, where a side road to the left leads to the villages of Mésa Lasithí and Mésa Lassitháki, while the main road continues on around the plateau, bringing one next to an approach road that leads up to the monastery of the Panayía Kroustallénia, which is perched in a splendid site high above the southeastern side of the plateau. The Kroustallénia is one of a pair of monasteries founded in 1543 by two pious sisters, Peladia and Theokliti Danasis, who were members of a group of refugees from Náfplion and Monemvasía resettled on the Lasíthi plateau by the Venetians after their towns had been captured by the Turks. During the nineteenth century the Kroustallénia was a centre of Cretan resistance against Ottoman rule, which led to attacks on the monastery by Turkish armies in 1823 and again in 1866. During the latter years of the nineteenth century the Kroustallenia had a renowned 'secret school', one of the admirable institutions where the monks kept Greek learning alive under the Dark Ages of Turkish rule.

From the Kroustallénia there is a path that leads eastward to the Katharó plateau, a hike of about two hours. This is a beautiful upland plain 8km long and 2km wide at an altitude of 1100 metres, with a number of villages scattered around that are inhabited only in summer. From the Katharó plateau one can walk on for another hour to an even more beautiful area called Choreftés, also known as Neraidokólyvoi – 'the Place Where the Nereiads Swim' – whose name suggests its bewitching charm.

The ring road around Lasíthi finally brings one to Psychró, a village on the western side of the plateau that has now become the goal of most excursions to the Lasíthi plateau, the attraction being the great cave above that is supposed by some to have been the birthplace of Zeus. A road leads up from the village to a car park and tourist pavilion, from where it is a steep climb of about a quarter of an hour to the Psychró Cave, one of the most remarkable sights in Crete.

The Psychró Cave first came to the attention of archaeologists in the late nineteenth century, with Arthur Evans visiting the site in 1894 and D. G. Hogarth making important discoveries there in 1899–1900. Hogarth's finds indicate that the Psychró Cave was used from the Middle Minoan era up until the Archaic period, and subsequent excavations have revealed that the cavern was once again in use during Graeco-Roman times.

Soon after its discovery the cavern at Psychró was identified by a number of scholars as the Dhiktaion Cave, known in Greek as the *Dhiktaíon Ántron*, which was one of the places believed in antiquity to be the birthplace of Zeus. Some authorities now believe that the Psychró Cave was originally a sanctuary of the Minoan mother-goddess, and that the cult of Dhiktaion Zeus was introduced there after the Mycenaean Greeks achieved dominance in the Great Island during the latter centuries of the Bronze Age. Besides being the birthplace of Zeus, the Dhiktaion Cave was the scene of a number of other Greek myths; these include the seduction of Europa by Zeus, the child of their union being Minos, the founder of the Minoan dynasty, who was said to have returned to this cavern every nine years to obtain laws from his father for governing the Great Island.

The entrance to the Psychró Cave is 1025m above sea level, and the mouth of the cavern can be seen from far away to the east as a gaping hole in the mountainside, making one wonder why it was not rediscovered until just a century ago. After passing through the narrow entrance, one emerges in the main cavern, which is 85m long, 40m wide, and has a maximum height of 20m. On the right side of the cave there are the remains of a temple that was walled off on that side of the cavern; the objects unearthed there, which are now on exhibit in the Iráklion Museum, date mostly to the Late Minoan period, c. 1550–1250 BC. On the left side of the cavern there is a passage that leads down to the lower part of the cave, where one sees wondrous stalagmites that have formed there across the ages, including one called 'The Mantle of Zeus', which mythology holds to be the petrified swaddling-clothes of the infant god. Surrounded by these stalactites, one is in a more receptive mood to consider the myths associated with this hallowed cave, evoking visions of the young warriors, the *Kuretes*, who danced around Rhea when she was giving birth to Zeus, clashing their shields together and shouting to drown out the cries of the baby. These *Kuretes* are believed by some to have been first goatherds to tend their flocks on the Lasíthi plateau, for mythology holds that Rhea's baby was nurtured by milk from the goat Amaltheia. The myth also says that Zeus was nourished on honey, and one of those who cared for him at his birth was the nymph Melissa, which in Greek means bee, a legend that has led some to suppose that the infant god was also looked after by the beekeepers of Lasíthi who kept their hives in the cave, fascinating ideas that somehow become much more believable down in the stalactite-surrounded depths of this ancient cave-sanctuary.

Psychró is also used as a base for climbers making the ascent of Madára, the highest peak of Mount Dhíkti. The climb from Psychró to the summits of Aféndis Christós and Madára takes eight hours, stopping en route at the mountain village of Limnakhoro, south of the Lasíthi plateau, where one can make arrangements to spend the night in the house of one of the villagers. One can make the ascent to the two summits more quickly from Ebaros, a village south-west of the Lasíthi plateau on the road from Iráklion to Áno Viánnos. For information concerning this and other climbs on Mount Dhíkti one should contact the Mountaineering Club in Iráklion.

After our visit to the Psychró Cave we returned to the car park and drove off in the rented car we had picked up in Iráklion. Then we drove down a short way to a roadside taverna that we had seen on the way up, a lovely place embowered in vines and surrounded by a flower garden, a venerable plane tree casting its shade over the courtyard where the tables were set. We were the only customers for lunch, and so after we had been served by the owner and his wife, Costa and Eleni, they sat with us and talked about our families and our lives as if we were old friends, which we were indeed even though we had just met. Then, after our meal, Costa brought out another carafe of his homemade wine and we drank to one another's health, as he and Eleni recited *mantinádes* for us and then sang some old Cretan songs, most of them dating back to Turkish and even Venetian times. And in the glow of the wine and their good company I let my mind wander as I looked out across the Lasíthi plateau, its farms and orchards still flourishing after having nourished human existence on this plain for some seven thousand years, the poetry and songs of our Cretan friends evoking for us once again the spirit of this ancient and surpassingly beautiful island.

6

SOUTH FROM IRÁKLION

Iráklion is an excellent base for visiting sites in central and southern Crete. These excursions can each be done in a day-trip from Iráklion, although those with more time to spare might want to stop off at one of the villages or beaches en route, where one finds a number of pleasant places to stay for a few days as well as some of the best swimming on the island.

A very popular excursion takes one southwest from Iráklion to the archaeological sites of Górtyna, Phaestós and Ayía Triádha, after which one can continue on to the south coast at the resort village of Mátala. Then afterwards one can drive back eastwards along the highway that cuts across the southern part of central Crete, making detours out to a number of places along the southernmost stretch of the Cretan coast between Cape Líthino and Cape Sidonía. Then the last part of this chapter describes an excursion taking one southeastward from Iráklion down to the south coast via Áno Viánnos, completing the third side of a huge triangle that includes all of central Crete aside from the places described in the previous chapters.

The first of the present excursions from Iráklion begins by taking one south-southwest through the verdant valley of Phinikiá, renowned for its vineyards that produce sultana raisins. At Stavrákia an alternative road branches off to the left to pass through the pretty village of Daphnés, while the main road goes on and passes through the village of Síva. The two roads rejoin one another near the vilage of Veneráto, where a side road leads up to the convent of Palianí. Palianí is probably the oldest convent in Crete, dating back to the first Byzantine period, which ended with the Saracen conquest of the Great

97

Island in AD 824. The earliest reference to the convent is in the year AD 668, when it is already called Palaía, or Old, of which its present name is an obvious derivative, and ancient architectural elements built into its structure indicate that the present building was erected on the site of an earlier edifice perhaps dating from late antiquity. The convent was destroyed by the Turks in 1821, at the beginning of the Greek War of Independence; at that time all but one of the nuns were slaughtered, with the single survivor, an old sister named Parthenia, making a miraculous escape. Parthenia then raised funds to restore the convent and when it reopened in 1826 she became the abbess, serving until her death in 1866, when she was reputed to be 133 years old. That same year the convent was destroyed by the Turks soon after the outbreak of the revolution of 1866, but it was later rebuilt and continues to function today. The nuns at Palianí support themselves by their sewing, knitting, embroidering and weaving, selling their fine work to those who visit the convent. One of the sites to be seen at the convent is the ancient myrtle tree that stands beside the south-east wall of the church; this is said to be more than a thousand years old, and tradition holds that at its foot there was discovered the miraculous icon of the Panayía Myrtidiótissa, whose discovery led to the founding of the convent. The feast day of the Virgin is still celebrated here on 24 September, a *paniyíri* that attracts people from all of the surrounding region.

Continuing along, one now passes the village of Avgenikí, where the road begins its long ascent to Ayía Varvára, a village on the south-eastern extension of Psilóritis. Off to the right here one can see Priniás, a mountain village approached by a road leading north from Ayía Varvára. About a mile to the northeast of Priniás one can see the most distinctive landmark of this region, the precipitous and flat-topped acropolis rock known as Patéla, whose summit is at an altitude of 686m. Archaeologists have discovered an ancient site on the acropolis hill, which they believe to have been a late Minoan shrine, though most of the remains found there, which are now in the Iráklion Museum, date from the Archaic period. Authorities are undecided as to the name of this site, some identifying it as Rhezania and others as Apollonia.

Within the valley between Priniás and Ayía Varvára there are some strange rocky excrescences known as '*Tis Grías ta Tiriá*', or 'The Cheeses of the Old Woman'. These rocks are said to cause the sudden and apparently inexplicable rainstorms that suddenly fall in this valley, giving rise to the proverbial saying that 'It's raining in

Ayía Varvára and even God doesn't understand.'

The road now brings one to Ayía Varvára, a very pleasant mountain village at an elevation of 600m. On entering the village one sees on the right the church of Áyios Profítis Ilías on a rocky eminence, a landmark of some renown, for tradition holds that this is the *omphalós*, or navel, the exact geometrical centre of Crete.

Beyond Ayía Varvára the road divides, with one branch leading off westward along the southern branch of Psilorítis through the villages, a second one leading westward to Megáli Vrísi and Áyios Thomás, while the main road, which is followed on the present excursion, heads southward toward the Mesará valley, passing its highest point at Vourvoulítis, at an altitude of some 650m. Once over the pass the road descends in a long series of hairpin turns called the Anegíri, from the turns of which one occasionally catches glimpses of the Libyan Sea far off to the south. Then finally the road comes down to the Mesará Plain, the most immense fertile area in Crete and its granary since ancient times, some 45km in length along its east-west axis and with an average width of only 8km. Then at 44km from Iráklion the road finally brings one to the village of Áyii Dhéka, the 'Holy Ten'.

Áyii Dhéka is named for ten Christians martyred here for their faith during the persecutions that took place during the reign of the Roman Emperor Decius. The saints were martyred at a place just to the south-west of the village centre, called Alóni, where a chapel dedicated to Áyii Dhéka is built over a crypt which local tradition holds to be the tomb of the martyrs.

The ruins of ancient Górtyna, known in modern Greek as Górtys, are scattered throughout Áyii Dhéka and the countryside to its west along the side of the road leading to Phaestós, the most prominent structures lying between the village and the river, known in antiquity as the Lethaios. One group of ruins, dating mostly from the imperial Roman era, straddles the side road that parallels the main road a short way to its south, going as far as another road that leads south through the village of Mitrópolis to Plátanos and then on to the south coast at Lebén (ancient Lebena), which was the original port of Górtyna. A second group of structures, which are mostly from earlier periods than the first group, lie just to the north of the main highway where it passes the side road to Mitrópolis and crosses the river, while across from these structures is the main theatre and the acropolis hill, where the Doric city of Górtyna was founded during the Dark Ages of the ancient Greek world.

Górtyna is renowned in mythology as the place to which Zeus

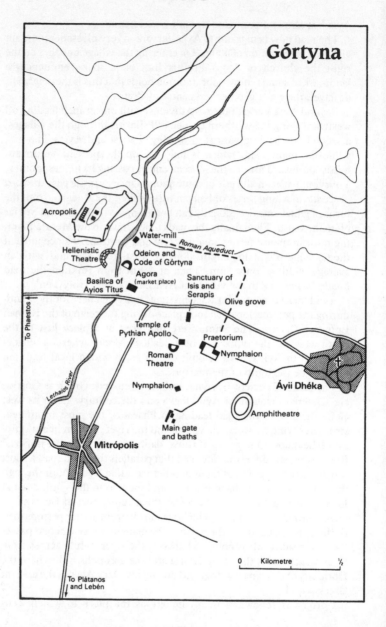

Górtyna

Acropolis

Water-mill

Roman Aqueduct

Hellenistic
Theatre

Odeion and
Code of Górtyna

Basilica of
Ayios Títus

Agora
(market place)

Sanctuary of
Isis and
Serapis

Olive grove

To Phaestos

Temple of
Pythian Apollo

Praetorium

Roman
Theatre

Nymphaion

Lethaíos River

Nymphaion

Áyii Dhéka

Amphitheatre

Main gate
and baths

Mitrópolis

0   Kilometre   ½

To Plátanos
and Lebén

brought Europa when he returned with her from Phoenicia to Crete, and where she bore him three sons: Minos, Rhadamanthys and Sarpedon. Europa was thereafter worshipped in Górtyna as a fertility goddess, eventually giving her name to the continent of Europe. Górtyna is mentioned by Homer in both the *Iliad* and the *Odyssey*. In the *Iliad*, it is one of the seven Cretan cities listed in the Catalogue of Ships, which describes the various contingents that joined the army of Agamemnon in the siege of Troy. And in the *Odyssey* it is mentioned in connection with the tale that Nestor relates to Telemachos about the adventures that he and Menelaus had on their homeward journey from Troy.

The 'walled' city of Górtyna mentioned by Homer in the Catalogue of Ships would have been on the acropolis hill on the right bank of the river. According to Strabo, who is referring to the period of Achaean supremacy on the Great Island, the three greatest cities on Crete were Knossós, Górtyna and Cydonía, the latter now known as Chaniá. A number of ancient writers, most notably Plato, believed that Górtyna was founded by settlers from the Pelopónnisos; this migration would have occurred toward the end of the Bronze Age, c. 1250 BC, when the Achaeans appear to have supplanted the Minoans as lords of the Great Island. Plato, in his *Laws*, writes that Górtyna was one of the best governed states in Crete, as well as being among the wealthiest and most powerful cities on the Great Island, its citizens held in high esteem. The city's constitution was in the fifth century BC incorporated in the renowned Code of Górtyna, which is the earliest known legislation in Europe as well as the most complete set of laws to have survived from ancient Greece. During the classical period Górtyna rivalled Knossós as the leading city of Crete. Then late in the third century BC Górtyna conquered Phaestós and its harbour at Mátala, giving the Gortynaians a second port in addition to Lebena. In 69–67 BC the Gortynaians sided with Quintus Metellus in his campaign of conquest in Crete, and so Górtyna was spared the destruction that was visited upon Knossós and other cities on the island. After this campaign Górtyna became the capital of the Roman province of Crete and Cyrenaica, and the Romans adorned the city with temples and other public buildings. Górtyna also became the first centre of Christianity in Crete, which began, according to tradition, when St Paul appointed Titus as bishop of the Great Island in c. AD 67. Górtyna continued to be the leading city of Crete during the early centuries of the Byzantine era, but after it was sacked and destroyed by the Saracens in 824 it never again regained its former stature. The village of Áyii Dhéka then grew up on the site during the Venetian and Turkish occupations, as the ruins of the ancient city became overgrown and covered with earth. A number of European travellers visited the site and described the ruins, but excavations did not begin until 1884 with the work of Halbherr and Fabricus, whose most dramatic discovery was the 'Great Inscription' containing the Law Code of Górtyna. The excavation of Górtyna has continued since then, unearthing the ruined edifices one sees today west of the village of Áyii Dhéka.

A pathway from the chapel of Áyii Dhéka leads south-westward toward the village of Mitrópolis, passing the Roman amphitheatre and bringing one to some baths and the remains of the main gate of Roman Górtyna, a vast city which, according to Strabo, had a diameter of 9.5km. Just to the north of the gate there are the ruins of a nymphaion, or monumental fountain, to which water was carried by the great Roman aqueduct, whose piers and arches one can still see curving around through the olive grove to the north, extending along the lower slopes of the hill toward the river. The other and more extensive ruins in this first group of edifices, all of which date from the imperial Roman era in their present structure, lie on either side of the road that parallels the main highway to its south. Walking along this road from the chapel of Áyii Dhéka, one first passes on the right another nymphaion, which stands next to the southern end of the aqueduct that once supplied it with water. The road goes through an S-bend at this point, and on its left side are the ruins of the Praetorium, the headquarters of the Roman governor of the province that comprised Crete and Cyrenaica. Continuing along, one passes on the right the ruins of the temple of Pythian Apollo, the centre of Górtyna and the principal sanctuary of the city. This was erected in the Archaic period on the site of a Minoan structure of which some traces still remain, and additions to the structure as well as extensive reconstitutions were made during the Hellenistic and Roman eras. A little farther along one finds on the right the ruins of the Roman theatre, and behind that and the temple of Apollo are the remains of a sanctuary dedicated to the Egyptian deities Isis and Serapis.

After seeing this first group of structures, one might then drive from Áyii Dhéka along the main highway to the near side of the bridge over the Lethaios, where on the right side of the road there is a car park from which one can explore the second group of ruins surviving from ancient Górtyna. The most prominent of these structures is the great basilica of Áyios Títos, which is just behind the car park. The original church on this site was probably built in the second century BC on the site of a martyrium dedicated to St Titus. The present basilica was erected during the reign of Justinian, 527–65, as evidenced by the imperial monograms of the emperor on the capitals unearthed in the ruins of the nave. The plan of the basilica is the classical cross-inscribed-in-a-square, a design that became archetypal for the churches of Byzantium, with a dome covering the intersection of the two arms of the cross. Two side chapels flank the central apse at the eastern end and these are prolonged as side aisles flanking the nave, with the edifice extended to the west by a narthex, through which the congregation entered. The best-preserved section of the basilica is its eastern end, where the great barrel-vaulted apse is flanked by two square tower-like structures that house the side chapels, with the outline of the nave still evident from the bases of the piers and the column-bases of the colonnades that once stood there. One of the side chapels still preserves fragments of the paintings in fresco that once adorned large areas of the church. This basilica was the centre of Christianity in Crete until it was destroyed by the Saracens when they sacked Górtyna in 824. The bones of St Titus and his other sacred relics were preserved at that time and later transferred to Khándaks, the present Iráklion, where they are now contained within reliquaries in the church of Áyios Títos there. The church of Áyios Títos in Górtyna does not seem to have been rebuilt after the Saracen sack, and when the Italian traveller Buondelmonti visited Crete in 1415 he found the basilica a total ruin. Excavation of the basilica began in 1900 under the Italian archaeologist G. Gerola, and at that time one of the side chapels was rededicated to the Panayía Kéra. The chapel is still used occasionally by the people of Áyii Dhéka, with services held there on the *paniyíri* of the Blessed Virgin, thus preserving the oldest Christian tradition on the Great Island.

Just beyond the basilica to the north is the unexcavated site of the Agora, the market place of ancient Górtyna. One of the edifices known to have stood in the Agora is a temple of Asklepios, which in the imperial Roman era was one of the most famous shrines on Crete. A statue of Asklepios that once stood in the Asklepion of Górtyna is now preserved in the Archaeological Museum of Iráklion.

Continuing on past the site of the Agora for a short way, one then comes to the Odeion, a building of semicircular plan that served primarily as a concert hall. The Odeion was erected by the Romans in the first or second century AD on the site of an earlier edifice dating from the Hellenistic era. When the Odeion was erected its Roman builders preserved the 'Great Inscription' that was preserved on a wall of the Hellenistic edifice, the famous Code of Górtyna. This inscription was discovered by the archaeologists who first excavated Górtyna, and it is now preserved *in situ* in a gallery behind the Odeion. The 'Great Inscription' seems to have been carved in the late sixth or early fifth century BC, and it may originally have been displayed in the Prytaneion, the town hall of Górtyna. The inscription consists of twelve columns of 52 lines each, a total of some 17,000 characters written in an archaic Doric dialect of Greek in the system known as 'boustrophedon', ('as the ox ploughs'); reading from left to right on one line and then right to left on the next, as one would plough a field. The Code of Górtyna preserves the ancient legal system of Crete that was so admired by Plato and other philosophers, serving as a model for Lycurgos and Solon when they drew up the constitutions of Sparta and Athens, respectively. The Code of Górtyna is also a rich source of information about life in the Great Island in ancient times, preserving the laws that tradition says were handed down by Zeus to Minos, when the King of Crete went to visit the god of Olympos at nine-year intervals.

Just beyond the Odeion on the river bank there is an old water-mill dating from the Venetian period. Apparently this mill was still in use up until about two decades ago, when water power was abandoned in favour of a modern gasoline engine, and the old mill was left to fall into ruin. It is an evocative sight, reminding one of the antiquity and continuity of everything associated with life on the Great Island.

Directly across the river from the Odeion, one can see the exiguous remains of the Hellenistic theatre. The theatre stands at the south-eastern foot of the acropolis hill of ancient Górtyna, which is best approached from Ambeloúzos, a village on the right bank of the Lethaios. Very little remains of the acropolis except for some fragmentary ruins of its ancient defence-walls. But the view is impressive enough for a romantic, for this is the 'walled city of Górtyna' mentioned by Homer in the *Iliad*, whose warriors journeyed all the way from the Mesará plain to the Trojan plain to join the army of Agamemnon in the siege of Troy.

After visiting Górtyna, we continued driving westward from Áyii Dhéka on the highway. Just after crossing the Lethaios we saw on the right side of the highway by the river bank the ruins of some ancient structures, identified as storage chambers used by the Gortynaians in antiquity. Two kilometres or so past Áyii Dhéka we passed the Agricultural School of the Mesará, where Cretan youths are taught modern methods of agriculture on a self-supporting farm, tilling the soil in what is probably the oldest farmland in Europe. Six kilometres farther along, the road goes through the large village of Míres, whose main street is lined with pleasant cafés where one might be tempted to stop for a drink before going on to Phaestós. Four kilometres beyond Míres a signpost indicates a road to the right that leads off to the nearby monastery of the Panayía Kaliviani, founded during the second Byzantine period. The monastery was adorned with frescoes, but these have all been destroyed, and the monastic church was totally rebuilt in the years 1911–24. The Kaliavaní is still a popular shrine, because it possesses a wonder-working icon of the Panayía discovered there in 1857, and pilgrims flock to the monastery on the *paniyíria* of the Virgin.

Four kilometres past the turn-off to the Kaliviani a signpost indicates a route to the left for Phaestós, bringing one along the far western end of the Mesára plain. Immediately after driving onto this road one can see the site of Phaestós on its commanding ridge overlooking the valley. The road then leads up to the car park of the tourist pavilion, from which one has a sweeping view of the surrounding countryside. Phaestós is the most superbly set of any of the Minoan sites on Crete. The ancient city looks out across the Mesára plain towards Mount Dhíkti and the mountains that surround the Lasíthi plateau, with the Geropótamos river winding its way westward through the most fertile area on Crete, bounded on the north by Psilorítis and on the south by the Asteroúsia Mountains, while off to the west one can see the Gulf of Mesára and the tiny port of Ayía Galíni. Looking towards the twin peaks of Psilorítis, the Saddle of Digenis, one can see just to their right and a little below the summit a large black hole in the mountainside; this is the Cave of Kamáres, where in Minoan times the kings of Phaestós brought votive offerings to Eileithyia, the ancient fertility goddess of the Great Island, thanking her for the bountiful products of the earth they had garnered from the rich farmlands that they surveyed from their palace above the western end of the Mesára plain.

Phaestós was one of the most renowned cities of ancient Crete, surpassed in importance only by Knossós. Tradition has it that Phaestós was originally ruled by Rhadamanthys, one of the three sons of Zeus and Europa, with the second son Sarpedon ruling in Mállia until he was defeated by Minos, who ruled supreme over all of Crete from his palace at Knossós. Rhadamanthys was renowned for his wisdom and the justice of his reign, and according to Greek mythology he and his brother Minos in their afterlife sat together as judges in Hades. Phaestós is one of the seven towns listed by Homer in the Catalogue of Ships in the *Iliad*, and it is also mentioned in the *Odyssey* in connection with the homeward voyage from Troy of Nestor and Menelaus. Phaestós was also the birthplace of the sage Epimenides, a contemporary of Solon who was one of the seven fabled wise men of antiquity.

Archaeological excavations at Phaestós began in 1900 under the direction of Federico Halbherr of the Italian School. These excavations have continued up to the present day, with Doro Levi directing the work of the Italian School at Phaestós from 1959–70. These excavations have revealed that Phaestós was founded on the site of a Neolithic settlement, with evidence of dwellings and artefacts dating back to c. 3000 BC. The Minoan era in Crete began c. 2600 BC, but it is not known whether the new settlers supplanted or merged in peacefully with the original Neolithic dwellers on the site. The first palace at Phaestós was erected c. 2000–1900 BC. This edifice, together with its associated building-complex, occupied an area of some 18,000 square metres, only slightly less than that of the great palace at Knossós, which had an area of about 20,000 square metres. The old Palace of Phaestós, as it is now called, was apparently destroyed by an earthquake c. 1700 BC, the same catastrophe that levelled Knossós and the other Minoan centres at the same time. A new and even grander imperial residence was soon afterwards erected on the same site at Phaestós, the so-called New Palace, incorporating some of the architectural members of the Old Palace in its structure, though some of the ruins of the earlier building remained covered with debris until they were unearthed by archaeologists in the present century. The New Palace would have been at the centre of life in Phaestós during the golden age of the Minoan world, but it was destroyed c. 1400 BC along with the palaces at Knossós and the other centres of Cretan civilization, perhaps by an earthquake. There is evidence that Phaestós continued to be occupied in the post-Minoan period, with some evidence of settlement there in the Mycenaean era. Phaestós seems to have emerged as a town once again during the Dark Ages of the ancient Greek world, but though it continued in existence into the Hellenistic era it never again regained the prominence it had in Minoan times.

Tours of Phaestós begin on the paved terrace below the Tourist Pavilion, an area at the north-western corner of the archaeological site known as the Upper Court. This was a part of the Old Palace that again

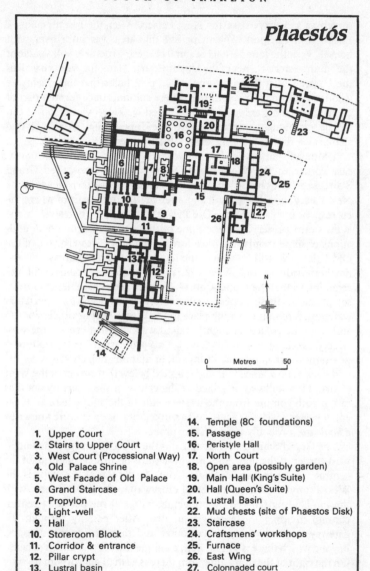

Phaestós

1. Upper Court	**14.** Temple (8C foundations)
2. Stairs to Upper Court	**15.** Passage
3. West Court (Processional Way)	**16.** Peristyle Hall
4. Old Palace Shrine	**17.** North Court
5. West Facade of Old Palace	**18.** Open area (possibly garden)
6. Grand Staircase	**19.** Main Hall (King's Suite)
7. Propylon	**20.** Hall (Queen's Suite)
8. Light-well	**21.** Lustral Basin
9. Hall	**22.** Mud chests (site of Phaestos Disk)
10. Storeroom Block	**23.** Staircase
11. Corridor & entrance	**24.** Craftsmens' workshops
12. Pillar crypt	**25.** Furnace
13. Lustral basin	**26.** East Wing
	27. Colonnaded court

served as a courtyard in the New Palace. After the resettlement of Phaestós in the post-Minoan period this area was built over with houses, with the foundations of some of these structures still visible at the southwestern corner of the Upper Court. Along the western wall of the Upper Court there is a row of 17 post-holes that once held the wooden columns of a colonnade. These columns once formed part of an arcade that covered the slightly raised walkway whose course can still be seen along the western edge of the Upper Court, passing several slab-graves dating from the early Christian period.

A Minoan stairway leads down from the Upper Court to the northeast corner of the West Court, from which the so-called Grand Staircase ascends to the left. Here one can see the western façade of the New Palace, which was built about ten metres to the east of where the corresponding façade of the Old Palace had been, the two levels of the West Court preserving the outline of the earlier edifice. The foundations of some rooms that once formed the north-western side of the Old Palace can still be seen at the foot of the Grand Staircase. At the northern side of the West Court, the successive courses of the retaining wall of the Upper Court have been set back in tiers to form a set of steps; these appear to have formed as seats for spectators watching ceremonies taking place in the West Court or processions to and from the palace. A slightly raised walkway that crosses the west court diagonally may in fact have been a processional path, leading at its southeastern end to the Propylon, or monumental entryway, of the Old Palace, now fenced off under a shed below that corner of the West Court. This walkway is joined at the centre of the court by another raised path coming from the western side of the site, where at its far end it passes a well or cistern and a sunken silo-like structure known as a *kouloura*, probably used to store grain.

The Grand Staircase leads up from the West Court into the northwest corner of the New Palace, whose ruins occupy virtually all of the central area of the archaeological site. At the top of the steps is the West Propylon, the monumental entryway to the New Palace, with the top landing flanked by projecting wings of the palace, a central column dividing the entryway in two. After passing through the gateway one enters in turn an outer and then an inner anteroom, beyond which there is a light-well, a unique feature of Minoan palaces. On the right of the inner anteroom there is a small guardroom used by the palace guards to control visitors to the palace; opposite to this on the north side is the entrance to a passageway which goes up three steps to a passage above that which turns back and brings one to a courtyard called the Peristyle Hall. Alternatively, one could continue straight ahead from the inner anteroom into the light-well, in the south-east corner of which there is a door, and after passing through here one can turn left to proceed to the Peristyle Court or go down to the right to the palace storerooms and to the north end of the Central Court. Approaching the Peristyle Hall by this latter route, one comes first to a long vestibule-corridor paved in gypsum. After passing through this anteroom one comes to the Peristyle Hall, an open courtyard surrounded by a portico and with a verandah on its north side looking out toward Psilorítis. The Peristyle Hall and its verandah were undoubtedly part of the complex of rooms that formed the residential quarter of the King of Phaestós, with the royal apartments forming the northern wing of the palace. In the central area of the Peristyle Court one can see the foundations of a Minoan house of the Prepalatial period, a structure that would have been levelled when the Old Palace was erected at the beginning of the second millennium BC.

After seeing the Peristyle Hall, one can return through its gypsum-paved anteroom and go down a flight of internal steps at its far end; this leads into the Lobby of the Magazines, a large chamber with two internal columns that opens off the western side of the Central Court near its northern end. This courtyard is so named because it probably served as a central office for the ten storage-magazines that flank the long corridor leading off from its western side. There are five of these magazines on either side of the corridor, the last one on the right at the far end still retaining its lintel and roof. Inside this chamber one can still see two *pithoi*, the giant urns that the Minoans used for the storage of grain, olive oil and wine; these date from the Middle Minoan II period, 1850–1750 BC, and were made for use in the Old Palace, remaining in place after the New Palace was erected.

One now enters the Central Court, whose origins date back to the time of the Old Palace, later becoming the central area of the New Palace. The courtyard is an immense paved area, 51.5m long and 22.3m wide; this is slightly smaller in extent than the great court at Knossós, but undoubtedly grander in its setting and design, with two tiers of alternating pillars and columns along its eastern and western sides, some of their bases still standing *in situ*. The south-eastern corner of the court is missing, having fallen down the precipitous slope of the hillside there, along with that quarter of the palace. The south-western quarter of the New Palace survives, the foundation walls of its labyrinth of rooms merging with those of the Old Palace, the latter extending somewhat farther to the west, their limit marked by the remains of the Propylon of the earlier palace. This part of the palace is separated from the north-western quarter of the complex by a long corridor that connects the West Court and the Central Court. The north end of the Central Court has a formal grandeur unique in Minoan architecture, with the central doorway leading in to the palace from the courtyard flanked by engaged half-columns and niches, the latter probably serving as sentry-boxes, for this was the main entrance to the Royal Apartments. A long and narrow corridor leads from this entryway into the open cloister known as the Court of the North Wing. Another corridor leads from the north-west corner of this courtyard to the Royal Apartments, whose foundation walls form the northernmost wing of the New Palace. The congeries of rooms whose foundations form the north-eastern corner of the archaeological site were chambers in the Old Palace, their specific functions unknown. The westernmost of these rooms was where the famous Phaestós Disc was found (see p. 47).

After completing an exploration of Phaestós one can go on to see the Minoan site at Ayía Triádha, which is about 3.5km farther to the west on the left bank of the Geropótamos River. Ayía Triádha was not a Minoan town, but rather a small palace or villa, along with its associated complex of buildings, perhaps the summer residence of the King of Phaestós and his household. The actual Minoan name of the site is unknown. The present name, which means the Holy Trinity, comes from the former village of Ayía Triádha, abandoned after most of its inhabitants were killed by the Turks in the revolution of 1897. A single Byzantine church of this village, dedicated to Ayía Triádha, survives to perpetuate the name of the village, standing on a hill to the south-west of the site. The site was first excavated by archaeologists of the Italian School early in the present century, just after the discovery of Phaestós. The finds from these excavations are now exhibited in the Iráklion Museum, the most remarkable being the famous Ayía Triádha Sarcophagus, with its vivid scenes of life here in Minoan times. Other notable discoveries include the Harvesters' Vase, the Chieftain's Cup, and the Rhyton of the Athletes.

The archaeological excavations have revealed that Ayía Triádha was first occupied, but only sparsely, during the Neolithic period; only fragmentary remains of very humble structures have been found dating from that time and from the Early and Middle Minoan periods (2600–1550 BC). The present structures at Ayía Triádha were first built c. 1550 BC, at about the same time as the erection of the New Palace at Phaestós, and that, together with the proximity of the two

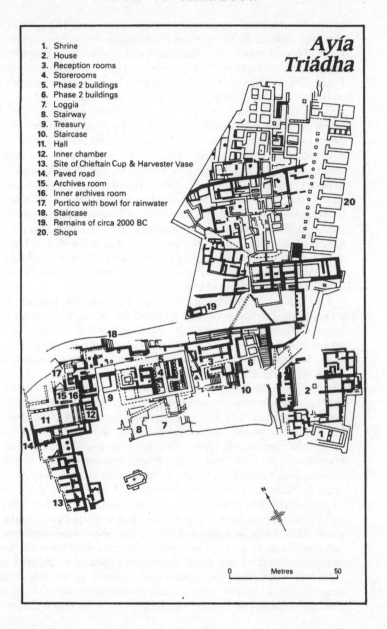

Ayía Triádha

1. Shrine
2. House
3. Reception rooms
4. Storerooms
5. Phase 2 buildings
6. Phase 2 buildings
7. Loggia
8. Stairway
9. Treasury
10. Staircase
11. Hall
12. Inner chamber
13. Site of Chieftain Cup & Harvester Vase
14. Paved road
15. Archives room
16. Inner archives room
17. Portico with bowl for rainwater
18. Staircase
19. Remains of circa 2000 BC
20. Shops

0   Metres   50

places, has led to the supposition that the villa at Ayía Triádha was a summer residence for the rulers of Phaestós, the site here being a very pleasant one on its hill above the lushest and most beautiful part of the Mesára plain at its eastern end, probably closer to the shore of the Libyan Sea in antiquity than it is at present. The imperial residence at Ayía Triádha was smaller and simpler in plan than the palaces at Knossós and Phaestós, without the central courtyard and spatial extent of those royal complexes. The villa at Ayía Triádha was destroyed c. 1400 BC, at about the same time as the destruction of the new palaces at Knossós and Phaestós and probably by the same catastrophe. After this catastrophe, toward the end of the Minoan III period, a simple rectangular building in four sections was built on the ruins of the Ayía Triádha villa, the earliest-known example in Crete of the megaron-type structure characteristic of Mycenaean Greece on the mainland. This Mycenaean settlement at Ayía Triádha appears to have died out during the Dark Ages of the ancient Greek world, and then during the Geometric period the site seems to have been set aside as a sanctuary dedicated to Zeus Welkhanos, the God of the Willow Tree, the principal deity of Phaestós.

The villa at Ayía Triádha occupies the southern half of the archaeological site, the various rooms of the edifice laid out on an irregular L-shaped plan. The Royal Apartments themselves were arrayed around the angle of the L, which forms the north-west corner of the lower half of the site; these chambers were approached by a ramp on the north-west side of that quarter of the site, where a staircase led to the *propylon* on the first floor, a monumental entryway that has now vanished. This opened into a courtyard that formed the north-western angle of the L, a vantage point from which the king and his household would have commanded a splendid view of the surrounding region. Six doors on the southern side of this courtyard opened into the main hall of the Royal Apartments, which were adorned with paintings in fresco, some of which are preserved in the Iráklion Museum. Beyond the inner end of the hall there are the remains of a light-well and then a room with benches around its walls, while just to the north there is a chamber that seems to have served as the royal archives, as evidenced by the clay seals found there with records dating to c. 1450 BC, about the time that the villa was destroyed. South of the Royal Apartments there is a congeries of chambers that formed the south-western quarter of the villa, with most of the surviving rooms being storage-magazines. A short distance to the east of the south-western corner of the villa is the little church of Áyios Yórgios Galatás, a chapel dating to the Venetian period, still adorned with frescoes of the fourteenth century.

The North Wing of the villa, forming the long arm of the L, has been much altered by the re-building that took place in Mycenaean times. One recognizable structure in this part of the villa is a storeroom with a central pillar, while another, farther to the east, is a Royal Apartment with a light-well and a *polythronon*. At the eastern end of the North Wing there is a staircase that goes down from the ramp that runs along the north side of the villa to the ancient road below that led to Phaestós. Off to the left of this as one descends is the East Wing of the villa, which seems to have been used to house servants and staff and also for cult-rooms, the southernmost building having been identified as a temple of the late Minoan III period. The open area between the East and West Wings is known as the Piazelle di Sacelli, the Square of the Holy Place, so-called by the Italian archaeologists because of the many *ex-voto* objects found there, including represent- ations of men, women, horses, oxen and a statuette of a Minoan ship, all of which are now in the Iráklion Museum, giving a picture of life at the Ayía Triádha villa in Minoan times.

The ruins in the northern part of the archaeological site are largely the remains of the town that developed at Ayía Triádha in late Minoan times. The most prominent structure here is the row of shops that extends along the western side of the site to the north; this is known as the Agora, and it served as the marketplace of Ayía Triádha in the Late Minoan III period. The labyrinthian complex of foundation walls to the west of this are mostly houses from the late Minoan town of Ayía Triádha.

About 150m north-east of the northern end of the Agora there are the ruins of two tombs of circular cross-section, similar to the *tholos* tombs of Mycenae. The tomb to the east is the older of the two, dating to the Prepalatial period (2600–2000 BC), while the other is from the Protopalatial period (2000–1700 BC). The Italian archaeologists unearthed about 150 skeletons in these two tombs, along with a rich board of funerary offerings, now in exhibit in the Iráklion Museum. They also unearthed a number of tombs of square cross-section a short distance to the south, and in one of these they discovered the famous Ayía Triádha Sarcophagus, with its vivid paintings in fresco depicting life in this town c. 1400 BC, when the Mycenaeans had apparently achieved dominance over the Minoans in the Great Island.

After visiting Phaestós and Ayía Triádha, one can then drive on to Mátala, a coastal hamlet on the eastern shore of the Gulf of Mesará.

During the past two decades Mátala has become the most popular summer resort on the south coast of Crete, the great attractions being its beautiful sandy beach and the extraordinary sandstone cliffs that bound its cove, honeycombed with ancient cliff-dwellings and rockhewn tombs, grottos that in recent years were re-inhabited by European and American hippies who camped out here to get away from the modern world.

During Minoan times Mátala was the principal port of Phaestós. Then, after the Gortynaeans captured Phaestós in c. 220 BC, Mátala became the harbour of Górtyna, with the town surviving on into Venetian times. Remnants of the ancient town of Mátala can be seen underwater off the sea-girt cliffs that bound the northern side of the cove. Just to the north one can see the cape known as Nysos, which is believed to be the rocky promontory referred to by Homer in connection with Górtyna, where the ships of Menelaus were wrecked on his homeward journey from Troy. As we sat on the beach at Mátala I recalled these memorable lines in George Chapman's translation of the *Odyssey*, evoking images of what this coast might have been like in Homeric times.

> There is a rock on which the sea doth drive,
> Bare, and all broken, on the confines set
> of Gortya, that the dark seas likewise fret;

Just to the north of Mátala there is another sandy cove at Komó Beach, the site of ancient Kommos. Excavations by the American School of Classical Studies during the past decade have unearthed very interesting Minoan remains at Komó. These include six houses of the Late Minoan period and numerous underlying foundation walls from the Middle Minoan period, as well as harbour-works and a stretch of an ancient highroad that may once have led to Phaestós. These finds indicate that Kommos must have been another port of Phaestós, probably a centre for the trade between the Minoans and the Egyptians.

There are other seaside resorts farther to the north and west on the Gulf of Mesará, the best-known being Kókkinos Pýrgos and Ayía Galíni, described in a later excursion from Réthymnon. The present excursion now goes on to describe the southern coast of central Crete from Cape Líthino to Cape Sidonía, including the hinterland as far north as the highway that crosses the countryside due westward from the Gulf of Mesará, where the Great Island achieves its greatest width.

The shore of the Gulf of Mesará extends in a great arc from Cape

Melíssa on the east to Cape Líthino on the south, seven miles below Mátala as the eagle flies. Then at Cape Líthino the Cretan coast bends abruptly through an angle of ninety degrees to head off due east along a precipitous shore that forms the southernmost rampart of the Great Island. The first port-of-call along this shore is Kalí Liménes, whose name in English means Fair Havens, ten km to the east of Cape Líthino. The best approach-road to Kalí Liménes from the southern highway turns south at Míres and passes through Pómpia and Pigaidákia, coming down to the sea a short distance to the east of the little fishing village.

Kalí Linénes may be the site of ancient Laséa, the port of Górtyna, although that Minoan harbour may be the smaller cove just to the east of the village. The cove at Kalí Liménes is protected on its western side by two almost-connected islands that jut out into the Libyan Sea, the outermost one being a bold headland terminated by a limestone cliff which must be a dramatic sight when the waves pound upon it in a storm. Captain Spratt, in his *Travels and Researches in Crete*, identifies Kalí Liménes as the haven where St Paul's ship took shelter when it was driven by a storm onto the southern coast of Crete, an adventure that probably occurred in AD 61 and which is described in *Acts of the Apostles*, 27; 9–26. There is a small seaside chapel in Kalí Liménes dedicated to St Paul, and tradition holds that this is where the Apostle made his first landing on Crete.

From the village a rough road leads north, coming in about 5km to the Monastery of the Panayía Hodeghétria, which is on the mountainous corner of land that projects out into the Libyan Sea between Mátala and Kalí Liménes to form Cape Líthino. The monastery is on the east slope of a mountain with an altitude of 379m, and from there one can clearly see the Nisi Paximádia, the two islets that float about 22 kilometres off from Mátala beyond the Gulf of Mesará. The monastery is dedicated to the Panayía Hodeghétria, whose sacred icon was once the protectress of Constantinople, paraded along the walls of Byzantium whenever the city was besieged. The monastery is still partly surrounded by its defence-walls, the main gate inscribed with the date 1568, and to the right of the entrance stands the historic defence–tower known as Xopatéras. This tower takes its name from the hero Xopateras, the nickname of a former monk named Father Ioassaf, who led a small force of Cretans here when the monastery was besieged in February 1829 by an army of 3000 Turks under the command of Suleiman Pasha. The Cretans defended the monastery until all had been killed except Xopateras, who fought on in the tower even when it had been set on fire by the besiegers. Then he battled with Turks hand-to-hand until he too was killed, after which his head was impaled and placed before the main gate as a warning against rebellion. The monastery has an interesting collection of old icons and sacred vestments, along with a number of memorabilia associated with its historic past.

From Kalí Liménes one can also take the road back to Pigaidákia and turn right there to visit the Monastery of Apezanés, which is near the village of Antiskári. This is a very old monastery which is still the scene of a very popular *paniyíri*, celebrated each year on 17 January, the feast day of St Anthony, when all the people of the surrounding region come to join in the festivities.

From Kalí Liménes there is a rough road leading eastward along the coast, passing the little seaside hamlets of Plateía Perámata and Papadogiánnis, finally coming to an end at Léndas. Léndas is a seaside hamlet near the site of ancient Lebén, whose ruins are scattered around the head of a cove bounded by two promontories, the one to the east known as Psamidhómouri and to the west Cape Léndas. Cape Léndas was in times past called Cape Leda, a variant of the Ancient Greek *léon* and the Phoenician-Semetic *leben*, both of which mean 'lion', a name arising from its resemblance to what Captain Spratt called 'a shaggy-shouldered, bluff-faced crouching lion . . .' According to one Greek myth, the cape is the petrified form of the lion who pulled the coach of Rhea, the mother of Zeus. Captain Spratt was also the first to identify and explore the site of ancient Lebena, which was first excavated in 1884 by archaeologists of the Italian School. These first excavations unearthed the remains of the Graeco-Roman city which began to emerge during the Archaic period, serving as the port of Górtyna, but more recent studies by the Greek archaeologist Alexiou have revealed evidence of an early Minoan settlement dating back to 2500–2000 BC.

Lebén was famed in antiquity for its shrine of Asklepius, the patron of medicine, which was founded around a spring noted for its curative powers. The spring and the remains of the temple of Asklepius are to be seen a short distance in from the head of the cove at its centre, surrounded by other structures associated with the healing shrine, which dates to the third century BC. Two columns of the temple still remain standing, flanking the altar at the eastern end of the sanctuary, where statues of Asklepius and his daughter Hygeia stood up until half a century ago, when they were destroyed by locals in search of hidden gold. At the northern side of the temple there is a marble stairway, with an arcade at its northern end and to its south a Nymphaion; these steps led down to a mosaic-paved treasury crypt called the Thesaurus, which was used to store valuable offerings presented to the temple by grateful patients who had been healed at the shrine. At the arcade was the Adyton, or inner sanctuary, in which the priests of the Asklepeion consulted with their patients and prescribed treatments for their illnesses. The sicknesses treated here included mental illness, and part of the programme including an imaginative analysis of dreams – psycho-analytic methods two millennia before Freud. The port and shrine at Lebén continued in existence up to the medieval Byzantine period, by which time the town was wiped out by the Saracen corsairs who ravaged the shores of the eastern Mediterranean in that era. Later reoccupation of the site is indicated by the eleventh-century church of Áyios Ioánnis that stands on the hillside to the east of the cove; this appears to have been built on the ruins of a Byzantine basilica of the ninth century, which in turn was constructed from the materials of some ancient structure. The church of Áyios Ioánnis is still adorned with frescoes dating from the fourteenth or fifteenth century.

While at Léndas one can also see the Minoan remains discovered by the Greek archaeologist Alexiou; these are 4km from the village at the base of Cape Léndas. These excavations have unearthed an early Minoan settlement dating c. 2500–2000 BC, with some of the objects giving evidence of the earliest-known trade between Crete and Egypt.

There are no roads along the south coast of central Crete between Léndas and Tsoútsouros, some 33km to the east, for the heights of Mount Kófinas rise precipitously in sea-girt cliffs, so that the only way to see this southernmost stretch of the Cretan coast is to hike it or to travel along it by sea, as I had once, long before, aboard an American troopship. Rough roads do come down to the sea at two places along this stretch of coast. The first of these is at Moní Koudoumás, about 25km east of Léndas, where there is an old monastery dedicated to the Koímisis Theotókou, the Assumption of the Blessed Virgin. The monastery perches above the sea directly under the highest peak of Mount Kófinas, which here reaches an altitude of 1231m. Some 7km east of Moní Koudoumás there is a tiny seaside hamlet called Trís Eklisiés, Three Churches; this can be reached by a rough road from Pýrgos, which is about halfway along the main highway that cuts across the southern part of central Crete just north of the Asteroúsia Mountains, reaching the sea just beyond Mírtos.

The eastern part of central Crete's southern shore is accessible by a rough coastal road that begins at Tsoútsouros Bay, which is approached by a side-road that leads off from the main highway near Kasteli|aná. Kastelianá is near the site of ancient Priansos, which was an important place during the Hellenistic period, one of thirty Cretan towns that signed a peace treaty with King Eumenes II of Pergamum (207–159 BC). Priansos had a port at the town of Inatos, which has been identified just east of the village of Tsoútsouros.

The eastern part of the southern coast of central Crete is accessible by a shore road that begins at the coastal hamlet of Tsoútsouros, where there is an excellent beach for swimming and camping. On the coast just east of Tsoútsouros archaeologists have discovered an ancient site identified as Inatos, with a cave-sanctuary dedicated to the fertility goddess. The dedicatory offerings found here are now in the Iráklion Museum; these include figurines of the Great Earth Mother, known in Crete as Eileithyia, as well as the figures of pregnant mothers and copulating figures, all symbolic of the fertility rites that were enacted in this cave-sanctuary in Minoan times.

The road from Tsoútsouros leads eastward around the bay of the same name, and then, after crossing the Anapodáris River, it goes around the western arc of Keratókambos Bay, passing through the coastal hamlet at Keratókambos. The road then veers inland to cross a river valley, after which it winds down to the seashore once again at Ayía Árvis, a coastal village at the end of a subtropical valley famed for its lush orange groves and banana plantations. Árvi, as it is more commonly known, has in recent years become popular as a summer resort, and now has a hotel and some seaside tavernas, a pleasant place to spend a quiet vacation on the south coast of Crete.

Árvi stands on the site of the Graeco-Roman town of Arvis, of which some pottery shards and architectural fragments have been found, along with a remarkable marble sarcophagus with sculptures in relief, described by Pashley in his *Travels in Crete*. The villagers told Pashley that they had used this sarcophagus and other remnants of the ancient town of Arvis in constructing their local church, dedicated to the Panayía. This church is referred to in the Basilicata map as La Madona di Arvi, and probably dates from the Venetian period. The church is believed to have been built on the site of a temple of Zeus Arbios; according to Pashley, the second name of the god here came from that of one of the nearby mountains where he was worshipped in ancient times. There is also a monastery dedicated to Áyios Antónios on the hillside above the gorge behind the village, a modern structure that has now been virtually abandoned by its community.

The coast road continues eastward from Árvi, passing the seaside hamlet of Faflángos, and then, after cutting across the base of Cape Sidonía, it comes to an end at Tértsa, a seaside village where there is a beach with a hotel and tavernas, another possibility for an out-of-the-way vacation on the south coast of Crete. Those wishing to explore the south coast of Crete eastward of this point must return to the main highway, which comes down to the coast just beyond Mírtos, after which it brings one to Ierápetra and then goes on into easternmost Crete. These parts of the Great Island will be explored in later itineraries, while the present one will conclude with a description of one more excursion through the southern part of central Crete, a drive that takes one south-east from Iráklion via Arkalokhóri and Áno Viánnos as far as Mírtos.

The village of Arkalokhóri is 32.5km from Iráklion on the road that leads south-east to Áno Viánnos and the south coast to Crete. The earliest mention of the village is in a Venetian census of 1583, and in late Ottoman times it was recorded to have about equal numbers of Christian and Moslem inhabitants. The village church, which is dedicated to the Archangel Michael, dates from the Venetian period, and is adorned with frescoes of the fourteenth or fifteenth century.

During the latter years of the Turkish occupation, the villagers in Arkalokhóri began finding antiquities in a nearby cave, attracting attention when they appeared in the market in Iráklion. When the Arkolokhóri Cave was excavated in 1931, the Greek archaeologist Khatzidhakis discovered a rich hoard of dedicatory offerings, including bronze double axes and a superb sword more than a metre in length, now exhibited in the Iráklion Museum. These finds indicate that the Arkalokhóri Cave was used as a sanctuary as far back as 2500 BC, with some authorities even suggesting that this was the mythological birthplace of Zeus. In any event, the Arkalokhóri Cave remained in use up until the late Minoan period, at which time the sanctuary was destroyed in an earthquake, which Spyridon Marinatos believes to have coincided with the catastrophic volcanic eruption that blew apart the Cycladic island of Santorini in c. 1450 BC.

Twelve kilometres beyond Arkalokhóri one passes through the village of Panayía, at an altitude of 350m, after which the road begins to wind upward around the south-western spurs of Mount Dhíkti. Some 2km beyond Panayía a turn-off leads south to the nearby village of Afráti, which is close to the site of ancient Arkhadia, also known as Arkhádes. Excavations on this site, which is on a hillside to the west of the village, revealed a large number of antiquities dating from the ninth and eighth centuries BC, indicating that Arkhadia must have been founded during the Dorian migration to Crete in the Dark Ages of the ancient Greek world. Arkhadia was destroyed by the Romans, but it was subsequently resettled and continued in existence up until the early years of the Christian era.

The road now winds its way southward, passing the villages of Ébaros, Thomadhianó and Mártha, after which it joins the main east-west highway across part of central Crete. Two kilometres farther along the highway passes Káto (Lower) Viánnos and then 2.5km beyond that it brings one to Epáno (Upper) Viánnos, better known as Áno Viánnos, a pretty village at an altitude of 550m and five miles north of the Libyan Sea, embowered amidst olive groves, vineyards and orchards. Áno Viánnos was the largest village in this part of Crete during Venetian times, with two of the local churches still remaining from the early part of that era, one of them dedicated to Ayía Pelayía and the other to Áyios Yórgios. Ayía Pelayía is adorned with outstanding frescoes, accompanied by an inscription recording that the paintings were done during a restoration of the church in 1360. Áyios Yórgios is also decorated with frescoes, which have a dedicatory inscription recording that they were done in 1401 by the Cretan painter Ioannis Mousouros.

The village is built on the same site and perpetuates the name of the ancient town of Viánnos, of which some archaeological remnants have been found. According to one Byzantine source, Stephanos Byzantios, Viánnos was the site of the legendary battle between Otus and Ephialtes, the giant twins that Ephimedia bore to Poseidon, though at the time she was married to Aloeus, King of Corinth. When the twins grew to their full gigantic stature they rebelled against the Olympian gods, defeating and capturing Ares, but then they were finally killed by Apollo. Pashley reports that he was shown a giant's tomb in Viánnos that tradition held to be the grave of Otus, probably perpetuating the memory of some ancient warrior-king who ruled in this region.

From Áno Viánnos one can drive down to the south coast at Árvi, while from Káto Viánnos there is a road to the coast at Keratókambos. One can also continue eastward from Áno Viánnos on the main highway, which finally comes down to the Libyan Sea at Mírtos, a village on the south coast that in recent years has become popular as a summer resort.

There are some interesting archaeological remains in the vicinity of Mírtos. On entering the town from the west the highway passes some ruins that have been identified as the remains of a Roman baths.

Fragmentary statues from the Roman period have also been found within the village of Mírtos, but systematic excavations have not been carried out there. Mírtos survived into modern times, mentioned in the Venetian census of 1583 and in the Turkish census of 1671. Viánnos was destroyed during World War II by the Germans, who executed all of the inhabitants whom they suspected of being partisans. The village was reconstructed after the war and in recent years it has begun to prosper as a summer resort.

One interesting archaeological site in the vicinity of Viánnos is at Pýrgos, which is on a hill east of the Kriopótamos River, on the opposite side of the bridge from the village. Archaeological excavations at Pýrgos have revealed that the site was inhabited as early as c. 2200 BC, while the principal remains visibly today are those of a Minoan villa dating from c. 1600 BC.

Three kilometres east of Mírtos there is another Minoan site known as Fournou Korifí, though its local name is Troúli. Archaeologists have unearthed evidence of an early Minoan settlement at Fourno Korifí dating from the period 2600–2200 BC. This settlement included more than ninety rooms, along with evidence that the inhabitants supported themselves through farming and the production of textiles, an interesting glimpse into the lives of those who dwelt on this site in Minoan times.

After seeing Mírtos and the archaeological sites in its vicinity, one can then drive on toward Ierápetra, passing the coastal villages of Néa Mýrtos, Ammoudáres, Néa Anatolí, Stómio and Grá Ligiá. Then one arrives at Ierápetra, a port town on the Libyan Sea at the narrow waist of the Great Island, where the present itinerary comes to an end.

7

FROM IRÁKLION TO
ÁYIOS NIKÓLAOS

Most visitors to Crete at some time during their stay drive along the
north coast of the island from Iráklion to Áyios Nikólaos, the
picturesque port and holiday resort on the Gulf of Merabéllo. The
main highway is the quickest and easiest way to go from Iráklion to
Áyios Nikólaos, but the present itinerary will also describe sketches of
the old coast road, along with detours and diversions to sites of interest
on either side of the main route as well as some of the beaches on the
northern shore, with those on the Gulf of Merabéllo noted in the next
two itineraries.

The coast immediately to the east of Iráklion has already been
described in an earlier itinerary, particularly the archaeological site at
Amnisós and the Cave of Eileithyia. At Amnisós one also finds the first
of the succession of good beaches that stretch along the coast east of
Iráklion, with others to be described later in the itinerary that follows.

Driving eastward from Iráklion, one follows the shore around the
seaward spurs of Kakón Óros, the Bad Mountain, with the islet of Día
floating offshore some ten km distant. Día is one of three game
preserves now set aside for the *agrími*, or *kri-kri*, the long-horned wild
goat that is one of the symbols of Crete, once free to roam the
mountains of the Great Island but now confined to this and two other
offshore islets.

Thirteen kilometres east of Iráklion one comes to Kókkini Kháni,
also known by its older name of Armylídhes. Here one finds an
archaeological site known as Nírou Kháni, where a large Minoan villa
was discovered in 1918–19 by the Greek archaeologist S. Xanthoudhidhis. The eldest shards found on this site date to the Middle Minoan

period, but the villa itself appears to have been erected in the late Minoan I period, c. 1550 BC. The building complex is so large and impressive, 100 square metres in area, that Xanthoudhidhis originally described it as a Minoan palace, although later archaeologists have classified it as a villa, though a very grand one indeed. Some forty chambers have been unearthed on the ground floor alone, along with corridors and two courtyards, and evidence has been found of stairways leading to an upper floor. The main entrance to the villa was from the eastern courtyard, on the southern side of which there seems to have been a theatral area for the celebration of religious festivals, as evidenced by the discovery there of a pair of 'horns of consecration'. From the northern end of the southern courtyard one entered the vestibule of the villa and then its great hall, which was apparently the centre of its residential quarter. A chamber just to the west of the great hall, known as the Room of the Four Double Axes because of the sacred weapons found there, seems to have been the principal sanctuary of the villa. A chamber beyond the great hall to the north-west is known as the Room of the Lamps, so called because of the four steatite lanterns discovered there, and to the north of this is a chamber known as the Banquet Hall, so identified from the frescoes that adorned its walls. Another chamber to the north-east of the banquet hall is known as the Room of the Three Altars, taking its name from three offertory tables where bloodless sacrifices were offered to the divinity whose idol and sacred symbols were apparently displayed here. Such altars were also found in other rooms, which led Sir Arthur Evans to suggest that the villa at Nírou Kháni was the residence of a Minoan ruler who was also a high priest, and that this dignitary used the offertory tables to dispense sacred objects such as miniature double axes to votaries of the cult over which he presided.

The villa at Nírou Kháni was apparently served by a port about a kilometre to the west of Kókkini Kháni, at a place known as Ayíi Theódorii from a ruined chapel of that name that still stands there. Xanthoudhidhis began excavations at Ayíi Theódorii in 1918, after which Spyridon Marinatos took charge and in 1926 discovered a Minoan settlement there, along with harbour works that can still be seen beneath the surface of the water in the ancient port. It is believed that the Minoan harbour at Ayíi Theódorii dates from the same period as the villa at Nírou Kháni, both places undoubtedly controlled by Knossós.

Continuing the drive eastward along the coast, at 15km from Iráklion one passes on the right the village of Goúrnes, opposite which there is now a large US military base. Three kilometres farther along a side-road to the right, signposted for Goúves, leads to the village and beyond to the hamlet of Skotinó, which is 6km from the highway. Skotinó, which means 'Dark Passages', takes its name from an enormous cavern originally known as the Grotto of Ayía Paraskeví, now better known as the Cave of Skotinó. At the entrance to the cave there is a chapel known as Áyios Nikólaos Skotinós, which was built in 1639 and dedicated to SS Nikólaos and Harálambos. On the west side of the cave entrance there are the ruins of a much earlier church, believed to have been dedicated to Ayía Paraskeví. The Cave of Skotinó has been thoroughly studied by the French archaeologist Paul Fauré, who has found evidence that the grotto was used as a religious sanctuary from the Middle Minoan period up until Roman times. Fauré believes that the cave-sanctuary of Skotinó was originally dedicated to the goddess Brytomartis, a deity whose Minoan name is one of the few words of that ancient Cretan language which can be understood, meaning 'sweet maiden'. Brytomartis seems originally to have been a moon deity, her cult often associated with that of Dhiktynna, the Cretan goddess who was the deification of Mount Dhíkti. Brytomartis was also associated with the Greek fertility goddess Artemis, who apparently was also worshipped in the Cave of Skotinó in ancient times.

Twenty kilometres from Iráklion the highway crosses the Aposelémis, a winter torrent that has its sources in the slopes of Mount Dhíkti that form the northern ramparts of the Lasíthi plateau. This strategic crossing, once a ford across the Aposelémis, has twice been the scene of battles in the struggle for Cretan independence, the first against the Venetians in 1273 and the second against the Turks in 1827, with 150 Greek rebels drowning in the river on the latter occasion.

Three kilometres beyond the bridge a road leads off to the south through the lush Langáda valley to the Lasíthi plateau, a route described in a previous itinerary. Then, 26 kilometres from Iráklion, one comes to Limín Khersonísou, a seaside village that has in recent years become a very popular resort because of its excellent beach. Limín Khersonísou occupies part of the site of ancient Khersonisos, which in Minoan times served as the port of Lýttos, the town continuing in existence throughout the Graeco-Roman era and up until the early Byzantine period. The most renowned edifice in ancient Khersonisos was its temple of Brytomartis, which has disappeared without a trace, except for an inscription of the first century BC found by Marinatos near the church of Áyios Nikólaos, which is built on the ruins of a basilica of the sixth century AD. Aside from this and another basilica of the fifth century AD, the only other remains of ancient Khersonisos are a Roman fountain and some fragments of the Roman harbour works. There is also a rock in the Gulf of Khersonisos whose form resembles a girl holding a basin on her head; this is known as Kóri, the Maiden, and is the subject of local legends, one of which says that it is a young woman who was petrified after being cursed by her mother for having kissed one of her own brothers.

Four and a half kilometres beyond Limín Khersonísou the highway passes Stalída, a seaside hamlet with an excellent beach and several hotels. Then some four kilometres beyond Stalída one comes to Mállia, whose superb beach has made it one of the most popular summer resorts on the north coast of Crete. But the very popularity of the resort, with the rise of new hotels and tourist facilities, has obscured the fact that Mállia is a very old village, dating back to Venetian times, when it was known as the Villa de Maglia. The local church of the Panayía dates back to the Venetian period, with two of its icons bearing the date 1495. The church is known locally as Galathiáni, from *gála*, the Greek word for milk. This name arises from an old tradition that the church was built from mud bricks made from earth mixed with milk that the local herdsmen had brought down from the Lasíthi Mountains to make a sanctuary for the Virgin.

Four kilometres east of Mállia village a side-road on the left leads to the archaeological site known as Mállia, though the actual name of the ancient settlement is unknown, unlike Knossós and Phaestós. Ancient Mállia is set in a beautiful site near the sea, surrounded by olive groves, carob trees and fruit orchards, with the Lasíthi Mountains rising in the background to the south. The ruins themselves are quite beautiful, and though the Minoan palace here has not been re-constructed as grandiosely as Knossós, it still has a natural grandeur that comes from seeming an integral and noble part of the landscape.

The Minoan palace of Mállia was discovered by Joseph Hadzid-hakis in excavations that began in 1915, with the French School of Archaeology taking over in 1922 and subsequently studying the site systematically. These excavations have revealed that the site was inhabited in Neolithic times, with the first palace erected c. 1900 BC, at about the same time as the Old Palaces at Knossós and Phaestós. The first palace at Mállia was also destroyed at the same time as those at Knossós and Phaestós, c. 1700 BC. Soon afterwards a second palace was built on the same site, and this survived until c. 1450 BC, when it

125

was probably destroyed in the same catastrophe that levelled the New Palaces at Knossós and Phaestós. Part of the site at Mállia was apparently re-occupied after the destruction of the New Palace, a development that took place in the Late Minoan III period. Aside from this late development, the Minoan palace at Mállia resembles in its general plan and decoration the imperial residences at Knossós and Phaestós, although a number of individual features here give this site its own distinctive character. Though the actual name of the Minoan settlement at Mállia is unknown, tradition associates the site with Sarpedon, brother of King Minos, for he was the legendary ruler in these parts. According to tradition, Sarpedon was defeated by Minos in a struggle for supremacy on the Great Island and forced to flee off to south-western Anatolia, where he and his followers founded a number of cities and established the country that the Greeks later called Lycia.

The usual approach to the archaeological site at Mállia brings one to the West Court, where an ancient raised walkway paved with large rectangular stone slabs leads across the open area beside the western façade of the Minoan palace. At the south-western corner of the palace complex one's attention is inevitably drawn to the eight *koulouras* in two rows of four each, the stone-lined circular pits that the Minoans used for the storage of grain. These and the raised walkway across the West Court date back to the first period of the palace, the latter probably serving as a processional way for imperial and religious processions. The entrance to the western side of the palace would have been approached about halfway along this pathway, where a long corridor leads into the labyrinth of rooms that are believed to have served as the royal apartments, while at the far end of the raised walkway one turned right onto another paved walk that leads to the northern entrance. But the main public entrance to the palace seems to have been at the centre of the south façade, where a paved corridor leads past a congerie of rooms on its right into the south-western corner of the Central Court.

The usual approach to the interior of the palace is via the paved path that leads to the northern entrance, in the course of which one passes the north-west corner of the complex, where one can see the foundation walls of the Old Palace. After passing through the remains of the northern entryway one passes into the North Entrance Hall. This vestibule is at the western end of a series of half a dozen storage magazines that form the northernmost end of the palace, with another group of similar storerooms forming the north-eastern corner of the complex. These chambers and another series of such magazines along

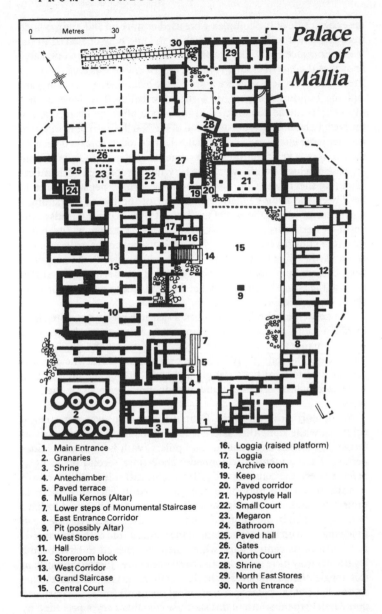

Palace of Mállia

1. Main Entrance
2. Granaries
3. Shrine
4. Antechamber
5. Paved terrace
6. Mullia Kernos (Altar)
7. Lower steps of Monumental Staircase
8. East Entrance Corridor
9. Pit (possibly Altar)
10. West Stores
11. Hall
12. Storeroom block
13. West Corridor
14. Grand Staircase
15. Central Court
16. Loggia (raised platform)
17. Loggia
18. Archive room
19. Keep
20. Paved corridor
21. Hypostyle Hall
22. Small Court
23. Megaron
24. Bathroom
25. Paved hall
26. Gates
27. North Court
28. Shrine
29. North East Stores
30. North Entrance

the eastern side of the complex were used to store oil and grain, which were contained in huge *pithoi*, such as the one now displayed in the North Entrance Hall. The North Entrance Hall leads to an open area known as the North Court. At the southern end of this area there is a later structure whose axes are askew to the main lines of the courtyard and the buildings around it, a structure believed to have been a Mycenaean shrine constructed in the period after the destruction of the New Palace. The south-west end of the North Court opens up into another large enclosure known as the Tower Court, so-called because the two rooms at its south-eastern corner are believed to have been in the base of a high watchtower. The labyrinthine complex of chambers adjoining the Tower Court at its south-western corner is believed to have been the King's Quarters, with one of the rooms containing a lustral basin. Just to the east of the Tower Court a corridor leads to the north-western corner of the Central Court, passing on its left a structure known as the Hypostyle Hall. This edifice has on its western end a narthex-like lobby with a central column, while the main hall has a colonnade of six pillars in two rows; it has been suggested that this was the palace kitchen, and that the royal dining room was directly above on the second floor.

One now enters the Central Court, a vast area measuring 48m along its north-south axis and 22m from east to west, an enclosure only slightly smaller than the main courtyards at Knossós and Phaestós. At the centre of the court there is an altar over a pit where sacrificial beasts are believed to have been slaughtered and then roasted on a grill in some sacramental ceremony undoubtedly presided over by the high priest.

At the northern end of the Central Court there was a portico of columns, while along the eastern side of the courtyard the arcade was formed by alternating columns and pillars, with both of these sides perhaps having identical colonnades above in a second floor. Post-holes between the columns and pillars on the east side of the courtyard indicate that there may have been a fenced-in enclosure there to protect the audience during the bull-games that are believed to have been performed in the Central Court. There also appears to have been a viewing-area on the second floor of the western side of the courtyard, just north of its central axis, where there is believed to have been a loggia that may have served as the royal enclosure. Just to the south of this 'loggia' there is a staircase that led up from the Central Court to the second floor of the palace. The area that opens off from the courtyard immediately to the south of this staircase contains a crypt preceded by a bench. Inside the crypt there are two pillars inscribed with double axes and other sacred symbols, and these, along with the evidence of animal bones, indicated that this was the site of secret rites accompanied by sacrifices.

At the south-west corner of the Central Court, where the paved corridor from the south entryway opens into the courtyard, there is a chamber that may also have been used for religious ceremonies. These ceremonies appeared to have focused on a circular stone there called the *kernos*, which has a large hollow at its centre and thirty-four smaller hollows around its periphery. These hollows are believed to have contained the *'panspermia'*, the first fruits of the bountiful Cretan harvest, placed on this stone altar as offerings to the fertility goddess of the Minoans.

Other rooms on the west side of the Central Court appear to have been used as cult-chambers, while the Royal Apartments seem to have been beyond these in the north-west corner of the palace. The rooms on the south side of the Central Court appear to have been used as workshops by the palace artisans, while the whole east side of the complex is made up of long and narrow chambers that served as granaries.

More recent excavations have unearthed a number of houses and other structures outside of the palace complex, undoubtedly part of the large Minoan town that developed around the imperial residence. One group of these structures can be seen under the corrugated roof just to the west of the north-western corner of the palace; this is known as the Hypostyle Crypt, and consists of a complex of houses, storage-magazines and benches, their function undetermined. Just to the north of the Hypostyle Crypt there is an immense area known as the North Court, measuring 40 by 29m, a quarter which from its foundations and the artefacts found there appears to have been the agora of the ancient town. West of the palace, behind the headquarters of the French Archaeological School, there is a covered excavation site known as Area Δ, which appears to have been a residential quarter of the Minoan town. About 75m to the north-west of this there is a site known as 'Quarter M', a large structure dating from the time of the Old Palace. This may have been an imperial residence, as evidenced by the sunken lustral basin found there, along with a store of archives written in hieroglyphics.

The most fascinating of the extra-palatial excavations at Mállia is a site about 500m north of the palace near the seashore. This is the so-called Chrysolakkos, the Golden Pit, an enormous rectangular mausoleum with several burial chambers, probably dating from the period of the Old Palace. The Chrysolakkos received its name from the numerous gold objects found there in early excavations, the most famous being a gold pendant in the form of two coupled bees, now on exhibit in the Iráklion Museum. This rich hoard indicates that the Chrysolakkos may have been an imperial tomb, perhaps built for the dynasty that ruled from the Old Palace at Mállia.

After passing the archaeological site at Mállia, the highway veers inland from the coastal plain and enters the wild gorge of Vrakhási, where at 43km from Iráklion one comes to the chapel of Áyios Yórgios Selínaris. This is a traditional stopping-place for those driving between Iráklion and Áyios Nikólaos, with travellers pausing to visit the chapel and afterwards stopping for lunch or a drink at one of the restaurants or cafés around the square. The chapel belongs to the Monastery of Selinári, now a home for the aged. Pilgrims from all over Crete congregate here for the great *paniyíri* of the monastery on 23 April, the feast day of Áyios Yórgios, when everyone in Greece named George celebrates his name's day. At such *paniyíria* it is customary to greet the celebrants by saying '*O pou Yórgos, kai malamá!*', 'Where you find George, you find gold!'

The Monastery of Selinári takes its name from Mount Seléna, whose highest peak, at an altitude of 1559m, rises about six km to the south-west. This peak was known in antiquity as the Mountain of Zeus Sellanius, which leads one to suspect that Ayios Yórgios Selínaris is a Christian reincarnation of an ancient Cretan deity, who became associated with Zeus in the post-Minoan times.

Most travellers continue from Selinári along the new highway to Áyios Nikólaos, but those with time to spare might be advised to take the old road, as in the present itinerary, which describes several interesting excursions en route. Following the old road beyond Selinári one comes next to the village of Vrakhási, 45km from Iráklion, perched on the southern slopes of Mount Anáviokhos at an altitude of 380m. After passing Vrakhási the valley of Skáfi Merabéllo suddenly comes into view, with Mount Stavrós rising to the left at an altitude of 794m, and on the right, at an altitude of 751m, Mount Kavalará, a lower peak of Mount Seléna.

Four kilometres beyond Vrakhási one can turn off onto a side-road for the village of Mílatos, which is 6.2km from the fork, situated about a kilometre from the north coast. Mílatos is the Doric form of Miletos, the ancient city that once flourished on the site of the present village. Archaeological excavations on the site of Miletos have unearthed a vase from the very end of the Late Minoan III period, c. 1400 BC, but nothing now remains of the ancient city itself. Miletos is mentioned by Homer in Book II of the *Iliad*, one of the seven Cretan cities that sent contingents to fight at Troy under the command of Idomeneus. Miletos was also the city from which Sarpedon left when he fled from Crete after his defeat at the hands of his brother Minos. According to tradition, the first city that Sarpedon and his followers founded in Asia Minor was Miletos, named for the native city of the Cretan colonists. Anataolian Miletos became the greatest of all the Ionian cities in Asia Minor, founding scores of colonies of its own and giving birth to the first three philosophers of nature in the Greek world: Thales, Anaximander and Anaximenes. But its founder, Cretan Miletos, faded into obscurity, and by Roman times the city no longer existed, having been destroyed by Knossós and Lýttus.

A turn-off to the left from the village, signposted for Spílio, or the Cavern, leads to the historic Mílatos Cave. In 1823 this cave served as a refuge for some 3700 Greek women, children and old people, who were besieged here by an army of 16,000 Turks under the command of Hasan Pasha. The Greek rebels in Merabéllo tried to break the siege, but they were hopelessly outnumbered, and so after holding out for two weeks those in the cave were forced to surrender to Hasan Pasha, who killed all of the old men and sold the women and children into slavery. A chapel dedicated to the Apostle Thomas was later erected in the Mílatos Cave, and each year on the anniversary of the 1823 massacre a memorial service is held there.

The road continues on past Mílatos to the seashore, where there are several restaurants that serve fresh fish caught by the local fishermen. Excavations here have revealed that this was the port of ancient Miletos, with evidence that the site was inhabited in Mycenaean times, though virtually nothing remains to be seen of this today. In any event, this is a perfect place to have lunch, and we spent a pleasant mid-day there while on our way from Iráklion to Áyios Nikólaos. Though there are no ruins here, the place is important in the pre-history of Crete, for the men of Miletos would have left from here when they went off to fight in Agamemnon's army in the Trojan War.

After the detour to Mílatos, one continues along the old road to Áyios Nikólaos, driving along the lush valley of Skáfi Merabéllo, whose name means literally the Trough of Merabéllo, indicative of its topography. Ahead one sees the villages of Latsídha and Voulisméni, and beyond them the town of Neápolis. Latsídha has two old chapels dating from the Venetian period; these are the Panayía Keragoniótissa and Ayía Paraskeví, both of them decorated with frescoes dating from the fourteenth or sixteenth centuries. Voulisméni is believed by some authorities to have been the site of the Roman town of Pannona, though other scholars place this in Monafátsi province. In any event, the present village of Voulisméni dates back to at least the Venetian period, when it was one of the largest towns in Merabéllo province. The village church, which is dedicated to both the Virgin and the Archangel Michael, has an inscription recording that it was restored in 1605.

Fifty-five kilometres along the old road from Iráklion one comes to Neápolis, which until 1904 was the capital of Merabéllo province, whose administrative centre is now Áyios Nikólaos. The original settlement, known then as the little village of Karés, dates back to the beginning of the Venetian occupation early in the thirteenth century. The most prominent figure produced by Karés was Petros Philargos, who was born there in 1340 and soon afterwards left a penniless orphan. The young boy was raised by the local Franciscan monks and sent for his education to their monastery school in Khándaks, where in 1357 he took monastic orders. Petros then continued his studies in Padua, Oxford and Paris, by which time he had become a distinguished teacher of philosophy, after which he travelled to Lithuania and converted the people there to Christianity, baptizing their ruler. The Duke of Milan, Giovanni Visconti, then invited Petros to his court and made him Ambassador, sending him on several diplomatic missions. The climax of his career came in 1409, when the Synod of Pisa elected him Pope as Alexander V. However he died in Bologna the following year and was buried there in the church of St Francis, where one can still see 'La Tomba di Alessandro V'.

In the meantime, Karés had been destroyed during the revolt of the brothers Psaromilingos against Venetian rule in 1341-7. Afterwards the town was rebuilt by the Venetians and called Villanova, known in Greek first as Neokhóri and then as Neápolis, all of these names meaning the New Village. Neápolis is renowned as one of the most progressive towns in Crete, noted for its fine School of Domestic Science and for its other educational institutions. It is also a very handsome town, its centre being the church of the Megáli Panayía with its charming square and gardens. From the square a road leads to the Monastery of Kremastá, which is about 2.5km from the town centre at an altitude of 360m. The monastery was founded in the last years of the sixteenth century, and during late Ottoman times it achieved considerable prominence because of its fine school and also because it was for a time the residence of the powerful Turkish governor of Lasíthi, the enlightened Kostis Adosides Pasha, who during the period 1867–71 made Neápolis the capital of Merabéllo and built numerous roads and public buildings.

Beyond Neápolis a road to the right leads to the Lasíthi plateau, while a short way farther along another road to the left brings one to the site of ancient Dreros. Archaeological excavations here have revealed that the site was inhabited as early as the Archaic period, with its earliest and most important edifice being the Temple of Apollo Delphinios, the Dolphin God, which dates to the seventh century BC. In this cult Apollo was represented as a dolphin, a form that the god assumed when he was guiding Greek mariners, particularly those who were embarked on the foundation of new colonies. The principal sanctuary in the Ionian city of Miletos in Asia Minor was that of Apollo Delphinios, which leads one to believe that perhaps the people of Dreros were associated with those of Cretan Miletos in the establishment of this colony on the Aegean coast of Anatolia. An altar filled with goat horns was also found within the temple of Apollo Delphinios in Dreros, a striking similarity to a sanctuary of Apollo in Delos known as the Keraton. According to tradition, the Keraton was built by Apollo from the horns of goats and other beasts slain at his shrine in sacrificial rites, and it was in front of this altar that the *Geranos* or Crane Dance was performed at the climax of the Delian Festival, symbolizing the flight of Leto before she gave birth to Apollo and Artemis. Tradition also holds that this dance was first performed at Délos by Theseus, who stopped there with his companions on their return voyage to Athens after having escaped from the labyrinth of King Minos on Crete. As Plutarch describes it, Theseus there 'danced with the young Athenians a dance that in memory of him, they say, is still preserved among the inhabitants of Délos, consisting of certain measured turnings and returnings, imitative of the windings and twistings of the labyrinth. And this dance . . . is called among the Delians *Geranos*, or the Crane Dance.'

Another fascinating discovery made in the temple of Apollo Delphinios at Dreros is a group of three statuettes of hammered bronze. This group is known as the Triad of Dreros, figures thought to be representations of Leto and her divine children Apollo and Artemis. The figures in the Triad are the earliest-known Greek statues of hammered bronze, and are now among the prize exhibits in the Iráklion Museum. Archaeologists have also discovered a second temple built at Dreros in the Classical period, and in early Venetian times its remains were built into the Catholic church of Áyios Antónios. Dreros remained a prominent city throughout the Archaic, Classical, and early Hellenistic periods, but then in 220 BC a political crisis divided its citizens and led to the eventual destruction of the city by its enemies. Another important find made among the ruins of Dreros are two bi-lingual inscriptions in Greek and Eteocretan, records that are of vital importance in the continuing effort to decipher the oldest-known language of the people who inhabited the Great Island before the coming of the Doric Greeks.

Resuming the drive eastward from Neápolis, one passes along the way a line of old windmills where a side-road leads to the coast and the resort village of Eloúnda, more easily approached by the road that leads along the coast of the Gulf of Merabéllo from Áyios Nikólaos. Continuing along, one then passes the villages of Nikithianó, Límnes, Khoumeriákos and Vrísses, as a splendid view opens up ahead of the Gulf of Merabéllo and its surrounding shores. The road then follows the streambed of the Xiropótamos River to the sea, passing the village of Xirókampos, and coming finally to Áyios Nikólaos, the picturesque port-town that has now become the most popular summer resort in all of Crete.

8

🔲🔲🔲

ÁYIOS NIKÓLAOS AND ITS ENVIRONS

Áyios Nikólaos, the modern capital of Lasíthi province, is a pretty and exceptionally picturesque port-town on the western side of the Gulf of Merabéllo. The civic centre of the town, the prefecture of Lasíthi, is on the promontory that forms the southern arm of the port; this occupies the site of Lato Pros Kamára, the harbour of the ancient city of Lato Etera, whose ruins are to be seen some five kilometres inland to the east of Áyios Nikólaos. Virtually nothing remains of Lato Pros Kamára, other than some fragmentary Graeco-Roman ruins that have been uncovered at several places in the outskirts of Áyios Nikólaos.

During the first century of Venetian rule the present site of the prefecture in Áyios Nikólaos was occupied by the Castle of Merabéllo, from which the Gulf of Merabéllo and its surrounding region took their name. This castle was erected in 1206 by Enrico Pescatore, Count of Malta, a Genoese adventurer who built or reconstructed fourteen castles on Crete within two years of the Capture of Constantinople by the Latin knights of the Fourth Crusade in 1204. Pescatore hoped thus to seize the Great Island and create there his own kingdom, but in 1212 he was forced to sign an armistice with Venice and abandon Castle Merabéllo and his other strongholds on Crete, whereupon the Venetians began their long occupation. The Castle of Merabéllo was badly damaged in an earthquake in 1303 and never completely rebuilt. It was then reduced to ruins after successive sieges by the Turks and the Venetians in 1645 and finally abandoned, though apparently fragments of the fortress survived until the end of the Ottoman period.

135

Áyios Nikólaos takes its modern name from a mariners' chapel dedicated to that saint on the seashore just to the north of the town. During Venetian times this settlement was named Porto di San Nicolo, while the harbour itself was called Mandráki. In 1870 the harbour was joined by a short canal to a small but very deep lake that now forms the inner port, a feature thus described by Spratt after his visit to Áyios Nikólaos in 1865:

> On the east side of the cove called the 'Mandragio' of St Nikolo is a small circular pool of brackish water, about 150 yards in diameter. It is separated from the sea by about twenty yards of low ground only; and yet this pool was found to have a depth of 210 feet in the centre – a depth which is not attained in the adjacent sea within two or three miles of the coast. But in the traditions of the natives of the locality, it was said to be unfathomable, and to communicate with the lower regions of troubled spirits. The sides of this hollow, beneath the surface of the pool, must constitute a precipitous funnel-shaped depression. Yet there is no appearance of its being a volcanic vent, or even the result of volcanic action, by any proximate igneous rocks being visible; and as it still has a small stream opening out of it into the sea, I think it was at one time the aperture of a larger source or subterranean river, which found its escape here from the heart of the mountains above.

Up until the early 1960s Áyios Mikólaos remained a quiet little port-town and provincial capital, but then it began to attract foreigners in increasing numbers, so that now it is an internationally-known resort. At last count Áyios Nikólaos had at least a dozen hotels, in addition to those at Eloúnda and other nearby beaches, and the waterfront is lined with restaurants, cafés, bars, boutiques and other touristic establishments catering almost exclusively to foreigners. And so when we first visited Áyios Nikólaos in the early summer of 1985 we expected to find that it had been spoiled, but we were pleasantly surprised to see that the hordes of foreigners had not marred the astonishing beauty of the port, which appeared to be as uniquely charming as it was in the old photographs that we had seen or in the accounts of earlier travellers we had read. Much of the quaint charm of Áyios Nikólaos comes from its bipartite port, the Voulismeni lake opening off the inner end of Mandráki harbour through a very short canal crossed by a little bridge, the deep lagoon giving the waterfront a faintly Venetian topography. Thus in the evening promenade at Áyios Nikólaos, the time-honoured *vólta*, one can walk along the periphery

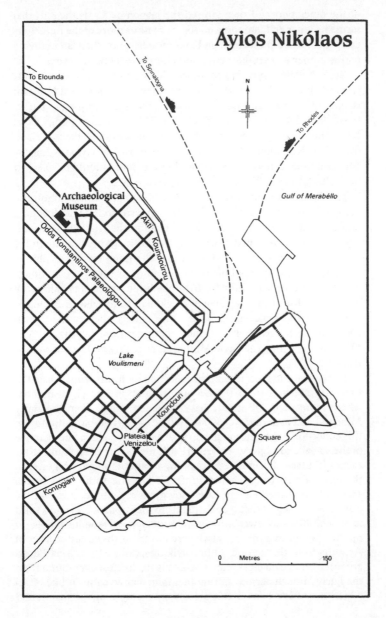

Áyios Nikólaos

of the outer port and then around the lagoon as far as the cliff that forms its inner end, stopping en route at one or more of the numerous cafés that line both the inner and outer waterfronts, then later moving on for dinner at a seaside restaurant elsewhere along the *paralía*.

Áyios Nikólaos now has more to offer visitors than just its cafés, restaurants and adjacent beaches, for its new Archaeological Museum is very interesting and quite attractive. The museum is five blocks from the north-west corner of Voulismèni Lake along Odós Konstantínos Palaeológou, which is itself three-to-four blocks inland from Aktí Koundoúrou, the seaside 'boulevard' of Áyios Nikólaos. The best time to go is late morning, but the hours should be checked beforehand at the office of the local tourist police.

The Archaeological Museum at Áyios Nikólaos exhibits antiquities discovered in recent years at various sites in eastern Crete, with objects found in earlier digs in this region housed in the Iráklion Museum. The antiquities range in date from the Neolithic age up until the end of the Graeco-Roman era, in addition to a charming exhibit of objects illustrating the folklore of the region up until relatively recent times. The most interesting exhibit from the Neolithic period is a phallic *idole* of red sandstone from the Cave of Pelekíta at Káto Zákros. Professor Costas Davaras believes this *idole* to be 'totally alien to the Cretan tradition', seeing parallels to it among figurines from Cyprus and Asia Minor representing the Great Mother, the fertility goddess of ancient Anatolia.

The largest and most important collection in the museum consists of funerary offerings from the necropolis at Ayía Photiá, near Sitía, where more than 250 graves have been unearthed from the Early Minoan I and II periods (c. 3000–2300 BC). One notable exhibit from this collection is a chalice in the form of a double cone, a fine example of the so-called Pýrgos ware, remarkable for having been found so far east of its place of origin near Iráklion; another is a spherical ewer in the form of a partridge, which Professor Davaras thinks may be the earliest bird-shaped Cretan vase known, an early predecessor of the numerous vessels of that type dating from the Bronze Age; and a third is a semi-lustrous ewer with an almost vertical spout, similar to pitchers found in Troy and elsewhere in the north-western corner of Anatolia from that period. Other striking exhibits from Ayía Photia are three bronze daggers, one of which is the longest ever found from the Early Minoan period; and another is an incised canteen-like vessel which may have been a cult-object, an example of the mysterious

Cycladic 'frying-pans' that may be abstract and magical representations of the Great Earth Mother.

Another outstanding pottery collection is from Fourno Korifi, whose site near Mírtos was described toward the end of the itinerary that concluded just west of Ierápetra (see p. 121). The most extraordinary object in this collection, which includes some 700 vases, is an anthropomorphic libation vase called the 'Goddess of Mírtos'. The vase is in the form of a legless bell-shaped body with a long goose neck and a weird ET-like head, with two long spindly arms emerging from the sides to embrace a smaller vessel, the female characteristics manifested in the tiny breasts which are merely two applied hemispherical lumps of clay, with the pubic hair represented by a painted grid of the same red colour and netted design as that depicting the woven garment in which she is clothed. This enigmatic vase is probably another cult-object symbolizing the Great Earth Mother, dating from the Early Minoan II B period.

Another style of Early Minoan II pottery exhibited in the museum is that of the famous Vasilikí ware, known for its site of origin on the isthmus of Ierápetra. As Professor Davaras describes the Vasilikí ware: 'This reddish-brown mottled pottery has a semi-lustrous surface with random mottling all over . . . The mottling is basically red with orangey and reddish-brown tones, with black spots and lighter areas. The decorative effects with its shining hues was unusually rich in variety and exceptionally attractive.' Two particularly fine examples of Vasilikí ware are exhibited in the museum; these are a 'teapot' with an incredibly long spout and a beak-spouted ewer, both found in the Early Minoan II B settlement at Mírtos.

The museum also has several important examples of gold jewellery from the Prepalatial period, most of which came from an Early Minoan II–III necropolis on the islet of Móchlos. Among the beautiful pieces in this collection are a hairpin in the form of a daisy, a lily-shaped bead, several sprays of foliate leaves once used as adornments for the hair of Minoan maidens, and a splendid golden diadem decorated in dot-repoussé with the figures of three *agrími*, the long-horned Cretan wild goats who still live in a game preserve on Ayíi Pántes, the tiny islet just outside the harbour of Áyios Nikólaos.

The museum also has a small but elegant collection of stone vases. Three of these are from the cemetery at Móchlos: a small cylindrical vase decorated with grooves made from multi-coloured limestone; a *pyxis* of the same stone and of similar design; and a 'sauce boat' of finely-veined limestone. Another unusual example is a 'tea-pot' of breccia, a leopard-like conglomerate stone, found in the necropolis at Gourniá, at the south-eastern end of the Gulf of Merabéllo.

One particularly fascinating group of exhibits in the museum is the collection of figurines and other votive-objects found in eastern Crete at mountaintop sanctuaries, a type of shrine that first appears at the end of the third millennium BC. These include the figures of men and women shown with their arms crossed or clasped to their breast in attitudes of prayer, including statuettes of several ladies with elaborate coiffures and headdresses that were popular in Minoan times. Other *ex-votos* include 'horns of consecration' in clay and plaster, a bull-head that was once part of a large libation vase; the naked torso of a female figure that may have been used as part of a fertility cult; and various representations of limbs and other parts of the human anatomy that may have been offered in thanksgiving to the mother-goddess for cures that she brought about.

There is also an interesting collection of pottery from the Late Minoan I B villa at Makrygialós in Sitía, an excavation carried out by Professor Davaras. One of these vessels is a beautiful marble chalice, apparently used in a Minoan communion-rite, some fifteen centuries before the beginning of the Christian era. Another striking exhibit in this collection is a clay alabastron decorated with the figures of two octopuses with their extended tentacles intertwined around the entire body of the vase, a dramatic work that is thought to be from one of the royal workshops at Knossós.

One of the most remarkable objects in the museum is the clay figurine of a female votary or priestess found at Myrsíni in Sitía, dating from the Late Minoan III A period. The lower half of the woman's body is represented as a short cylinder with a cross painted beneath the base, another haunting precursor of Christianity. The upper half of the figure represents the woman with her hands clasped together at her breasts in prayer, with a pious expression evident in her eyes though her face is an almost featureless abstract sculpture, a work of remarkable power for all of its apparent simplicity.

There are also on exhibit in the museum two objects bearing inscriptions in the as-yet undeciphered Linear A script. One of these is a clay bar of the Middle Minoan II period found in the palace of Mállia, with an inscription in Linear A on all four of its faces, some of them ideograms representing various types of vases. The second object is a gold pin with a miniscule inscription in Linear A on one side, consisting of eighteen characters, while on the other it is decorated with an incised design in the form of a bramble with rich foliage; this superb jewel was purchased in Brussels in 1981 and presented as a gift to the museum, its provenance remaining unknown.

The museum also has an important collection of Mycenaean pottery, unearthed in a number of chamber tombs of the Late Minoan III A/B period. These include: an incense burner decorated with painted horns of consecration; an amphora painted with the figures of birds; another amphora painted with the forms of hanging lyres; a *kalathos*, or basket-like vase, which in its form and decoration is obviously an imitation of a real woven basket; a funnel-like libation cup decorated with papyrus leaves and other designs; an elegant high-footed *kylix* with a spiral design; a stirrup-cup decorated with the undulating tentacles; an amphora with scenes depicting a dense foliage of papyrus leaves; and a cult-object consisting of three joined vessels, with small birds in relief perched on the lips of the vases, undoubtedly representing the epiphany of a goddess.

One particularly evocative collection consists of objects from the Bronze Age, including bronze weapons, tools, ritual objects and bronzeware for daily use. These include large daggers with ivory handles, the *elephanti dedemena* referred to in contemporary Linear B tablets in Mycenaean Greek; spear or javelin points; double axes, which seem to have been used for cutting wood rather than as sacred ritual objects, though some of them may have been *ex-votos*; and a basin with a single handle, an example of the Bronze Age craftsmanship that was so admired in later times.

One interesting series of exhibits is the collection of terracotta sarcophagi and funerary urns. Two of the sarcophagi are in the shape of old-fashioned bathtubs, an unusual form found only on eastern Crete and in the ancient Ionian city of Clazomenae on the Aegean shore of Asia Minor; the first of these is decorated with the figures of birds, while the second has octopuses with elongated undulating tentacles outside and dolphins on the inner surface. One extraordinary exhibit in this collection of funerary pottery is a Late Minoan III C burial which was transferred *in toto* from its site at Kryá; as Professor Davaras describes it, this is 'a rare example of an infant inhumation in a *pithos*, which was placed inside a kind of miniature *tholos* tomb. With great difficulty this unique tomb from the end of the Bronze Age was transferred in its entirety to the Museum without displacing a single stone, excepting the narrow slab at the front which closed off the mouth of the *pithos*.'

The Dark Ages of ancient Crete are represented in the museum by a haunting collection of figurines from Vrakhási, dating from the beginning of the first millennium BC. Two of these are clay votive figurines, weird abstract representations of the human face and form evoking images of ancient Minoan rites of religious magic. These anionic statuettes appear to be imitations of sacred wooden figurines representing the fertility goddess, similar to the 'xoanons' known to have been venerated during the Geometric period. A third such figure is in the form of a bell-bottomed vase whose upper half is in the form of a woman with tiny exposed breasts, with a strange removable head that is more vulpine than human.

Other interesting objects of the Post-Minoan age are Creto-mycenaean funerary offerings found in a chamber tomb at Miletos, one lovely item being a spouted gypsum jug of the Late Minoan III A period. Other objects found in the same tomb include a few fragments of amber from the Baltic, an exceptional rarity on Crete, and a miniature ivory crocodile, evidence of contacts between the Great Island and Egypt.

Also of interest are the so-called 'daedalic' figurines of the seventh century BC; these are named for Daedalus, the legendary artisan and inventor who worked for King Minos. Three daedalic figurines are exhibited in the museum, one of them a beautiful bust of a woman that serves as the cover for a cylindrical vessel. The maiden's forehead is adorned with a fringe of curls and her face lighted up in a faint Giaconda smile, representing the dawn of the Archaic age on Crete.

There are also a number of terracotta reliefs from the Archaic period on display in the museum. One of these, found at Tourtoúli, Sitía, shows a young warrior striding forward while he leads a smaller youth by the hand, evidently his reluctant captive. This is believed to represent a scene from the Achaean conquest of Troy, showing Achilles leading the captive Troilus, the youngest son of Priam. Other Archaic sculptures in the collection were found at Oloús, an ancient city on the isthmus joining the main Spinalónga peninsula-island to the mainland near the north-western end of the Merabéllo Gulf. Two of these are large busts of female figures, probably representing goddesses, with both maidens having elaborate coiffures and beaming in archaic smiles. Among the other objects found at Oloús there are some interesting votive figurines; a siren, or maiden-faced bird; a votive rooster; a goddess or priestess wearing the tall conical headdress known as a *polos*; and a *kourothropos*, a young woman tenderly holding a baby to her breast, looking very much like the Virgin and Christ child, yet another prefiguration of Christianity on the Great Island in ancient times.

One last exhibit of considerable interest, though macabre, is a skull with a gold wreath representing olive leaves affixed to its cranium. This skull was found in a cemetery at Potamós, which in antiquity would have been part of Lato Pros Kamára, now the town of Áyios Nikólaos. Exhibited along with the skull is a silver coin that had been placed in the mouth of the deceased, the traditional fare paid by the dead to the boatman Charon, who ferried them across the River Styx to the Underworld. The coin is a silver tetradrachma from the Cretan town of Polyrhínia minted by the Emperor Tiberius, thus dating the burial to the period of his reign, AD 14–37. Also here is a superb aryballos, which was found at the feet of the deceased; when in life he would have used this vessel as a container for the olive oil with which he annointed himself after exercise in the *palaestra* of Lato Pros Kamára.

Most of the tourists who visit Áyios Nikólaos go on to Eloúnda, the most popular beach-resort on Crete, which is an eleven-kilometre drive to the north along the coast of the Gulf of Merabéllo. Along the last stretch of the drive one commands a magnificent view of the north-western shore of the gulf, where the long peninsula-island of Spinalónga extrudes out from a narrow isthmus and extends for some four kilometres to the north parallel to the coast, a narrow inlet of the sea that is virtually a salt lake, its narrow entrance partially blocked by the tiny islet of Nisí Spinalónga, the Venetian fortress that in times past was used as a leper colony.

The isthmus joining the Spinalónga peninsula to the mainland was the site of Oloús, which in antiquity was the port of Dreros. During the pre-Hellenic period Oloús was apparently known as Olontion, a name that has survived in the present Eloúnda. The isthmus on which Oloús stood was higher and much wider in antiquity, and much of the city was submerged in the surrounding sea during the general subsidence that lowered and narrowed this neck of land to its present dimensions. Part of the harbour of ancient Oloús can still be seen beneath the surface of the sea in the shallow waters off the isthmus on a calm day, and other remnants are visible on and around the neck, the most prominent being in a field about 100m from the shore where archaeologists have unearthed an early Christian basilica with a mosaic pavement decorated with marine scenes.

The name Spinalónga was originally applied by the Venetians to the whole of the peninsula that extends north from the isthmus, but today it is used to designate the little islet off its northern tip, where a ruined Venetian fortress still guards the entrance to the inlet. Apparently there was a fortress on Spinalónga island in antiquity, its purpose being to protect the entrance to the harbour of Oloús. This ancient fortress seems to have been still standing in 1574, when Venetian military engineers first surveyed the islet with a view to build more modern fortifications there in order to protect their port at Eloúnda. One of the engineers built a model of the ancient fortress before it was destroyed to make way for the present Venetian stronghold, and this miniature replica of the classical castle can still be seen in a museum in Venice. The present Venetian fortress was completed in 1579 by Jacopo Foscarini, the Proveditore Generale at the time. The fortress on Spinalónga was one of the most formidable of the Venetian castles on Crete, with an armament that in 1630 comprised thirty-five cannon of various sizes. The fortifications on Spinalónga were so impregnable that the Turks were unable to capture the islet in 1669, when they took Candia to complete their conquest of Crete, and the fortress there remained in Venetian hands until 1715, when it was finally surrendered to the Ottomans along with two other offshore castles elsewhere on the Great Island. The fortress was then occupied by the Turks to protect their shipping in the harbour, and a Turkish village developed on the islet.

The Turkish community on Spinalónga remained until 1903, when the Cretan government announced its decision to turn the island into a leper colony, whereupon all of the Moslem families who had been living there fled to the mainland opposite, to be repatriated to Turkey two decades later. Spinalónga then became a refuge for the lepers who had been living as pariahs elsewhere on Crete, eking out a miserable existence in shantytowns outside the walls of Candia or huddling in caves in the mountains. With government help, the lepers then repaired the dilapidated houses on Spinalónga and created their own self-contained community there, with a hospital, church, and even tavernas where they could eat together, enjoy themselves, listen to music, and dance, just as Cretans did elsewhere on the Great Island, though here on their quarantined island they were doomed to disfiguration and painful death. The leper colony, which reached a maximum population of about four hundred, remained on Spinalónga until 1957, when those who were still there were moved to a hospital in Athens. In the years since then the island of Spinalónga has been opened up to the public, and one can still see the abandoned village of the leper colony there within the walls of the Venetian fortress.

One of the most popular excursions from Áyios Nikólaos is to Kritsá and Lató. The initial approach to both sites is via the highway that leads to Sitía and Ierápetra; then about a kilometre out of town one turns off onto a road that leads to the village of Kritsá, which is some 12km from Áyios Nikólaos. Both sites are signposted, with the first coming into view about a kilometre before reaching the village, where one sees the whitewashed church of the Panayía Kéra standing serenely alone in the midst of an olive grove.

Panayía Kéra, the church of the All-Holy Lady, is believed to have been founded in the thirteenth century, the date of its central nave, with the two side aisles and the supporting buttresses at their flanks added during the following century, when the interior was adorned with the superb frescoes that make this the greatest monument of Byzantine art in Crete.

Before examining the frescoes in detail, one might first pause to study briefly the architecture of the church. The church is almost square in plan, except for the three semicircular apses that form the eastern ends of the central nave and its two flanking side aisles. The original thirteenth-century edifice consisted of the central nave and its surmounting dome, which is supported by four piers and carried on the high cylindrical drum characteristic of late Byzantine churches. This single-aisled church was dedicated to the Assumption of the Blessed Virgin. The first of the two side aisles to be added (in the fourteenth century) was the southern one, dedicated to Ayía Ánna, followed by the erection of the northern aisle, dedicated to Áyios Antónios.

The frescoes that adorn the interior of the church are dated in the same chronological order as the structure of the three main lateral sections of the edifice, with the paintings in the central aisle remaining from the original decoration of the thirteenth century, while the side aisles were apparently painted during the early part of the fourteenth century, part of the brilliant cultural renaissance that took place in Byzantium under the Palaeologus dynasty, its effects felt even in Venetian-controlled Crete. The main iconographic themes in the church reflect the dedication of its three parts, particularly the south aisle. There the domical vault of the apse is filled with a bust of Ayía Ánna, while in the upper zone of the aisle itself there are scenes from the life of her daughter, the Blessed Virgin, based on the Apocryphal Gospels, while the lower zone has representations of saints. However, the traditional decorative scheme is interrupted in the northern aisle, where the main subject is the Second Coming of Christ, while the vault of the central aisle is covered with scenes depicting the Ascension, with Christ Pantocrator in the crown of the arch above the *víma*, or holy altar, and in the lower zone of the apse behind it the fragmentary figures of the Co-Officiating Hierarchs. But this very brief outline merely suggests the main iconographic themes of the fresco decoration of the Panayía Kéra, where one afternoon we caught a brief glimpse of the brilliant religious visions of Byzantium in the last centuries of the Empire, immortalized here in this magnificent little church amidst the vast olive grove that fills the verdant Kritsá plain.

Two kilometres farther along, just before the main asphalt road enters the village of Kritsá, a signposted dirt road to the right leads off to the site of ancient Lato Etera, a drive of some 4km past the turn-off. This brings one to the archaeological site, known locally as Goulás, with the ruins spread over the twin peaks of a double acropolis hill and the saddle that extends between them. These ruins were first explored by Spratt, though he incorrectly identified this as the site of Oloús, rather than Lato Etera, an identification that was established by the excavations of the French School in 1899–1900.

Lato Etera was founded in the post-Minoan era, probably at the time of the Doric migration to Crete during the Dark Ages of the ancient Greek world. It became the dominant city in the region during the Archaic period, flourishing on through the Classical and Hellenistic periods. Lato Etera had its port at Lato Pros Kamára, which was on the site of the present town of Áyios Nikólaos, with the two places treated as one administrative unit. The principal deity in both Lato Etera and Lato Pros Kamára was the fertility goddess Eileithyia, a cult which the original settlers here undoubtedly inherited from the Minoans they found dwelling in this region at the time of the Dorian migration.

The most interesting and important part of the archaeological site at Lato Etera is the quarter around the *agora*, or market-place. Wycherley, in his *How the Greeks Built Cities*, found this to be the archetypal example of the *agora* of an Archaic town, with strong Minoan traditions. The other civic institutions of Lató are scattered close around this irregular-shaped market square, including the *Prytaneion*, or town hall, as well as a *stoa*, an *exedra*, a sanctuary, a stone circle believed to be a threshing-floor, and a broad flight of steps leading up to a platform that may have been a theatral area, where the stumps of two columns still stand *in situ*. The view from the upper part of the site is superb, looking out over the Kritsa plain to the western shores of Merabéllo.

After visiting Lató one might continue on into Kritsá, one of the largest villages in Crete, set in a lovely location amidst the green sea of carob trees and olive groves in the Kritsá plain, at an altitude of 300m. Kritsá is renowned for its local folk handicrafts, examples of which are displayed outside many of the village houses. While in Kritsá one might also ask directions to two other frescoed Byzantine chapels in the vicinity of the village. One of these is the church of Áyios Yórgios Kavousitiótis, whose wall-paintings are believed to be from late thirteenth/early fourteenth century; the other is Áyios Ioánnis Theológos, whose frescoes have a dedicatory inscription dated 1370.

The most popular of all the archaeological excursions from Áyios Nikólaos is to Gourniá, a Minoan site at the south-western end of the Gulf of Merabéllo. This drive brings one along the Áyios Nikólaos-Sitía highway past one of the most beautiful coastlines in Crete, a succession of scenic promontories, inlets and sandy coves, with several excellent places to swim, the best-known being Ístro and Pachiá Ámmos.

There are also several interesting diversionary excursions one can take on the way from Áyios Nikólaos. Just before Ístro, 13km out of Áyios Nikólaos, a side-road to the right leads off via Kaló Khorió to the south-western end of the Dhíkti range and then down to the southern coast of Crete, with a branch-road from Kalemáfka leading to Ierápetra. Those driving this way might take the opportunity of visiting the archaeological site at Vrócastro, south-east of Kaló Khorió, where one can ask directions or engage a guide. 'Vrócastro' is a shortened version of 'Evreócastro', meaning the 'Fort of the Jews', a name that one occasionally finds applied to ancient ruins in Greece and Asia Minor. The site at Vrócastro was excavated in 1910–12 by Edith Hall of the University of Pennsylvania, who found there remains dating from the Middle and Late Minoan eras as well as from the Geometric period. Minoan remains have also been found at five other sites in the vicinity of Kaló Khorió, namely at the places known locally as Kopránes, Masikókhorta, Priniátikos Pýrgos, Káto Arnicó and Amygdháli, the latter being an Early Minoan site also excavated by Miss Hall.

Six kilometres beyond the turn-off to Kaló Chorió on the Áyios Nikólaos-Sitía highway there is another turn-off to the right that leads to the Convent of Faneroméni, a six-kilometre drive up into the steep hills above the coast at the south-western end of the gulf. Faneroméni was founded no later than the fifteenth century, when a nunnery was built around a grotto where a local miraculously discovered a sacred icon of the Panayía Theotókou, the Mother of God. The cave-sanctuary dedicated to the Virgin at that time is still functioning, its walls adorned with fragments of its original late-Byzantine frescoes. The convent is also a superb site for looking out over the whole of the Gulf of Merabéllo, one of the most magnificent marine landscapes in all of Greece.

Nineteen kilometres out of Áyios Nikólaos one finally comes to a turn-off signposted for Gourniá, whose site is just beside the old coast road. This is one of the most appealing archaeological sites in Crete, set on the gentle slopes of a low mound just below the higher hills that rise up from the southern shore of the Gulf of Merabéllo, which is here indented by a little bay that was probably the harbour of the Minoan town. And Gourniá is all the more charming because here one is not looking on a grand imperial palace or villa but an ordinary Minoan town, its narrow cobbled streets still winding through the labyrinthine maze of foundation-walls that survive from its houses and public edifices, a romantic sight that strongly evokes the vanished life of this ancient place.

Gourniá was first excavated in 1901–4 by Harriet Boyd-Hawes, who found that the site was settled at the beginning of the second millenium BC, with the town flourishing c. 1600 BC and continuing in existence until c. 1450 BC, when it appears to have been destroyed in the same catastrophe that brought down Knossós and the other great centres of Minoan civilization on Crete. There is some evidence that Gourniá was inhabited again in the period 1300–1200 BC, but if so the settlement was a small and short-lived one, perhaps squatters living among the ruins of the once-great Minoan town. In any event, Gourniá never revived after the Bronze Age, and in subsequent times its ruins were buried and the town so completely forgotten that there are no references to it in ancient sources. Even the Minoan name of the town is unknown, the present place name stemming from the little stone troughs called *goúrnes*, which were found in large numbers during the archaeological excavation of the site, virtually every house having one outside its door, here again evoking the vanished past of this ancient place.

The ancient town of Gourniá is laid out very much like the large villages one sees today in the Cretan mountains, with small houses crowded together chockablock along a few narrow cobbled lanes on a hilltop site. These ancient lanes divide Gourniá into four unequal and irregular quarters, with the main street extending north-south just inside the western periphery of the town, a second street bordering the

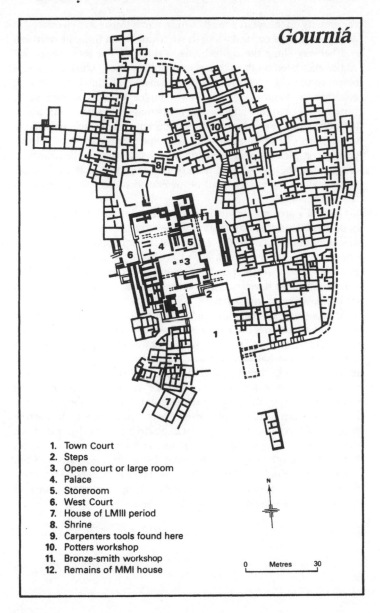

Gourniá

1. Town Court
2. Steps
3. Open court or large room
4. Palace
5. Storeroom
6. West Court
7. House of LMIII period
8. Shrine
9. Carpenters tools found here
10. Potters workshop
11. Bronze-smith workshop
12. Remains of MMI house

N

0 Metres 30

community on the west, a third cutting across from east to west well in on the northern side, and a fourth stretching down from the northern end halfway along the central axis of the site. The most important edifice excavated on the site is the so-called palace, which is perhaps more accurately identified as the mansion of the local Minoan governor of Gourniá. This is a complex of apartments, halls, storerooms, corridors and stairways opening off a small court about halfway along the southern stretch of the street that runs uphill along the western side of Gourniá. The large open area to the south of this palatial complex has been identified as the principal public courtyard or *agora* of the town. A sanctuary has also been identified about halfway along the western half of the east-west cross-street, north of the palace complex.

Gourniá's greatest archaeological interest lies not in its individual buildings but in their contents, for the town appears to have been a hive of industry, with the houses of its inhabitants yielding an astonishing number and variety of artifacts, tools, implements and products related to their various trades and commercial activities, which appear to have included agriculture, stock farming, fishing, building, weaving and pottery.

After visiting Gourniá one can return to the new coastal highway and continue driving towards Sitía. Two kilometres or so beyond the turn-off to Gourniá one passes Pachiá Ámmos, a little port-town with a good beach that has now become a popular summer resort. Then, some 4km past Pachiá Ámmos, the highway brings one to the first of the two crossroads that extend across the narrow eastern end of the Great Island from the Aegean coast to the southern shore and the Libyan Sea, with the lateral highway here cutting across the narrow isthmus to Ierápetra. This route will be described at the end of the itinerary that follows, which takes one around easternmost Crete, beginning with the stretch of highway from the crossroads to Sitía, where from the heights one can look back on the Merabéllo Gulf and the splendour of promontories and coves along its coast, the town of Áyios Nikólaos sparkling on the western shore.

9

◫◫◫

EASTERN CRETE

Eastern Crete has a quite distinctive character of its own, differing from the other regions of the Great Island in its appearance, topography and even in its people, whom some writers in both modern and ancient times believe to be the Eteocretans, the descendants of the Minoans.

Be that as it may, eastern Crete is different, and this change is immediately apparent when one drives eastward along the Áyios Nikólaos-Sitía highway beyond the crossroads where the lateral highway cuts south-west across the isthmus to Ierápetra, and as one leaves behind the coastal plain south of the Merabéllo Gulf and begins ascending the north-western foothills of the Sitía Mountains.

The first village that one comes to along this route is Kavoúsi, about 6km past the crossroads and 28km out of Áyios Nikólaos. Kavoúsi is used as a base by those climbing Aféndis Stavroménos, the highest peak in the Sitía Mountains (1476m). There are also three chapels in and around Kavoúsi that date from the late Byzantine period, as well as a small Post-Minoan archaeological site named Cástro, also excavated by Harriet Boyd-Hawes. The latter site is one of the places mentioned by John Pendlebury in his *Archaeology of Crete*, where he writes that

> after the break up of the Bronze Age civilization we find the castles of the robber barons on the rocky eyries of Karphí, Kavoúsi, Vrócastro, and the Zákros Gorge. No consideration of a water supply is shown. The one concern is inaccessibility.

And with that chilling note one suddenly catches a glimpse of life in the Dark Ages of ancient Crete, sheer terror driving the Eteocretans to this and other remote crags to escape from the murderous invaders who had driven them from their homes, probably fleeing from the Dorian Greeks who migrated from the Pelopónnisos to the Great Island early in the first millennium BC.

From Kavoúsi onwards the road takes one *en corniche* along the northern edge of the Sitía Mountains, with spectacular views of the beautiful coast that travel brochures refer to as the Cretan Riviera. An excellent place from which to enjoy this view is Plátanos, 7km beyond Kavoúsi, where there is a roadside spring with several outdoor tavernas and cafés. From Plátanos one can see the small island of Pséira floating about three kilometres offshore just to the north, and some two miles to the south-south-east of this is the tiny islet of Móchlos, almost connected to the far side of the cape that forms the eastern limit of the Merabéllo Gulf. Móchlos was originally connected to the cape, but a subsidence of the earth separated it from the mainland at some time in antiquity, probably in the first millennium BC. The American archaeologist Richard Seager excavated both Pséira and Móchlos in 1907–8, finding evidence of settlements there that flourished from the Early through the Late Minoan eras, contemporary with the nearby town of Gourniá. The Greek archaeologist Nikolaos Platon has more recently found remnants of harbour works in the shallows off Móchlos, which along with Pséira apparently had trade connections with Egypt and other countries in the Middle East during Minoan times. But the most important finds in Móchlos have been in the tombs excavated there, from which a rich hoard of stone vases and other funerary objects have been unearthed, with some of the most beautiful pieces now exhibited in the Áyios Nikólaos Museum. One can make an excursion to Pséira and Móchlos by boat from Áyios Nikólaos. One can also drive to the village of Móchlos, on the mainland just opposite the isle of Móchlos, taking a side-road that leads off from the highway just before Sfáka, 5km past Plátanos, a drive of an additional 7km beyond the fork. There are also hotel facilities in the village of Móchlos, where one can spend the night before or after sailing out to visit the archaeological site on the isles of Móchlos and Pséira.

Returning to the highway, one passes next through Sfáka, a large village at an altitude of 200m, after which the road begins to ascend once again, coming next to Tourlotí, a hamlet dating back to Venetian times. Half an hour's walk from Tourlotí there is a hilltop site named Kastrí, where archaeologists have excavated the ruins of an ancient town of the Post-Minoan period. Beyond Tourlotí a turn-off to the left leads to the nearby village of Myrsíni, where tombs of the Post-Minoan II period have been excavated in recent years.

Continuing on beyond Tourlotí, one comes next to the twin villages of Mésa Moulianá and Éxo Moulianá, which are set in fertile valleys whose vineyards produce the famous Moulianitika wine. Near Mésa Moulianá there is an ancient site excavated in 1903 by Xanthoud-hidhis, who found there interesting funerary objects dating from the Mycenaean and Early Geometric periods. The most fascinating of these finds is a vase with a painted scene depicting a mounted warrior, now in the Iráklion Museum; this is the earliest-known depiction of a horseman on Crete, undoubtedly a Mycenaean lord, one of the few glimpses of life in that era on the Great Island. The village church of Ayía Triádha in Mésa Moulianá had frescoes of the Venetian period, as does the chapel of Áyuos Yórgios in Éxo Moulianá.

Continuing along the highway, one comes next to Khamézi, a village set at an altitude of 380m, 63km from Áyios Nikólaos. Xanthoudhidhis has also excavated an archaeological site at Khamézi, unearthing a Middle Minoan structure that he believes to be a castle surrounded by the satellite buildings of a farming community. However, more recent researchers have led Nikolaos Platon to theorize that this may be a peak-sanctuary of the Middle Minoan I period, with the main sanctuary in the circular building and various cult-rooms in the other buildings.

The present village of Khamézi goes back to Venetian times, when it was a fief of the Kornaros family. This was the family that produced Vicenzos Kornaros, the seventeenth-century poet and playwright who wrote the great epic poem, *Erotókritos*, and also the *Sacrifice of Abraham*, the finest play produced by the Cretan renaissance. Kornaros is believed by some scholars to have been born in Khamézi, though others hold that his birthplace was Piskokéfalo, a village south of Sitía.

A short distance beyond Khamézi the highway bypasses the large village of Skopí, after which it descends to the coastal plain and brings one to the pretty town of Sitía, set at the western end of the beautiful Bay of Sitía. Sitía is the largest town in eastern Crete and the fifth most populous community on the Great Island, after Iráklion, Chaniá, Réthymnon and Ierápetra, serving as capital of the Province of Sitía. But when Spratt passed this way in 1855 Sitía was virtually abandoned, with only the ruins of a Venetian fortress standing on the present site of the town.

All of this changed just fifteen years after Spratt's visit, for in 1870 the Turks rebuilt and repopulated Sitía, which thereafter served as capital of Sitía Province during the last years of the Ottoman occupation of Crete, continuing as the provincial centre after the Great Island became part of Greece. Today Sitía is the most modern of the four large towns on the Great Island, with virtually nothing to remind one that this is one of the most ancient cities on Crete. The name of the town was originally Itia, or Etea, which in ancient times served as the northern port for the more important inland city of Praesós. Itia was noted as the birthplace of Myson, one of the seven sages of ancient Greece. The only traces of ancient Itia to be found in the town are some excavated tombs of the Middle and Late Minoan periods, as well as the fragmentary ruins of Roman buildings and an early Christian basilica. The town and its port continued in existence throughout the Graeco-Roman and Byzantine eras and on into the Venetian period, when it came to be called Sitía. Thenceforth the surrounding province was organized under the name of La Sitia, from which Lasíthi is derived, though that name is now applied only to the beautiful plateau on Mount Dhíkti. During the latter Venetian period the town of Sitía was thrice devastated; first levelled by an earthquake in 1508, then sacked in 1538 by the Ottoman pirate-admiral Barbarossa; and then in 1651 the entire community and its fortress were deliberately destroyed by the Venetians so that they would not fall into the hands of the Turks. The town was virtually abandoned for more than two centuries after that time, until the Turks rebuilt it as their provincial capital in 1870. Today all that remains of medieval Sitía is the ruined fortress on the north-eastern side of the town above the port. The fortress was originally built by the Byzantines at some time after their recapture of Crete from the Saracens in 961. It was then rebuilt by the Genoese war-lord Enrico Pescatore when he took over Crete early in the thirteenth century, only to be captured by the Venetians in 1212 when they gained complete control of the Great Island. The Venetians held the fortress until they abandoned Sitía in 1651, after which it was demolished along with the rest of the medieval town, which was known as Voúrgos, whose name survives in that of the quarter around the ruined castle. Apparently there were still some ruins of the ancient city left when Spratt explored the site in 1855, but these must have been destroyed or built over when the Turks rebuilt the town in 1870.

Although Sitía is a completely new town, with none of the medieval quaintness of Chaniá or Réthymnon, it is nevertheless quite charming, and its people are noted for their friendliness and hospitality. The situation of the town is splendid, its houses clustering in amphitheatral tiers on a low eminence overlooking the Gulf of Sitía, its waterfront lined with restaurants and cafés, giving it a very Mediterranean atmosphere.

Sitía is liveliest at the time of its Raisin Festival, which is held annual on 30 August, celebrating the gathering of the year's crop of sultana raisins, the principal agricultural product of the Sitía region. This festival is accompanied by general festivities throughout the town, including public performances of folk dancing and Cretan music. This festive atmosphere and the friendliness of its people make Sitía a pleasant place to spend a holiday, with several good beaches in the vicinity of the town, and it is also a very convenient centre for exploring the interesting sites on the eastern end of Crete.

A very popular excursion from Sitía is to Káto Zákros, the most important Minoan site in eastern Crete. This excursion can be combined with visits to the Toplú Monastery and to the famous palm-fringed beach at Vai, as well as to several minor archaeological sites en route. These places can all be seen in a single day's outing from Sitía, with time for lunch and a swim at Vai or one of the other beaches along the way, although those with time to spare might want to spend the night at Zákros or Palaícastro, where there are hotels and restaurants as well as good beaches.

This excursion first takes one eastward around the bay of Sitía, with dramatic views of the north-easternmost tip of Crete and the little archipelago to its north, the Nísi Dionisiádes. About 7km out of Sitía the highway comes to a by-pass that leads to the village of Ayía Photiá, where a Minoan necropolis was uncovered in 1971, one of the objects unearthed at that time being the beautiful biconical chalice now on exhibit in the Áyios Nikólaos Museum. Then, about 14km from Sitía, after the highway turns inland at the eastern end of Sitía Bay, one passes a side-road that leads to the Toplú Monastery to Vái and the archaeological site of Ítanos, which will be visited later on the present itinerary.

After passing this turn-off, the highway takes one across the base of the tapering peninsula that extends out to form the north-easternmost extension of the Great Island and brings one to Palaícastro, close to the far side of the peninsula, where the present itinerary turns right for Zákros (with the main road to the left leading to Vái and Ítanos, and a secondary road continuing straight ahead to the archaeological site at Petsofás).

From Palaícastro one follows the highway as it winds its way generally southward through the valleys near the eastern end of the

Great Island as far as Azokéramos, where the route suddenly turns westward and brings one up into the hills to Adravásti, after which it descends as it goes south as far as Áno Zákros, the uppermost of the twin villages of Zákros. This is one of the prettiest and most picturesque villages in eastern Crete, and might want to pause here at a café or taverna before going on to the archaeological site at Káto Zákros, the lower of the two villages, which is 7km farther along on the south-eastern shore of the island. On the final approach to Káto Zákros one sees off to the left the crags that rim the wild canyon known as the Valley of the Dead, so called because of the Minoan tombs and graves unearthed there. Then finally the road brings one down to the village of Káto Zákros and the archaeological site, which is set above the sandy cove that was once the port of the Minoan town.

Spratt was convinced that the ruins at Káto Zákros were the remains of Ítanos, but modern scholars have identified the site of that ancient town at Erimoúpolis, just north of Vai below the south-eastern tip of Crete. The ancient name of the Minoan town at Káto Zákros is unknown, and today it has come to be called by the same name as the village, a community that dates back only to Ottoman times. But it is possible that 'Zákros' may be derived from 'Za-ka-rou', the name of the Sea People who invaded Palestine in the thirteenth century BC, perhaps also settling in this south-eastern corner of Crete at the end of the Bronze Age.

The first archaeological exploration of the ruins at Káto Zákros was made in the closing years of the last century by the Italian archaeologists Federico Halbherr and Luciano Mariani. In 1901 the English archaeologist D. G. Hogarth began excavating on the slope of the hill to the north-east of what is now the main site, unearthing about ten houses of the late Minoan period, along with important finds from the Mycenaean age as well. Then in 1961 Nikolaos Platon began exploring the site, attracted there by the numerous gold objects that had been found there in previous excavations, and the following year he began a systematic excavation of Zákros, a project supported by Harriet and Leon Pomerance of New York, with the work continuing to the present day. These excavations have revealed that there was a major town and seaport here in Minoan times. Platon had unearthed a palace exceeded in size on the Great Island only by those at Knossós, Phaestós and Mállia. Thus it appears that the site at Zákros was one of the major centres of Minoan civilization, with its port on the south of the Great Island putting it in touch with Egypt and other countries in the Middle East.

Platon's excavations have shown that the first settlement dates back to at least the Prepalatial period, c. 2600–2000 BC, as evidenced by tombs and graves excavated in the Valley of the Dead. The first palace at Zákros is believed to have been built early in the second millennium BC, with parts of it unearthed beneath the New Palace, which was erected c. 1600 BC. The New Palace seems to have been severely damaged c. 1500 BC, perhaps by an earthquake, but it appears to have been rebuilt immediately afterwards, only to be finally destroyed altogether in c. 1450, a catastrophe that may very well have been linked with the seismic explosion of Santorini at that time, when Knossós and the other great centres of Minoan civilization also suffered total destruction. The catastrophe that finally destroyed the New Palace at Zákros seems to have given warning of its onset, because apparently the populace had sufficient time to flee, but they seem never to have returned to the site, except for some partial resettlement on the ruins in the Post-Minoan period. In fact, the ruins of the New Palace were so completely covered over with earth after the final catastrophe that they were never looted, and so archaeological excavation of the site has unearthed a rich hoard of treasures and also objects of daily use that would otherwise have long since vanished. Thus we have a particularly detailed record of life in this thriving Minoan town at the peak of its glory. Some of the most beautiful and interesting of these finds are exhibited in the Archaeological Museum at Iráklion, in the gallery devoted to the Palace at Zákros.

Like the other imperial residences on Minoan Crete, the palace at Zákros was a veritable labyrinth, with 250–300 rooms extending over 6500 square metres on two, or even possibly three, storeys in some parts of the site. The lay-out and design of the palace complex at Zákros are similar to those at Knossós, Phaestós and Málli, with a large central court surrounded by a maze of royal apartments, sanctuaries, cult-rooms, magazines, storage-rooms, work-rooms, halls, corridors, stairways and light-wells, the latter being the hallmark of Minoan architecture. The main entrance to the palace at Zákros was on the north-east side of the complex, where a paved road from the harbour entered the town. After entering the town one passed through a service courtyard and then a corridor that brought one into the north-eastern corner of the main courtyard, the large rectangular open area near the southern side of the archaeological site. The royal apartments are believed to have been on the eastern side of the courtyard, with the king's room flanking it at the centre and the queen's room just to the north of that, the royal bathroom a short way

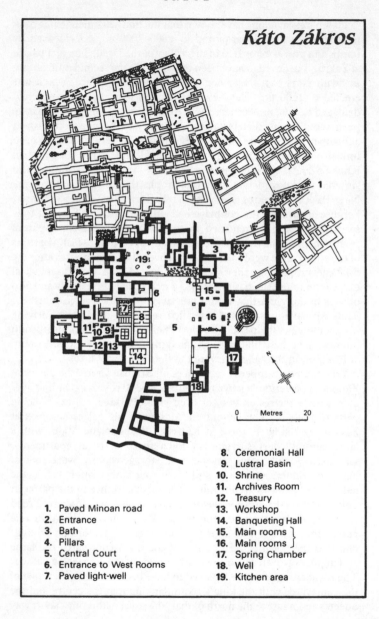

Káto Zákros

1. Paved Minoan road
2. Entrance
3. Bath
4. Pillars
5. Central Court
6. Entrance to West Rooms
7. Paved light-well
8. Ceremonial Hall
9. Lustral Basin
10. Shrine
11. Archives Room
12. Treasury
13. Workshop
14. Banqueting Hall
15. Main rooms ⎫
16. Main rooms ⎭
17. Spring Chamber
18. Well
19. Kitchen area

further along just beyond the north-eastern corner of the court. Just east of the king's room there is a circular cistern, and south of that there is a well with a fountain, with a second well at the south-east corner of the courtyard, while off the southern side of the courtyard there were apparently workshops, studios and perhaps a sitting-room for the royal family.

The grandest rooms in the palace are those on the west side of the courtyard. At the north-western corner of the courtyard there was a lobby with a staircase leading to the upper floor, while to the south of that, across a lateral corridor, was the great chamber known as the Hall of Ceremonies (the bases of three columns still stand along its central axis), and opening off that to the south between two piers was the Banqueting Hall. The Hall of Ceremonies would have been where the king presided over the religious and civic ceremonies associated with Minoan life, with the rites followed by a great feast in the Banqueting Hall. West of these two great halls there is a maze of smaller chambers that served as cult-rooms, archives, and storage-rooms along with a shrine and a room with a lustral basin. North of these there is another collection of rooms identified as magazines and other service areas, with a large room off the north-west corner of the central court apparently serving as the palace kitchen.

North of the palace itself there is an equally large area of excavations, where one sees the foundations and other remains of the town that abutted the palace on that side. These were probably houses and commercial buildings used by the ordinary people of the Minoan town, many of whom would have been employed down at the harbour in commerce with Egypt and Phoenicia, while others would have worked in the palace itself, one of the great centres of Minoan civilization.

After visiting the palace at Zákros one might relax with a swim and then afterwards lunch at a taverna on the beach below Káto Zákros. Afterwards one can then drive back to Palaícastro, to visit several minor ancient sites in the vicinity of that crossroads village. One of these is the Minoan site known as Palaícastro, which is about 2km to the east of Palaícastro village on the shore of Grándes Gulf, the bight bounded on the south by Cape Pláka and on the north by the hydra-headed peninsula that forms the north-eastern tip of Crete. This site was explored in the years 1902–4 by R. C. Bosanquet of the English Archaeological School, who unearthed a large Minoan settlement of numerous small houses standing chockablock along two narrow intersecting streets, looking very much like the village one sees today in Crete. Bosanquet also discovered here ruins of a sanctuary of the Hellenic era which he identified as the famous temple of Dhiktian Zeus, which is known from an inscription to have been located in far-eastern Crete. This temple and other ruins of the Hellenic era at Palaícastro may be remnants of the ancient town of Dhragmos. Today the site is part of the seaside hamlet of Agáthia, where there is a good beach with an outdoor taverna.

One can continue eastward on the road that passes Agáthia and drive as far as Petsofás, an archaeological site on the peak of a steep hill out near Cape Pláka. The site at Petsofás was discovered in 1903 by J. L. Myres of the English Archaeological School, who found here an open-air peak-sanctuary of the Middle Minoan period. Myres was led to this identification by his discovery of numerous *ex-voto* statuettes of men and women there in postures of prayer, similar to figurines found at other Creten peak-sanctuaries of that period. Some of these peak-sanctuaries are now replaced by Christian chapels, usually dedicated to Prophítias Ilías, the Prophet Elijah, thus perpetuating an ancient Creten religious tradition, where the local men and women can be seen in the same attitudes of prayer as in the statuettes representing their Minoan predecessors.

Returning to the crossroads at Palaícastro village, one can now head north along the main road that leads to Vái and Ítanos, which after 6km passes the turn-off that leads back to the Toplú Monastery and the main road to Sitía. Two kilometres past the fork one comes to the turn-off for Vái, which is down on the seashore another kilometre farther along. Vái is one of the most beautiful beaches in all of Crete and certainly the most unique, its stretch of pink-white sand fringed by an extraordinary grove of palm-trees, making this look like a tropical lagoon on a South Sea island. But its exotic beauty has attracted hordes of tourists to Vái, so that it has become very overcrowded in summer. Thus on our own visit to Vái we stopped only for a brief swim and stroll along the beach to enjoy the extraordinary spectacle of its surrounding grove of palm-trees, after which we fled from the crowds of tourists and went on to visit Ítanos, which is about one and a half kilometres to the north, beyond the Vái turn-off.

The site of ancient Ítanos is at the north-western corner of the Grándes Gulf, at the base of the serpentine peninsula that ends in Cape Síderos, the easternmost tip of Crete. The site is known locally as Erimoúpolis, or the Deserted Village.

The earliest reference to Ítanos in historical sources is in Book IV of the *Histories* of Herodotus. There Herodotus tells of how an expedition of colonists from the island of Théra, now known as Santoríni, were guided to Libya by a fisherman from Ítanos named Corobius, who helped them found the city of Cyrene on the North African coast in 630 BC. Stephanos of Byzantium writes that the original name of the town was Itanos Phinikas, and that it was founded by the Phoenicians. But the origins of Ítanos must be much earlier than the Phoenician era, for its strategic location on the north-eastern tip of Crete would have made it a natural place for the Minoans to establish a port, putting them in commercial contact with Anatolia, the Middle East, and Eygpt, and archaeological evidence indicates that this was the case. The French Archaeological School excavated the acropolis and necropolis of Ítanos in 1950, finding evidence of a Minoan settlement and of continued habitation there in Hellenic times. The most informative evidence concerning the history of Ítanos in Graeco-Roman times is in the form of inscriptions, one of which is preserved today in the Toplú Monastery. The Toplú inscription records that in 146 BC the people of Ítanos asked for help from King Plotemy VI of Egypt against Praesós, the most powerful city of eastern Crete, which at that time was at war with Ierápythna (present-day Ierápetra). The plea must have been successful, for Ítanos was left in peace during the war, which concluded in 145 BC when Ierápytna destroyed Praesós and took over the lands that their enemy had possessed in eastern Crete. This gave Ierápytna a common border with Ítanos and brought those two towns into conflict, particularly concerning the administration of the sanctuary of Dhiktian Zeus, a shrine where all of the people of eastern Crete worshipped together despite their continuing conflicts with one another, their bond undoubtedly being that they were all Eteocretans. The conflict between Ierápytna and Ítanos continued intermittently until 58 BC, when the Romans began their occupation of Crete, after which all internal disputes on the Great Island ceased under the mantle of the *Pax Romana*. Ítanos continued in existence throughout the Roman period and on into the medieval Byzantine era, but then in about the ninth century AD the town was utterly destroyed, probably by Saracen pirates, after which it was never again rebuilt or resettled. Today all that remains are some scattered ruins, including the foundations of an early Byzantine basilica, the fragmentary ruins of the Hellenistic defence-walls on the acropolis, and the excavation-pits of the archaeological digs that unearthed the Minoan settlement and its necropolis, along with some underwater ruins of the port of ancient Ítanos.

Ítanos is the end of the line so far as roads are concerned in the north-east corner of Crete, and those who wish to explore the peninsula beyond it to Cape Síderos and around the cape to the northern coast will have to do so on foot or by boat. At the time of our visit to Ítanos we contented ourselves with reading Spratt's description of the peninsula and the Nísi Dionysiádes to its north, the little archipelago still commonly known as the Yanisádes Islands.

> The north-east extremity of Crete extends towards the islands of Caso and Carpatho as a narrow promontory, formed of three distinct peninsulas, two of which are almost islands, and the terminal peninsula forms the present Cape Sidero or Sidaro. Five or six miles to the west of Cape Sidero, and directly opposite the Sitia Bay, but seven miles distant from the latter, are the Yanisades Islands, four in number, all high and bold rocks of limestone. A long narrow channel separates the two southern islands; and although with too deep water to anchor in it, and the channel is used as a shelter by coasting-craft that know it, such as the sponge-divers, and was used by the Barbary and Greek corsairs who frequented this neighbourhood in very recent times. A small drip of water exists in a cave there, which is sufficient for supplying a few men; and this has favoured the use of it as a hidden and favourable position for pouncing upon the passing trader . . . On turning Cape Sidero to the south a fine bay opens, with two or three islands off it; and a small snug cove is also seen entering into the cape itself, forming an equally convenient retreat for a corsair or pirate of ancient days. The anonymous coast-describer ('Stadiasmus') evidently calls this headland Cape Salmone, as he mentions this port, and states that it had a temple to Minerva.

Spratt also points out that Salmone is mentioned in Chapter 27 of the *Acts of the Apostles*, which describes St Paul's voyage in AD 61 and tells of how his ship passed this cape on its way to its eventual anchorage at Kalí Liménes, or Fair Havens, on the south coast of the Great Island. As one reads in *Acts* 27: 7–8: 'And when we had sailed slowly many days, and scarce were come over against Cnidus, the wind not suffering us, we sailed under Crete, over against Salmone; and hardly passing it, came unto a place which is called the Fair Havens; nigh whereunto was the city of Lasea.'

After exploring the north-eastern corner of Crete, one can head back towards Sitía via the road that passes the Toplú Monastery, which is 6km beyond the fork that one passed earlier on the way out to Vái and Ítanos. This monastery, one of the oldest and most famous in Crete, preserves its old Turkish name of Toplu Monastir, the Monastery with Cannons, because in Venetian times it served as a fortress, one of the main strongholds of eastern Crete. The actual name of the monastery is the Panayía Akrotiriáni, Our Lady of the Cape, named for one of the nearby promontories on the north-east coast of Crete.

The Toplú Monastery is believed to have been founded in the second half of the fifteenth century. The present monastic building is thought to have replaced an older and smaller monastery dedicated to Áyios Isídhorus, destroyed by Turkish corsairs c. 1460–70. When the present monastery was founded it was constructed in the form of a fortress, for the Turks and others continued to raid the coast of Crete up until very recent times. Above the main gate of the monastery there is an opening which is called 'The Murderer' because through there the defenders hurled missiles and poured boiling oil down on those who were trying to force their way through the entryway. The present monastery seems to have been founded by the Kornaros of Sitía, the distinguished family that gave birth to Vicenzo Kornaros, author of the *Erotókrito*, the Cretan national epic. Another notable member of that family was Ioannis Kornaros, who in 1770 painted the extraordinary icon known as the 'Greatness of the Lord', which still adorns the monastic church, a work of art that is considered to be the last great masterpiece of the Cretan renaissance. Also to be seen in the church is the historic Toplú Inscription, recording the appeal that the people of Ítanos made in 146 BC to King Ptolemy VI of Egypt, asking him to protect them from their enemies in Ierápytna (now Ierápetra). This inscription was discovered in 1834 by Pashley when he visited the Toplú Monastery, where the stone was being used as an altar-table in the chapel of the Holy Cross, which accounts for the partial effacement of the record. Pashley convinced the monks at Toplú to preserve the inscription by setting the stone into the façade of the monastic church, where it remains to this day, one of the most important epigraphical records on the Great Island, further adding to the interest of this venerable monastery.

After visiting the Toplú Monastery one continues westward along the same road by which one approached it, coming back to the main highway again 3km further along. One can then drive back along the highway to Sitía, this time heading westward along the shore of the gulf, with a splendid view of the town of Sitía and the promontory to its north, Ákri Vamvakiá.

Another interesting excursion takes one south from Sitía across the waist of Crete to the Libyan Sea. One can then drive westward along the southern coast as far as Ierápetra, from where one can cut back across the isthmus to the Gulf of Merabéllo, thus completing a tour around eastern Crete.

At the very beginning of this excursion, just 3km south of Sitía, one comes to the village of Piskoképhalo. This is the same route that Spratt took when he headed south from Sitia in 1855, and it is remarkable how little the scenery has changed since then, despite the intrusion of the modern world into the arcadia of old Crete. As he writes:

> The valley of Sitia penetrates towards the south more than half across this part of the island, and beyond the village of Episko Kephalo. It is confined between rocky cliffs of white tertiary strata and little cultivation, but overshaded in part by wild olive and plane trees, under which a pretty, refreshing rivulet murmurs along in its course, turning now and then a water-mill of some solitary inhabitant.

Some scholars believe that the village of Piskoképhalo was the birthplace of Vicenzos Kornaros (see p. 153) though others think that he was born in Khamézi, learned opinion being about equally divided between the two places. In any event, Piskoképhalo dates back to at least 1583, when it is first mentioned in a Venetian census, and it was even then a fief of the Kornaros family. This distinguished clan also gave birth to Andreas Kornaros, whose last will and testament, dated 1611, is an important source for the history of Crete in the Venetian period, mentioning, among other facts, that he had bequeathed a large sum of money for the support of the Toplú Monastery.

There are a number of minor Minoan sites in the vicinity of Piskoképhalo. One of these is approached via Káto Episkopí, which is about a kilometre from Piskoképhalo, with the archaeological site another 2km beyond that hamlet, on a hill named Zoú. Zoú was excavated by Nikolaos Platon, who discovered here a Minoan villa dated c. 1600 BC, a sumptuous residence with rooms on several levels connected by both ramps and stairways. Platon also unearthed at Zoú a Minoan necropolis of the Neopalatial period.

A second minor Minoan site in the vicinity of Piskoképhalo is at Achládia, which is some 6km to the west, approached by a side-road from the main highway that eventually crosses the Sitía Mountains and leads down to the Libyan Sea. Archaeological excavations in Achládia have unearthed a settlement surrounded by Cyclopean walls, apparently a farming village of the Neopalatial period, which included living-quarters, storerooms, and stables, along with a sanctuary. Archaeologists have also uncovered another Minoan settlement about half an hour's walk from Achládia, a village that seems to have been inhabited in the Neo-Palatial and Post-Palatial periods, with a *tholos* tomb dating from the latter era.

Continuing along the main highway south of Piskoképhalo for another 7.5km, one reaches a turn-off to the left that winds its way up toward the hamlet of Néa Praesós, a distance of some 4km from the main road. Just outside the village to the east one comes to the site of ancient Praesós, once the most powerful city in eastern Crete.

Praesós was first explored in 1884 by the Italian archaeologist Federico Halbherr, who discovered there a large number of clay idols and some unique inscriptions in a hitherto-unknown language. They were in Greek characters, written *boustrophedon* ('As the Ox Ploughs'), but the language was non-Hellenic. Some scholars believe it to be Eteocretan, spoken by the surviving Minoan people in the mountains of eastern Crete in the centuries after the Great Island was taken over by the Dorians. This theory is supported by the testimony of Strabo, who quotes an earlier source, named Staphylus, explaining that in Crete 'the Dorians occupy the part towards the east, the Cydonians the western part; the Eteocretans the southern; and to these last belongs the temple of Dhiktian Zeus; whereas the other people since they are more powerful dwell in the plains.'

Praesós was the principal town of the Eteocretans in the post-Minoan era, controlling the sanctuary of Dhiktian Zeus, a cult that they had inherited from their Minoan ancestors. It had harbours on both the north and south coasts of Crete, the town being strategically located in the centre of the eastern peninsula of the Great Island, with Etea serving as its port on the Merabéllo and Stiles on the Libyan Sea. The principal Dorian city in eastern Crete was Ierápytna, the present Ierápetra, which was the major rival of Praesós in Graeco-Roman times. This rivalry between the two cities climaxed in 145 BC, when Ierápytna destroyed Praesós at the end of a war for dominance in eastern Crete. Praesós was never again rebuilt or resettled, and thenceforth the Eteocretans disappear from history, ending the long twilight of Minoan civilization on the Great Island.

Further excavations of Praesós and its vicinity began in 1901 under the direction of R. Carr Bosanquet of the English Archaeological

School in Athens. One finding of this investigation was that the region around Praesós was inhabited as early as the Neolithic period, which on Crete ended c. 3000 BC. The excavations also revealed that the present ruins of Praesós represent a town founded soon after the end of the Bronze Age, with the original Minoan settlement, now vanished, having been somewhere close by – its precise location is yet unknown. The present town of Praesós would have been founded by the Eteocretans, who, judging from the inscriptions discovered here, seem to have preserved their old language and customs in eastern Crete for a millennium after the collapse of Knossós and the other centres of Minoan civilization. The ruins of Eteocretan Praesós occupy three acropolis hills, with the highest of them, a natural stronghold, being the core of the oldest part of the town, while one of the other two eminences served as a peak-sanctuary, standing outside the circuit of defence-walls. The excavators also discovered the necropolis of Praesós, which seems to have been used from the Mycenaean era down to Hellenistic times. One tomb, discovered in 1935 by the Greek archaeologist Mavroidis, revealed a very interesting burial, a Praesian athlete interred with all of his trophies, including a Panathenaic amphora from the period 560–500 BC, a prize awarded to winners at the games in Athens during the Archaic period. Thus it would appear that the Praesians, while still preserving their Eteo-cretan heritage, had by the Archaic period been so integrated into Greek culture as to participate in one of the principal festivals of Athens, which at the time was at the dawn of its golden age.

Those with time to spare might search out three minor archaeological sites in the region around Praesós. One of these is Tourtoúli, at the summit of Mount Profítis Ilías, where a Minoan villa has been unearthed along with some fragmentary frescoes. A second site is at Fatoulas, where a vaulted Minoan tomb has been excavated; and at a third, which is a few kilometres off to the south-west at Sklávi, another Minoan tomb has been found.

After visiting Praesós one can return to the main highway and continue driving towards the south coast. Alternatively, one can continue on the side-road that passes through Néa Praesós, eventually coming to the mountain village of Chandrás, at an altitude of 450m, where one has a choice of several routes. One of these is to drive on to the mountain village of Zíros, at an altitude of 440m. This village dates back at least to Venetian times, and the local church of Ayía Paraskeví is decorated with frescoes that are believed to be the last wall-paintings done during the Cretan renaissance. From Zíros one can continue on by a secondary road that leads down to the Libyan Sea at Xerókampos, from where the route continues around the south-east corner of Crete and leads back to Epáno Zákros. Another secondary road from Zíros leads down to the Libyan Sea at Goúdouras, a coastal hamlet on the Bay of Makrí Yiatos where there is a good beach. The road continues westward along the southern coast, and on the western side of Makrí Yialos Bay it passes the Monastery of Kapsá. This establishment is actually dedicated to Áyios Ioánnis Pródromos, St John the Forerunner, with the name Kapsá probably being the surname of the founder of the monastery. The monastery is thought to have been founded in the middle of the fourteenth century, originally consisting of a small cave-sanctuary surrounded by a few monastic cells. The original monastery was destroyed by Turkish corsairs in 1471, but it was rebuilt in Venetian times. The most famous resident of the monastery was a monk named Gerontyoannis, or Old John, who was born in 1799, retiring to Kapsá in his later years after an adventurous youth, soon becoming famous for his piety and his miraculous cures. The widespread popularity of Gerontyoannis attracted numerous pilgrims to the monastery and added to its endowment, so that it became a widely-known shrine. The Kapsá Monastery still attracts large crowds of visitors at the time of its annual *paniyiri* on 29 August, the feast day of St John, one of the most popular last-summer festivals in eastern Crete.

The coast road continues westward beyond the Kapsá Monastery and joins the main highway from Sitía just before that route reaches the Libyan Sea at Análipsi. Those who have followed the main highway down from the turn-off at Néa Praesós will have enjoyed some of the finest highland scenery in eastern Crete, driving down the valley between the two ranges of the Sitía Mountains, with views opening up ahead to reveal the southern coastal plain stretching westward to the Ierápetra isthmus, with the islets of Koufonísi, to the east, and Chrisí, to the west, floating three to five kilometres offshore in the Libyan Sea.

After Análipsi, the main highway continues westward along the shore to Ierápetra, passing a succession of excellent beaches, the best-known of which are those at Makrygialós, Koutsourás, Férma, Koutsounári, and also in the vicinity of Ierápetra, which one finally approaches across the coastal plain that opens out on the southern side of the isthmus that connects eastern Crete to the rest of the Great Island. The scenery along this stretch is less interesting than it is elsewhere along the south coast, for here the Sitía Mountains recede inland and then finally give way altogether at the isthmus, where the modern town of Ierápetra clusters around the promontory where the ancient city of Ierápytna stood.

Ierápetra is the fourth largest city on Crete, the most populous community on the southern coast of the Great Island, capital of the isthmian province that bears its name, Ierápetra is the southernmost town in modern Greece, with a definite North African air about it, its sun-drenched white and pastel houses clustering around the old Venetian fortress that still guards its port. Ierápetra also has reminders of its Turkish past, principally the minaret of an Ottoman mosque and an old *cheshme*, or street-fountain. The local museum has a small but interesting collection of archaeological finds, including some from Ierápytna, the ancient predecessor of the present town. But there is nothing left standing of ancient Ierápytna itself, though many edifices from the Roman era still survived as late as the sixteenth century, including a *naumachia*, or fortified harbour, and several *thermae*, or Roman thermal baths. One of the antiquities of Ierápytna that can still be seen today is the headless statue that still forms part of the Bembo Fountain in Iráklion. This was removed from Ierápetra in the Venetian period.

No systematic excavation of Ierápetra has ever been made. It is believed that the name of its predecessor, Ierápytna, is Doric in origin, probably founded during the Doric immigration to Greece during the Dark Ages. During its early years Ierápytna was under the shadow of Praesós, then the most powerful city in eastern Crete. But during the Hellenistic period Ierápytna rose to power and finally crushed Praesós in 145 BC. Thenceforth Ierápytna became the dominant power in the region, controlling the south-eastern coast of Crete from Tsoútsouros to the eastern end of the island. Ierápytna continued to dominate eastern Crete until the end of the Hellenistic period, finally falling to a Roman army under Quintus Metellus in 67 BC, the diehard Cretans fighting a last stand on the isthmus under the command of their general, Lasthines. Ierápytna was in ruins at the end of this battle, but the Romans rebuilt the town on a grander scale than before, and it flourished throughout the Imperial era and on into the Byzantine period. The town was destroyed by a Saracen raid in AD 824, but apparently it was rebuilt during the second Byzantine period, for it was again a considerable city during the Venetian occupation, when it was capital of the castellany of Ierápetra.

The fortress that now guards the port was built in 1626 by Francesco Morosini. It is an impressive structure, 50m long on its eastern and western sides and 25m in length on the north and south, armed with five large cannon and 180 smaller guns. But the fortress was held by the Venetians for only a little over two decades, after which it fell to the Turks in 1647 when its commander Mouatsos surrendered after a short siege. Mouatsos himself managed to escape, but the other defenders and many of the townspeople were put to the sword by the Turks, despite assurances that they would go unharmed if they surrendered. The Turks then rebuilt the town, which during the Ottoman period served as capital of the easternmost province of Crete. Ierápetra remained a backwater during the Ottoman period, the one historical incident of note during that time being Napoleon's overnight stay there in June 1798, after his expedition against Egypt. The house in which he supposedly slept is still standing in the town.

Ierápetra is a pleasant place to spend a few days while travelling in eastern Crete, with many tavernas and cafés in the town and on the excellent beaches nearby. The climate is distinctly tropical, the North African coast being only 230 miles distant across the Libyan Sea. Ierápetra is also a convenient centre for visiting sites on the south-eastern coast of Crete, the most interesting one in the near vicinity being the Minoan ruins at Mírtos, which were described in a previous itinerary. Another interesting excursion takes one westward from Ierápetra, passing Grá Ligiá 5km out of town and then 2km further along turning right onto a side-road, which leads up into the south-eastern ramparts of the Dhíkti range. This road brings one up as far as Máles, a mountain village perched at an altitude of 580m. Máles dates back to Venetian times, when it was the largest village in the castellany of Ierápetra, and there are still two local churches remaining from that period; these are the Panayía, dating from the fourteenth century, and Áyios Nikólaos, which was built in the seventeenth century. One can continue on from Máles and drive on a secondary road that winds up through the villages still higher up on the mountain, whose two main peaks tower just off to the north-west: Aféndis Christós to an altitude of 2141m and Madára at 2148m.

Ierápetra is also the port of embarkation for the two lonely little isles that lie off the south-eastern coast of Crete. The nearest of them is Chrisi, which is about 12km south-south-east of Ierápetra, and the other is Koufonísi, which is five to seven km south of Ákra Goudoúra, the large promontory that forms the south-eastern rampart of Crete. Koufonísi is the more interesting of the two, particularly since the recent discovery there of part of a theatre and other fragmentary ruins of an ancient town, near the actual village of Koufonísi. The island is by far the largest in the little archipelago, which in antiquity were known as the Leucae, the White Islands.

After visiting Ierápetra we drove back across the isthmus toward the Merabéllo Gulf, passing the village of Káto Khorió about halfway along the route. Then, just 3km south of the gulf, we turned left onto a side-road that almost immediately brought us to the village of Vasilikí. This village has given its name to the nearby archaeological site, where an early Minoan settlement was discovered in 1904 by Harriet Boyd-Hawes, with Richard Seager continuing the work in 1906. These excavations revealed that the site at Vasilikí was inhabited as early as 2500 BC, with the settlement later developing around a building complex that may have been a small palace or villa, which dates from the period 2300–2100 BC. The excavations also unearthed large quantities of a very distinctive pottery that came to be known as Vasilikí ware, superb examples of which are exhibited in the Iráklion Museum. As Professor Sakellarakis describes this pottery: 'the pottery of the Vasilikí style . . . is characterized by a bold new shape with the elongated neck, or "spout". The dramatic surface decoration of red and black patches has been produced by uneven firing. It is clear that the potter's wheel is now in wide use.'

After visiting Vasilikí we returned to the main road, which 3km further along brought us to the Gulf of Merabéllo. There we turned left and began driving westward around the shores of the gulf towards Áyios Nikólaos, having completed our tour of eastern Crete.

10

███ ███ ███

IRÁKLION TO RÉTHYMNON

After our tour of eastern Crete we drove back along the coastal highway to Iráklion, where we spent the night. Then the following morning we started off again, beginning our exploration of the region between Iráklion and Réthymnon, the central stretch of Crete's northern coast, and taking in the area which lies between the Aegean coast and Mount Ídha, better known to the Cretans as Psilorítis.

The new highway between Iráklion and Péthymnon is far faster and more direct than the old routes connecting those two towns, two parallel routes that wind their ways through the villages south of Psilorítis, with the southern road taking one up to the highest villages on the northern tier of the mountain. Most tourists travelling along the northern coast take the new highway, which is less than 80km in length between Iráklion and Réthymnon, a drive that can easily be done in an hour or less, taking one past a succession of beach resorts. But some travellers still prefer to take the old roads between Iráklion and Réthymnon, for these routes give one a more intimate glimpse of the villages and countryside in this part of Crete, which one would miss speeding along the super highway past modern holiday villages. And so the present itinerary is a composite of both the new highway and the old roads, pointing out the places of interest along the parallel routes between Iráklion and Réthymnon.

The routes leading westward from Iráklion all leave town through the Chania Gate. Outside the city to the west the routes diverge, with the old road curving in towards Psilorítis, one of them going high along the northern slope of the mountain via Anóyia to Pérama, where it joins the middle road, while the new super highway first curves

171

around the western side of the Gulf of Iráklion and then turns left to pass the Bay of Ayí Pelagía, after which it heads westward as it goes past the Bay of Fódhele and then the turn-off to the birthplace of El Greco, an itinerary described in the excursions from Iráklion. Seven kilometres farther along the highway passes the village of Síses, where a side-road to the left leads inland to the middle and upper roads, eventually taking one up to Anóyia, the largest and most interesting village on the slopes of Mount Ídha. From Anóyia one can continue up to the Nídha Plateau and the Idaean Cave, as described in one of the excursions from Iráklion, and from there one can climb up to the highest peak of Mount Ídha, Psilorítis itself, at an altitude of 2456m. Psilorítis is one of the most majestic sights on Crete, dominating the whole landscape in the region between Iráklion and Réthymnon, looking like the veritable symbol of the Great Island. As John Pendlebury wrote about his ascent of Psilorítis and the peaks of the other two great mountains of Crete, quoting an old *mantináda*:

> To have stood on Ida, on Dikti and on Aphendes-Kavousi in the clear shrill wind and to have toiled through the hot little valleys with that unforgettable smell of herbs is an experience the memory of which nothing can ever take from you.

> When you go to Crete, Cretan, greet Crete for me,
> Greet me from the mountain, aged Psiloritis.

From Anóyia one can also go on to Axós, a mountain village 7km to the north-west, where a transverse route connects the upper and lower roads, leading down the Mylopótamos valley. A signpost indicates the way towards the site of ancient Axós, mentioned by Herodotus, which is situated on a steep acropolis high above the village. Axós was first settled in the Late Minoan III period, c. 1400 BC, but the ruins one sees today are of the town founded there probably in the eighth century BC, of which fragments of the defence-walls remain, as well as antiquities on display in the Iráklion Museum. The site of Axós was discovered in 1835 by Robert Pashley, who identified the ruins from the ancient coins and inscriptions he found there.

From Axós a transverse route connects the upper and lower roads, joining the latter at the confluence of the two streams of the Mylopótamos River, where one passes the village of Garázo. From Garázo the middle road heads down the Mylópotamos valley, joining the upper road just before the large village of Pérama, which is only a six-kilometre drive from the main coastal highway.

After passing the Bay of Fódhele, the coastal highway leads

westward at some distance from the sea, passing through the narrow coastal strip between the Aegean and the range known as Kouloúkunas, the ancient Mount Tallaion, which is separated from Psilorítis to the north by the Mylopótamos valley. About halfway along this stretch of highway one sees off to the south the old Monastery of Vósakos, dedicated to the Tímios Stavrós, the True Cross, a fortress-like edifice probably dating to the Venetian period. The highway reaches the shore again at the Bay of Balí, named for the coastal village of Balí, approached by a turn-off to the right. Balí stands on the site of ancient Astale, of which little is known other than its name; whatever ruins there are remain unexcavated. There is a good beach at Balí, and one might be tempted to stop there for a swim on the way from Iráklion to Réthymnon.

Just beyond the turn-off to Balí, another turn-off to the left leads in 1km to the Monastery of Áyios Ioánnis. Two kilometres beyond that the highway comes to a crossroads, with the branch to the right leading back to Balí, while the road to the left leads inland by several routes to Pérama, as does another turn-off to the left 6km farther along the highway, at the village of Skepastí. Three kilometres beyond Skepastí a turn-off to the right leads in 2km to the coastal village of Pánormos, which lies at the northern end of the road from Pérama.

Pánormos was formerly known as Ruméli Castélli, the European or Roman Castle, taking its name from an ancient fortress that once stood there but has now all but vanished, though fragments of the castle and the city that it once guarded were still standing when Pashley and Spratt explored this coast. According to Spratt, Pánormos was formerly the principal port for the Mylopótamos valley, of which Axós was in ancient times the capital, and for that reason the fortress here was also known up until recently as Castle Mylopótamos.

The fortress at Pánormos was still in use in Venetian times, and in 1341 it was besieged by Cretan rebels, who failed to capture it. the fortress and the town were sacked in 1538 by the Ottoman admiral Barbarossa, but they were afterwards rebuilt by the Venetians. Pánormos was captured by the Turks in 1647, and thenceforth the fortress was more or less abandoned and allowed to fall into ruins, its last fragments virtually vanishing in fairly recent times. Archaeological excavations in 1947 at the nearby site of Ayia Sophia revealed the foundations of a large Christian basilica of the fifth century AD, a remnant of the Byzantine town of Pánormos.

From Pánormos one can drive south to Pérama, a distance of 6km, for there are several places of interest in the vicinity of that village. One of these is the famous Melidhóni Cave, which is approached by the side-road that leads eastward from the Pánormos road just before it reaches Pérama. After 4km this road takes one to the village of Melidhóni, beyond which a signpost directs one to Spílion, the Cave, taking one another 2km farther along to a little chapel. The Melidhóni Cave is just a few metres further along to the left, with the entrance down to the right in the crater.

The Melidhóni Cave has the status of a national monument in Crete, because of the terrible tragedy that occurred there during the Greek War of Independence. In late September of 1823, when the surrounding countryside was being ravaged by a Turkish army led by Hüseyin Pasha, son-in-law of Mehmet Ali, the Ottoman ruler of Egypt, some 300 Christian Greeks took refuge in the Melidhóni Cave, most of them women, children and old men, for the men of military age were fighting as partisans elsewhere in Crete. Hüseyin Pasha besieged the cave for several days, during which time those inside refused to surrender and inflicted casualties on the Turks when they tried to force their way in. Finally, on 3 October 1823, the Turks stopped up the entrance to the cave and set brush fires in the openings that led into the cavern, filling it with smoke and asphyxiating all of those inside. Pashley heard the story eleven years later from an old man named Manoli Kermezakes, who was one of the first to enter the cave after the Turks left, the other two being men whose wives and children had taken refuge within the cavern. The other two men died shortly afterwards, leaving Manoli alone to tell the tale to Pashley.

The bones of those who died in the Melidhóni Cave have long since been gathered up, now resting in an ossuary in the large inner cavern. An altar has also been erected there as part of a Christian cave-sanctuary, where a memorial service is held in memory of the martyrs each year on the anniversary of the massacre.

The Melidhóni Cave had also been a religious sanctuary in classical times, dedicated to the worship of Tallaean Hermes. This was a local Cretan cult in which the Greek god Hermes was associated with the mythical figure Talos, the giant known as the Man of Bronze. There are many legends concerning the origins of Talos, but the most prevalent one is that he was created by Hephaestus and then presented by Zeus to King Minos, who employed him to guard Crete. Thus the bronze giant strode around the periphery of the island thrice a day, hurling huge boulders at any ship that approached the Great Island. This was the terrible threat that Jason and his shipmates forced when they sailed by Crete on their long voyage home from Colchis, having stolen the Golden Fleece with the help of the sorceress Medea. The scene is described by Apollonius of Rhodes in his epic poem, the *Argonautica*, when the *Argos* approached Crete:

Talos, the man of bronze, was seen upon a peak to stand;
And thence he rocky fragments cast, nor suffer'd them to land.

But Talos had one flaw, for his life depended on a bronze nail that closed the opening in an artery in his leg. When Medea learned of this she drugged Talos and drew out the nail from his leg, after which the *ichor* drained out of the giant and he died, whereupon the Argonauts sailed safely by the Great Island.

Another interesting place in the vicinity of Pérama is Eléftherna, a post-Minoan site some 5km to the south as the eagle flies, but more than twice that distance by road, approached by the route through Prinés. Four kilometres south of Pérama the road passes Margarítes, which has long been noted for its fine local pottery, and one might stop here to look at the examples for sale in the village shops. Six kilometres beyond Margarítes, after passing through Kinigianá and then turning east, one then comes to Prinés, where a secondary road leads north to the new village of Eléftherna, which is near the ancient site of the same name.

Eléftherna was discovered in 1855 by Spratt, who remarks that Pashley missed identifying the site of the ancient city when he passed through the same region twenty-one years before. The remarkable thing about Eléftherna is its almost impregnable site, which made it an ideal place for a fortified settlement during the Dark Ages of the ancient Greek world, when the post-Minoan population of the island fled to such mountaintop eyries to escape from the Dorian Greeks. But, despite the apparent impregnability of its position and defences, Eléftherna fell to the Romans under Quintus Metellus in 67 BC. According to one account, the Romans sapped the great tower blocking their way by pouring vinegar on its walls under cover of night, thus dissolving the bonding between its stones and causing it to collapse, whereupon the besiegers made their way through the breach and captured the town. The breach that the Romans made in the great tower is still evident, never having been enlarged or repaired, for after this defeat the town lost its independence forever and disappeared from history.

Spratt found a number of structures and antiquities in and around Eléftherna, including the foundations of house walls, two churches of early date, the platform of a temple, a mutilated statue, and two bridges, one of which still survives, a splendid structure of the classical period. One interesting find subsequently made at Eléftherna is a weather-worn bust of a *kouros*, an idealized representation of a young man personifying Apollo, now on exhibit in the Iráklion Museum. The Eléftherna *kouros* dates from the decade 630–620 BC and is a good example of the sculpture of the Late Daedelic period in archaic Cretan art.

After seeing Eléftherna one returns to Pérama, where one can either take the old road toward Réthymnon or drive back to the new highway at the Pánormos turn-off, with most travellers taking the latter route. The two routes join at Stavroménos, 8km past Pánormos on the new highway, which halfway along that stretch passes the summer resort at Lavris, where there is a good beach and hotel facilities. At Stavroménos, which is on the boundary between the provinces of Mylopótamos and Réthymnon, one can take a side-road via Loútra to the famous Arkádhi Monastery, a drive of about 20km. This takes one up into the hills that form the north-western ramparts of Mount Idha, where at the road's end, and 500m up, one comes to the great Monastery of Arkhádi, the most celebrated monument in the modern history of Crete.

The Arkhádi Monastery is believed to have been founded during the second Byzantine period, which began in 961 when Nicephorus Phocas recaptured Crete from the Saracens. The monastery subsequently expanded, and during the sixteenth century the establishment was reorganized and expanded, with a new and larger monastic church completed in 1587. The monastic church, which was built by the abbot Klimis Hortatzis, was designed in the rococo mode then popular in Europe, and today its façade represents the finest example of that architectural type still extant in Crete. Arkhádi was one of the centres of Greek culture during the Cretan renaissance. Its monks preserved a rich heritage of ancient manuscripts, but many of these were looted and destroyed during the Ottoman occupation, with the monastery being sacked by the Turks after the fall of Réthymnon in 1645. Attempts were made to protect Arkhádi by declaring it a 'Stavropígiako' monastery, administered by one of the patriarchates of the Orthodox Church, with a decree to this effect being issued in 1700 by Meletius Pigas, Patriarch of Alexandria. This preserved Arkhádi from further attack until 1866, when the monastery became a centre of resistance in the Cretan rebellion against Ottoman rule. In the autumn of that year the Christians of the surrounding region took refuge here along with a band of Cretan partisans and the resident monks, who had armed the monastery with two cannon and two field-artillery pieces, muskets and shot, as well as horses for their cavalry. At the beginning of November the Turks besieged Arkhádi with an army of 16,000 troops and artillery, under the command of Mustafa Pasha Giritlis (the Cretan). The besieged then numbered 964: 259 Cretan partisans, 40 monks armed with muskets, and the remainder women, children and old people. The Turks began their assault on 7 November with an artillery barrage that by the following day had destroyed the main gateway, leading to a hand-to-hand battle between the Turks and the defenders. Even when all seemed lost there was no question of surrender, and at the last possible moment the Abbot Gabriel gave orders to one of the partisans, Constantine Giamboudakis, to set a fuse to blow up the magazine where all of the powder and ammunition were stored, and when that exploded it killed all of those in the surrounding area, Cretans and Turks alike. Only a handful of the besieged managed to escape; 114 were captured and enslaved; more than 800 were killed in the explosion or in the fighting before and afterwards. The Turks lost about 3000 dead and 1500 wounded. The explosion at Arkhádi was heard throughout the world, with Garibaldi and Victor Hugo espousing the cause of Cretan independence along with many others, gaining unprecedented support throughout Europe for the rebels. Nikos Kazantzakis later made Arkhádi the subject of his most powerful novel, *Freedom or Death*, whose title became the rallying-cry for Cretans in later rebellions against the Turks and later still in their resistance to German occupation during World War II. The monastery at Arkhádi is now a national shrine, and each year the heroism of those who died there is commemorated on 7 November, with people from all over Greece in attendance, including leading members of the Cretan and Greek governments.

A tourist pavilion has now been set up at the Arkhádi Monastery for the convenience of the many foreigners and Greeks who visit there each year, with the forty or so resident monks providing hospitality for those who wish to stay there overnight as guests, with beds for ten and dining facilities in the refectory. One enters through the western gate, which was destroyed by the Turkish artillery on 7–8 November 1866, with the heaviest fighting taking place in its immediate vicinity. After passing through the gate and the western stoa one enters the courtyard, with the rococo façade of the monastic church straight ahead. This is a two-apsed structure, with the left side of the sanctuary dedicated to the Metamorphosis of Christ and that on the right to SS.

Constantine and Helen, the founder of Byzantium and his mother. A small museum has been set up in chambers off the south-east corner of the courtyard, with memorabilia of the siege of 1866 and other important events in the history of the monastery. One can also see the cell of the Abbot Gabriel, which is in the end room at the north-western corner of the monastery. And the most dramatic sight of all is the roofless powder magazine at the north-eastern corner of the monastery, where the Abbot Gabriel had Constantine Giamboudakis light the fuse that blew up Arkhádi rather than surrendering to the Turks, thus immortalizing all of those who died here in the cause of Cretan independence.

After visiting Arkhádi, one returns along the same road by which one approached the monastery, then turning left at Loútra onto another road which in 6km brings one out onto the coastal highway at Plataniás. Plataniás is the most popular resort in the vicinity of Réthymnon, with numerous hotels and restaurants along the beach that stretches off from here in both directions along the coast. Turning westward onto the highway, one comes next to Perivólia, 2km further along, where one now turns off onto the shore road that in 2km brings one into Réthymnon, which many believe to be the loveliest town in all of Crete.

11

RÉTHYMNON

During our summer in Crete we visited Réthymnon a number of times, for it was just an hour's drive from our *pýrgos* in Chaniá, and we passed through the town whenever we were headed for Iráklion and points east. And so we came to know Réthymnon very well, and soon fell in love with the town, particularly the old quarter down by the medieval port, where venerable Ottoman and Venetian houses line streets that have not changed in centuries, leading one back into the vanished past of this ancient place.

Réthymnon has never been subjected to a systematic archaeological survey, but random excavations have turned up evidence that the site was inhabited in late Minoan times. The principal finds indicating pre-Hellenic settlement come from an excavation made in 1947 in the suburb of Mastabá, where a rock-hewn grave was discovered with pottery dated to the Late Minoan period, c. 1350–1250 BC, with the vases now on exhibit in the Réthymnon Archaeological Museum. Other than these chance archaeological finds, the main evidence for the pre-Hellenic origins of the town is its name, which is given by various ancient sources as Réthymnos or Réthymna, with the -*mnos* and -*mna* endings being common among toponyms in Greece dating back to the time before the arrival of the first Greek-speaking people, perhaps originating with the Carians or other Anatolian races who may have crossed over from western Asia Minor early in the Bronze Age. Although the name Réthymnos is pre-Hellenic, the first direct evidence of its use is in coins minted by the city in the fourth century BC. Most of these coins have the head of either Apollo or Athene on one side and a trident or dolphins on the other, with the name of the city indicated by the letters RI or RITHY. The god-heads indicate that Apollo and Athene were the principal deities of Réthymnos, with the trident and dolphins symbolizing the sea as the principal source of the city's wealth, from commerce and fishing. Inscriptions also record that Réthymnos had a sanctuary of Rokkaia Artemis, a local Cretan cult in which the goddess was worshipped for her power in healing rabies! The principal source for information on this unique cult is the Roman writer Aelian, who tells the tale of a fisherman of Réthymos to whom Artemis revealed a cure for rabies, which he treated by applying a potion made from the crushed entrails of the *hippócampos*, or sea-horse. The cult of Rokkaia Artemis survived as late as the fourth century AD, as evidenced by inscriptions now exhibited in the Réthymnon museum, but then the triumph of Christianity ended that and all other pagan beliefs in Crete, though the crushed entrails of the *hippócampos* were undoubtedly applied to dog-bites for long afterwards in the town, and perhaps are still used today in local folk medicine.

Little is known of the history of Réthymnon during the Byzantine era, except that the town was destroyed by the Saracens and then rebuilt after the reconquest of Crete by Nicephorus Phocas. Réthymnon first begins to appear in the full light of history during the Venetian era, when it emerged as the third largest town on Crete, a position that it still retains today. This is evidenced by the fact that from the thirteenth century onwards Réthymnon was forced to outfit four galleys for the Venetian fleet, while Chaniá rigged eight galleys and Candia thirteen. The Rethymnaeans played a leading role in the many Cretan rebellions against Venetian rule, as they would do again in the equally numerous uprisings against the Turks during the Ottoman occupation. The Rethymnaeans also distinguished themselves as scholars, writers and artists during the Cretan renaissance. One notable Rethymnaean during this cultural revival was Marco Musuru (1470–1517), who taught Greek at the universities of Rome, Padua and Venice as well as being a close friend of both Erasmus and Giovanni de Medici, who became Pope Leo X. Musuru, together with his Venetian colleague Aldus Manutius, founded one of the first publishing houses in Venice, putting out first editions of classics that had survived from ancient Greek literature. Another Rethymnaean in Venice during the Renaisance was Zaccharia Calergi, whose edition of the *Greek Etymological Dictionary* in 1499 was the first modern European work to be published in ancient Greek. Rethymnaeans also distinguished themselves in the Great Island itself during the

Renaissance, most notably the hagiographers Emmanuel Tzane and
Lampardi, the playwright George Hortatzis, the sculptor Frampeneti,
who created the elegant Morosini Fountain that still adorns Iráklion,
and the poet and historian Marinos Tzane Bounialis, author of an epic
entitled *The Cretan War*, describing the Turkish conquest of Crete in
the years 1645–69. Bounalis writes that in his day Réthymnon was
known as 'the old Athens', since Athens itself had not yet emerged
from the Dark Ages of Turkish occupation that it endured until the
Greek War of Independence (beginning in 1821). But the Turks
eventually ended the cultural renaissance in Crete as well, beginning
with their invasion of the Great Island in September 1645. Réthymnon
fell to the Ottoman forces at the end of November of that same year,
and Khándaks, the modern Iráklion, eventually surrendered in
1669. Thus began the Ottoman occupation of Crete, which was to last
until the final years of the nineteenth century, a terrible period that
represented another Dark Age in the history of the Great Island. But
Rethymnaean culture survived those centuries and remained alive
during the difficult decades that followed, particularly the German
occupation in World War II. Thus Réthymnon today is renowned as
the intellectual capital of Crete, still producing outstanding scholars
and writers, the most recent figure of note being Pandelis Prevelakis,
who died in his beloved home town in the spring of 1986. One of the
many works written by Prevelakis is his *Tale of a Town*, an affectionate
description of old Réthymnon that is now available in an English
translation, evoking the spirit of one of the most remarkable towns in
Greece. Another more recent work is an excellent guide to Réthymnon
written by A. Nenedakis, which we used constantly when strolling
around the streets of the town during the summer of 1986. As
Nenedakis writes in the Introduction to his work:

> Rethymno is a small town in the centre, approximately, of the
> north coast of Crete. It is more typically Greek than any other city
> in Greece; at least, it retains – as few of the known ancient cities of
> the Greek domain do – the colour and spirit of all the eras that
> recede deep into the past. . . .

The most prominent monument of old Réthymnon is the Fortezza,
the mighty Venetian fortress that surmounts the acropolis hill on the
northern promontory of the town. The peninsula that connects this
promontory to the mainland was in antiquity only a very narrow spit of
land, filling out during the course of centuries through the constant
deposit of alluvial earth carried down from the mountains by the

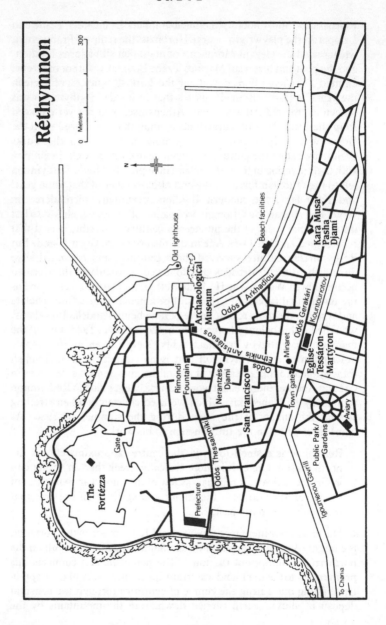

Réthymnon

0 Metres 300

N

Old lighthouse

Beach facilities

Archaeological
Museum

Odós Arkhadíou

Kara Musa
Pasha
Djami

Odós Gerakári

Kountourotov

Odós Ethnikís Antistáseos

Minaret

Rimondi
Fountain

Nerantzés
Djami

Odós

San Francisco

Town gate

Eglise
Tessáron
Martyron

Gate

The
Fortézza

Odós Thessaloníki

Public Park/
Gardens

Aviary

Igoúmenou Gavríil

Prefecture

To Chania

elements and filling up the harbour, also creating the long sandy beach that stretches from the port out beyond the eastern limits of the town. Nenedakis quotes Onorio Belli's statement that in his time, 1586, there were ruins of an ancient temple still standing on the promontory. That was just four years after the completion of the Fortezza, which was begun in 1573 and built on the site of an earlier fortress called Palaeócastro. Today nothing remains of the earlier structures, though these and other ancient ruins may be buried beneath and within the Fortezza itself.

The Fortezza is an immense structure, and it took us the whole of one blazing-hot July afternoon to explore it all from within, saved from sunstroke only by occasional retreats to the shade of a little café that one enterprising local had set up under a plátanos tree within its grounds. From the tree's dappled shade we studied the architecture of the old fortress and read about its history.

When the Venetians first took over Réthymnon they inherited the old Byzantine fortress on the promontory, Palaeócastro, which may actually have been a rebuilt Graeco-Roman castle, as well as a line of defence-walls that surrounded the town. These fortifications were undoubtedly in ruins by the beginning of the thirteenth century, and so the Venetians would have repaired them, but they did not feel the need to strengthen the town's defences until the Turkish threat appeared on the horizon. The first large-scale Turkish raid on the Great Island came in 1538, when an Ottoman fleet under Hayrettin Pasha, the infamous Barbarosso, conquered the Cyclades and ravaged the northern coast of Crete, sacking Réthymnon and carrying off most of its surviving population into slavery. Réthymnon had barely recovered from this catastrophe when it was raided again in 1562, this time by an Ottoman fleet commanded by Uluch Ali, known to the Turks as Kilich Ali Pasha. These raids showed that the defences of Réthymnon were hopelessly inadequate, and so the Venetian town council, known as the 'Magnifica Communita', began considering plans for a new fortress. The first plans submitted to the town council were by the Venetian military engineer Michele Sammicheli, who had built the defence-walls of Khandaks. But Sammicheli's plans seemed too expensive to implement, and so the town council instead chose a less elaborate design drawn up by another Venetian military engineer named Palavitsini. Construction of the new fortress, the Fortezza, began on 15 September 1573, and by the summer of 1577 all sides of the fortifications had been completed except for the seaward walls, which were finished in the following year. Then in 1580 work began on filling in the interior of the fortress with earth to raise it close to the level of the ramparts, after which construction started on the various structures in the citadel, which included a grand palace for the governor, barracks for the garrison, administrative buildings for the staff, storerooms for food, magazines for ammunition, cisterns for drinking water, a hospital to care for the sick and wounded, and houses for those of the townspeople who might choose to live within the fortress, though only three or four dwellings were actually built, and finally a chapel where those in the Fortezza could attend divine services. All of these structures appear to have been erected by 1582–83, as evidenced by a report sent to Venice by the security officer in charge of the Fortezza at the time.

The Turkish invasion of Crete began in early September 1645 with their attack on Chaniá, which fell after a siege of two months. The Ottoman forces then attacked Réthymnon by both land and sea, their army burning all of the villages and farms in the vicinity. The Venetian forces and their Sklavounian and Dalmatian mercenaries tried to stop the Ottoman army at the outer defence walls of Réthymnon, but the Turks broke through and the surviving defenders retreated to the Fortezza, where they joined the permanent garrison and the people of the town, whose population was then about 8,500. Thus began the Turkish siege of Réthymnon, with the Ottoman fleet bombarding the Fortezza from the sea and their army attacking it from the peninsula that connected it to the mainland. The defenders were at a grave disadvantage, for many of the leading officers of the Venetian forces in Crete had been killed in the defence of Chaniá and in the earlier fighting around Réthymnon, but they fought back valiantly, killing and wounding several thousand Turks during the siege. But meanwhile conditions within the citadel became intolerable, as an epidemic of cholera broke out among the thousands of townspeople and soldiers crowded together in the fortress, until finally the Catholic bishop of Réthymnon pleaded with the commanding officer to surrender the Fortezza, which thus fell to the Turks at the end of November 1645 after a siege of twenty-three days.

After the surrender of the Fortezza, the surviving soldiers of the Venetian garrison and some 1,500 townspeople managed to escape aboard ships, while the remainder of the populace were taken captive by the Turks, with the women and children being sent off to be sold at the slave market in Istanbul. Ten of the most beautiful women and children captured at the fall of Réthymnon were presented as a gift to the Sultan, Crazy Ibrahim, who brought them into his harem in

Topkapi Palace, the imperial pleasure-dome in Istanbul. Among these captives were three daughters of a priest named Vorias from Mylopótamos, the youngest of them, who was three years old at the time she entered the Harem in 1646, being given the Turkish name of Rebia Gülnüs, the Rose of Spring. Rebia Gülnüs lived to become the wife of Sultan Mehmet IV and mother of the Sultans Mustafa II and Ahmet III, and today she is buried in an imperial Ottoman mausoleum in Istanbul.

After the fall of Réthymnon many of the Turkish forces settled in the town, later to be joined by Cretan refugees when the Ottoman conquest of Crete was completed with the capture of Khandaks in 1669. Thus Réthymnon became an ethnically-mixed town, with Christian Greeks living side-by-side with Moslem Turks. But the two groups did not live in peace, for the Cretans rebelled frequently against Ottoman rule, particularly in the nineteenth century, and the Turks responded with reprisals against the Christian population, with the Bishop of Réthymnon himself being hanged by the Ottomans in one such local massacre. At times these massacres and other persecutions lowered the Christian population of Réthymnon to a small minority of the total number in the town, with the Cretan Greeks fleeing elsewhere or converting to Islam, although these tendencies changed during the latter years of the Ottoman occupation. But when Pashley visited Réthymnon in 1834 the town was still predominantly Turkish:

> The present population of Rhithymnos is upwards of three thousand souls, of which only about eighty families are Christians. Here the character of the bazaars, and streets, which are better than those of Khania, is entirely Turkish.

Relics of the Ottoman occupation can be seen today in Réthymnon, where a few mosque domes and minarets still form a distinctive part of the old town's character, along with the baroque beauties of Venetian arches, doorways, and a street-fountain. However, the spires of Greek churches now far outnumber all of these relics of foreign dominion, here and elsewhere on the Great Island, and the Fortezza still dominates the old town from the ancient acropolis hill. The only Turkish monument on the Fortezza itself is a domed mosque in the centre of the citadel, an Ottoman structure which seems to date from the mid-sixteenth century, probably built soon after the capture of Réthymnon. The interior of the dome has an extraordinary mosaic revetment of tiny multi-coloured tesserae quite unique in Ottoman architecture, and there is also a superb *mihrap*, the niche in a mosque that indicates the direction of Mecca, with the top of the niche decorated with a finely carved stalactite design. Otherwise the Fortezza is completely Venetian in its architecture and appearance, the only other reminders of the Ottoman past here being the few Turkish domes and minarets that one can see in the town below when admiring the sweeping view of Réthymnon and surrounding country-side from the ramparts of the old fortress.

The oldest and most interesting part of Réthymnon is the quarter around the port, as well as the streets that lead off it from it to the south. The port itself is exceptionally picturesque, with old pastel-painted houses clustering around the crescent harbour, which is closed on its outer side by a breakwater with a lighthouse at the end, the quay lined with the colourful caiques of the local fishermen. Most of the old houses along the quay have now been converted into restaurants, and there are few settings more romantic than here, particularly on a moonlit evening, when there is a haunting Venetian atmosphere about this medieval port.

There are a number of interesting relics to be seen in old Réthymnon, the best approach to them being the street that leads into the town from the southern end of the Venetian harbour, beginning as Odós Néarchou, its name then changing after the first intersection to Soulíou and a little farther on to Ethnikís Antistáseos. At the first intersection one comes to a quaint structure known as the Loggia, the principal Venetian building still standing in Réthymnon. This is a handsome Palladian edifice of square plan with three arched openings in the surrounding arcade, and with a central doorway on each of the sides approached by a short flight of marble steps. The Loggia is believed to date from the late sixteenth or early seventeenth century, and was originally designed as a meeting-hall for the gentry of Venetian Réthymnon. During the Ottoman period it was converted into a mosque, with the base of the minaret still visible at the rear of the building, and with some of the old Turkish tombstones from its graveyard arrayed in the garden to the side. The Loggia is now used to house the Archaeological Museum of Réthymnon, with exhibits from local sites as well as from excavations elsewhere in Réthymnon province, including bronzes from a Roman shipwreck discovered off Ayía Galíni. The most interesting of the local antiquities are those found in 1947 at Mastabá, the area behind the Gymnásion Appenón, just south-east of the Public Park. These are from a rock-hewn grave of the Late Minoan C period, c. 1350–1250 BC, and include a large krater, three amphorae, a large kylix and fragments of three other vases. These are the oldest objects ever found in Réthymnon, and are the first evidence of the ancient city of Réthymnos, which appears from these objects to have been founded at the very end of the Bronze Age.

Just a block to the west of the Loggia, on Odós Palaeológou at its intersection with Odós Thessaloníki, one finds the last of the old Venetian street-fountains still standing in Réthymnon. This is the Arimondi Fountain, a beautiful Renaissance structure consisting of four Corinthian columns, with their capitals and architrave framing three panels in which water flows from the mouths of three lions in relief. The fountain dates from 1623 and is named for Alvise Raimondi, who at the time was the Venetian Rector of Réthymnon, and who during his tenure in office built a number of other street-fountains in the town, of which only this single lovely example remains. The fountain was originally sheltered from the elements by a domed fountain-house, of which three of the four supporting pillars still stand along with a fragment of the cupola. The fountain is still functioning, though now water emerges from the mouth of only one of the lions, but the sight of the local women filling their amphorae here evokes memories of what Réthymnon might have been like in Venetian days, when the Italian Renaissance touched this and other towns on the Great Island.

Walking south from the fountain for one block, one comes to the edifice known as Nerantzes Djami, whose most striking feature is a tall and slender minaret of exceptional beauty. The large edifice beside the minaret was originally a Venetian church named Santa Maria, mentioned in records as far back as 1227. The church was converted into a mosque soon after the Turkish conquest of Réthymnon in 1645, becoming first Hüseyin Pasha Djami, and later Nerantzes Djami. The minaret dates to the mid-seventeenth century and is one of the finest of its kind in Greece, said to be a copy of one of the minarets of the mosque of Sultan Selim II at Edirne, the supreme masterpiece of the great Ottoman architect Sinan. One should also notice the magnificent doorway at the end of the former church nearest the minaret, where an arched entryway is framed by two pairs of Corinthian columns complete with their capitals and architrave, framing two pairs of niches, a beautiful neoclassical relic of Venetian Réthymnon.

A little farther down the main north-south street, which is here known as Odós Ethnikís Antistáseos, one comes to the church of San Francisco, another splendid survivor from Venetian Réthymnon. The church had fallen into ruins in the late Ottoman period, but in recent years it has been undergoing restoration and is now being used as a concert hall, a particularly beautiful setting for such a purpose.

There are also a number of beautiful Venetian doorways along this and the other streets of Réthymnon's old quarter. There is an exceptionally fine one at number 154 Odós Arkhadíou, the first street in from the shore road. There a pair of Corinthian columns with their capitals, architrave and pediment frame a portal with an engaged circular arch springing from two fluted piers, with a floral relief adorning the semicircle above the door. This superb portal appears to date from the first half of the seventeenth century, when Renaissance architecture as well as art and literature flowered in Venetian Réthymnon.

Returning to Odós Ethnikís Antistáseos, continue on towards its intersection with the main east-west avenue of modern Réthymnon. One short block before the street reaches the avenue it crosses Odós Gerakári, where on the near corner to the left there stands another Turkish minaret, but the Ottoman mosque to which it was attached has now disappeared. Beyond the minaret, on the last short block of Odós Ethnikí Antistáseos before it reaches the main avenue, the street passes through an arched portal. This is the Porto Guoro, the last surviving gateway from the old Venetian defence-walls of Réthymnon, known to the Greeks as 'I Megáli Pórta', the Great Gate. This gate was part of the fortifications that the Venetians erected around the lower town of Réthymnon in the second half of the sixteenth century, when the threat of a Turkish invasion of Crete appeared imminent. The gateway takes its name from Giacomo Guoro, who was the Venetian Rector of Réthymnon at the time. The gateway was once surmounted by a pediment adorned with a relief depicting the winged Lion of St Mark, symbol of the Serenissima, the Serene Republic of Venice.

The itinerary now turns left onto Odós Gerakári, a very picturesque old street that takes one eastward parallel to the main avenue. On the second block along this street one passes behind the cathedral known as the Eklisía Tessarón Martýron, the Church of the Four Martyrs. This is named for the four Retzepi brothers – Manolis, Nikolaos, Yorgios and Angeli – who were martyred in Réthymnon in 1824 during a Turkish massacre of Christians.

Continuing along Odós Gerakári for about 500m beyond the turning, one sees on the left the minarets and domes of an old Ottoman mosque, Kara Musa Pasha Djami, the last stop on this itinerary. This fine structure was originally a Franciscan monastery dating from the Venetian period, converted into a mosque soon after the Turkish conquest of Réthymnon in 1645. The Venetian origins of the edifice are most evident in the beautiful neoclassical entryway and in the ogive arches of the interior, a square area covered by nine domes, the most Ottoman elements being the domes themselves and the minaret. The old mosque is now the headquarters for the Director of Byzantine Antiquities in Réthymnon, and there are plans for converting the edifice into a museum devoted to the history of the town during the Byzantine period. In the meantime, the old mosque and its courtyard are evocative reminders of both the Ottoman and Venetian periods in the history of Réthymnon, seven centuries of foreign occupation represented here in the architectural elements of a single edifice.

The most exciting time to be in Réthymnon is during its annual wine festival, which is celebrated in the public park each year at the end of July. We caught the last day of the festival during the summer of 1986, when we arrived in Réthymnon on our way back to Chaniá after having toured the eastern part of Crete. The town was packed, for people had come from all over Crete for this festival, a welcome sight to see Greeks far outnumbering foreigners in summer, and we were very lucky when we obtained the very last hotel room in the town because of a last-minute cancellation. We were exhausted after our long tour of eastern Crete, but we quickly showered and hurried over to the public park, which was throbbing with the sound of Cretan music, with musicians, singers and folk dancers performing on stage and crowds of celebrants dancing amongst themselves in various parts of the green, with local wine being served from barrels at several strategic places. Taking our jug of wine and our two glasses, we tried to find a table. But they were all full and so we found a seat on a park bench and had our own private party there with snacks we had brought along from our trip, sitting happily through the whole of the evening and on into the *óres mikrés* – the small hours – listening to the happy sounds of song, music and dance as the people of Réthymnon celebrated their annual Dionysian festival. The memory of that night touches me now as I write, but alas I am thousands of miles from that wonderful town.

12

§§§

SOUTH FROM RÉTHYMNON

The modern Prefecture of Réthymnon coincides almost exactly with the old Venetian Territorio de Rethimno, comprising the region between the peaks of Mount Ídha on the east and those of the White Mountains on the west, extending from the Aegean to the Libyan Sea. The Prefecture consists of four provinces, with that of Réthymnon marking up the north-west quarter, Mylopótamos the north-east, Áyios Vasílios the south-west and Amári the south-east, the latter stretching in from its salient on the Libyan Sea into the centre of the region. Most of Mylopótamos Province has already been included within earlier itineraries, and so the present chapter will cover the other three provinces of the Prefecture, describing a series of excursions that bring one south from Réthymnon across the west-central quarter of Crete to its southern coast.

The first of these itineraries begins by taking one eastward along the coast to Perivólia, where one heads south on the road that leads to the Amári valley, the heart of the south-eastern province of the Réthymnon Prefecture. This road brings one up along the valley of the Sfakoriakó, reaching an altitude of 340m at the village of Prasiés, 11km from Réthymnon, with Mount Vrísinas looming just to the west at an altitude of 858m.

At Prasiés there is a turn-off to the right leading around the northern side of Vrísinas, while 3km farther along the main road to the south there is another turn-off to the right leading around the southern flank of the mountain. The first village to the west of Prasiés on the northern side of Vrísinas is Hromonastíri, where there is a very old church dedicated to the Panayía Kéra. This church is believed to date from the second Byzantine period, perhaps erected soon after the recapture of Crete from the Saracens in AD 963. Some of its original frescoes are still visible. The Panayía Kéra is one of six old churches in Hromonastíri mentioned by Guiseppe Gerola in his magisterial work, *Monumenti Veneti nell' Isola di Creta* (1905–32), but the other five are in ruins. Gerola's catalogue lists these among 850 Byzantine churches that were still standing in Crete at the beginning of the present century, with 281 of these in the Prefecture of Réthymnon alone, one of the rich heritages of this region of Crete. The catalogue also lists a Byzantine chapel of St John in Sellí, one of the villages on the south side of Mount Vrísinas, but its date is not given. An early Byzantine basilica has also been discovered at Karé, on the south-western slope of the mountain. Another interesting discovery has been made a short way to the east of Karé, at Onithé, where Nikolaos Platon has unearthed two houses from the Archaic period, perhaps part of the ancient town of Phálanna, which is believed to have been on the south slope of Vrísinas.

Continuing on beyond Prasiés and the turn-off to the villages south of Mount Vrísinas, one soon crosses a tributary of the Sfakoriakó, its stream here forming the boundary between the provinces of Réthymnon, to the north, Áyios Vasílios, to the south-west, and Amári to the south-east. The road then crosses the main stream of the Sfakoriakó a short way farther along, after which it follows the stream-bed of an upper tributary of the river, here only a winter torrent, as it leads one into Amári province. Twenty-five kilometres out of Réthymnon the road passes the tiny village of Vení, too small to be indicated on any of the modern highway-maps of Crete, but mentioned in Gerola's catalogue as having a Byzantine chapel dedicated to Áyios Antónios, and also with a monastery known as Moni Vení. This insignificant little hamlet apparently dates back to ancient times, for it is believed to be the birthplace of the poet Rhianos, who flourished in the latter part of the third century BC. As Peter Jay writes of him in his edition of the *Greek Anthology*:

> Rhianos came from a small town in Crete. The *Suda* says he was originally a slave. He was active perhaps in the second half of the third century; he wrote lengthy epic poems – five titles are known – and edited Homer. This suggested that he worked at Alexandria. Ten epigrams survive, mainly dedicatory and pederastic. The most interesting is the ironic thank-you poem given here.

Archinos, this retsina-bottle contains
Precisely half pine-resin and half wine.
Cuts from a leaner goat, I've never seen
(Though Hippocrates who sent them, the dear man
Deserves *every* thanks).

Thirty-two kilometres out of Réthymnon the road brings one to Apóstoloi, a picturesque mountain village perched at a height of 500m at the head of the Amári valley, which stretches off from here to the south-east, bounded on the east by the great massif of Psilorítis and on the west by the smaller range of Kédros, whose summit is at 1777m. This is one of the loveliest and most fertile valleys in the Great Island, a lost paradise hidden away here in the mountains of central Crete, its pretty villages set up among the hills like captive constellations, looking from a distance as if they had not changed in their appearance since antiquity. Apóstoloi is one of five villages that cluster here at the north-west tier of the Amári valley, the others being Thrónos, Klisídi, Kalóyeros and Génna. These five villages are all within the former bounds of the ancient city of Sývrita, whose site is just north of Thrónos, with fragments of its walls and a gateway still standing. Sývrita was once the most powerful city in this part of Crete, its domains extending over much of what are now the provinces of Amári and Áyios Vasílios. These regions were known in antiquity as the Sývriti, with Amári being then known as High Sývritos and Áyios Vasílios as Low Sývritos.

There is a greater concentration of Byzantine churches in the villages of the Amári valley than anywhere else on Crete, particularly on the road that extends around the eastern side of the valley, beginning at Apóstoloi, although there are also a number on the road that goes around the western side, via Gerakári. The two routes link up once again at the main highway near the south coast. The following is a listing of some of these old churches, with information gleaned from Gerola's catalogue and other sources.

At Apóstoloi there is a church of Áyios Ioánnis dating from the fourteenth/fifteenth century, and beneath that the mosaic pavement of an early Byzantine basilica. At Thrónos there is a church dedicated to the *Koimisis tis Panayía*, the Dormition of the Virgin; this is dated to the thirteenth century, and there are inscriptions of 1491 and 1558, indicating restorations at those dates. In Génna the church of Áyios Onouphrios has a frescoed scene of the Crucifixion dating to 1330. Kalóyeros has two churches with frescoes of the fourteenth century.

Starting down along the road that runs along the eastern side of the valley, one comes to Moní Asomáton, where there is a church dating from the second Byzantine period, with many old icons from that era. At Moni Asomáton one can take a detour that leads to Amári, the little capital of the eparchy. The road to Amári passes Monastiráki, near which archaeologists have discovered an ancient site at Kharakas, with a settlement clustering around a palatial structure of the Minoan era. One then comes to Amári, which has been the capital of the valley since Venetian times, once a gathering-place for the nobility of the island. At Amári the church of the Asómatos has frescoes of 1225, the oldest-dated wall-paintings known on Crete. Amári also has the church of Ayía Ánna, which is among the oldest in Crete, dated 1250, and the 'Sameito' church, built in 1385, as well as Ayíi Theódori, which dates from 1588, and the old churches of Áyios Ioánnis and Áyios Phótios, both of uncertain date.

Returning to the main road at Moni Asomáton, one now drives down the eastern side of the Amári valley to Vizári, west of which there are the ruins of a large town dating from the Roman period, as well as the remains of an early Byzantine basilica. This ancient town survived up until the medieval Byzantine period, when it was destroyed by a Saracen raid, as evidenced by the Islamic coins found in its destruction-fill. Two kilometres beyond Vizári the road brings one to the crossroads village of Fourfourás, where there are two old churches: Áyios Yórgios, dating to 1411, and Ayía Paraskeví, which dates from 1515.

At Fourfourás one can make a short detour up to the village of Platánia, which is 3km to the north on a branch-road that leads back to Moní Asomáton under the massif of Mount Ídha, whose main peak at Tímios Stavrós towers just to the east, at an altitude of 2456m. Platánia has an old frescoed church of the Panayía, which tradition holds was founded soon after the fall of Constantinople in 1453. There are also three noted caves in the vicinity of Platánia, all on the slopes of Psilorítis. The lowest of these is known as Dígenes, at an altitude of 820m; the second is Kissóspelios, at 1000m; and the third and highest is the Cave of Pan, at 1750m. This latter cave was revered in antiquity as the abode of the god Pan, whose pan-pipes are still played by the Cretan shepherds who tend their flocks on these mountains.

Returning to Fourfourás, one now drives south through the lower part of the Amári valley, a region known as Abadía, passing the villages of Kouroútes and Níthafris, where the route joins the road that has come down the western side of the valley. Taking the south fork at Níthafris, one passes the old church of Ayía Paraskeví, and then a short way farther along one comes to Apodoúlou, with an old frescoed church dedicated to Áyios Yórgios. This brings one to Plátanos, where the left fork leads off along the southern tier of Mount Ídha to Zarós and Ayía Varvára, a route described in an earlier itinerary, while the right fork leads down to the south coast. Keeping to the left on main roads beyond Plátanos, a drive of 14km brings one to Timbáki, the southernmost point on the present itinerary, with the road continuing on to Phaestós and the southern coastal region of central Crete. Otherwise there is nothing of interest to detain one in Timbáki, a large village that dates back to Venetian times, but which was destroyed during the rebellions at the end of the Ottoman occupation, and which was devastated again by the Germans during World War II.

The present itinerary now starts back westward along the coast from Timbáki, turning off to the left after 2km and then driving another km down to Kókinos Pýrgos, a coastal hamlet on the Libyan Sea that has now become a summer resort. There is an even more popular resort farther west at Ayía Galíni, approached from a turning 6km further along the main highway Ayía Galíni is a pretty spot with an excellent beach, but its popularity as a resort has now made it very overcrowded during the summer season, and so those who want to swim in more secluded surroundings might explore the shore farther along the coast to the west, for there are no roads along the shore between here and the Préveli Monastery, the next major point of interest on this itinerary. In Ayía Galíni itself, aside from the beach, the only place of interest is the old church of the Panayía, which probably dates to the Venetian period.

After leaving Ayía Galíni, one now takes the left fork outside the village, which takes one northward for about 5km up the right bank of the Platís, a river which flows down from the Amári valley through the coastal plain here to the Libyan Sea. Then the road turns westward along a tributary of the Platís, taking one from the province of Amári into the province of Ayios Vasílios, which extends from here all the way along the coast to the White Mountains and the Prefecture of Chaniá. About 5km farther along a turn-off to the left leads to the large village of Mélambes, on the way to which there is another turn-off onto a rough road that leads out to the coast at Cape Mélissa; on the right at this point there is also a turn-off that leads back to the southern end of the Amári valley. Continuing along the main road, one now passes between Mount Kédros and two lower coastal mountains, the first named Vouvál, at an altitude of 947m, and the second Sidérotas, whose summit is at 1136m. The road now heads north-westward along the western side of Kédros, whose summit hovers above at 1777m, passing the villages of Kría Vrísi, Platanés, Akoúmia (where another rough road leads down to the coast near Cape Mélissa), Akoúnta and Kisós. The latter two villages are reached by turn-offs at the same crossroads, with the one to the left leading to Akoúnta and then off to the coast, while the one to the right goes to Kisós and then around the northern flank of Kédros to Gerakári, which is on the road that goes around the western side of the Amári valley. Then 5km farther along the main road one comes to the large and cheerful village of Spíli, a strategic spot to stop for a coffee at one of the cafés along the main street. Spíli is renowned for its extraordinary public fountain, a relic of Venetian days, with water pouring from the mouths of nineteen sculptured lions into a trough and out over the edge in a cascade. While in Spíli one should visit its old chapel of the Metamorphosis, another relic of Venetian days. Spíli also has a good view of Mount Kédros, whose peak is off to the south-east.

After Spíli the road heads westward along a tributary of the Megapótamos, and 5km farther along it joins the main highway that leads south from Réthymnon to the Libyan Sea. Turning left at the crossroads, one heads south through the village of Koxaré. Beyond Koxaré the road enters the dramatic Kourtaliótiko gorge, at the beginning of which the Megapótamos river rises from a spring beside the chapel of Ayios Nikólaos. At the end of the gorge the road turns westward and comes to the village of Asómatis, heading towards the coastal resort of Plakiás. But the present itinerary takes a detour left onto a turn-off that leads back to the Megapótamos, heading south along the river toward Moní Préveli. On the approach to the site the road crosses the Megapótamos on a bridge dating from the Venetian period, passing the abandoned tower that once housed Moní Préveli. Then one finally comes to the new Préveli Monastery, whose monastic buildings are in two groups, one high above the Libyan Sea and the other down in the valley of the Megapótamos.

The original monastery here was founded in the mid-seventeenth century, with one tradition holding that the founder was a refugee from the village of Prevelianá Monofatsíou, near Iráklion, though another legend says that it was the foundation of a noble Byzantine family named Prevelis. In any event, the monastery was dedicated to St John the Theologian, who is depicted in an ancient Byzantine icon that is preserved in the monastic church. After the Ottoman conquest of Crete many Christian youths sought refuge from Turkish persecution by becoming monks at Préveli. Préveli was a centre of learning in Ottoman times, with its monks establishing secret schools in the local villages to keep Christian Greek culture alive, training youths who would themselves later become monks and teachers. Préveli also became a centre of Cretan resistance to Ottoman rule, and in 1866 the Turks retaliated by burning the monastery to the ground. Préveli was rebuilt later in the Ottoman period, the present monastic buildings dating from that time. The monastery again became a centre of Cretan resistance during the German occupation in World War II, with the monks sheltering British and Commonwealth soldiers until they could be taken off by Allied submarines. George Psychoundakis writes of this in the *Cretan Runner*, a chronicle of his activities as a guide and courier for the British Intelligence forces during the German occupation: 'The news of submarines approaching Préveli had reached all ears, and wherever English were hidden, their protectors made haste to guide them that way.' When the Germans learned of this they occupied the monastery, with the Abbot Agathangelos escaping just in time and making his way to North Africa. After the end of World War II the British forces presented a pair of silver candlesticks to the monastery as a token of gratitude, and these are still treasured in Préveli today, shining symbols of Cretan heroism in World War II.

After visiting Préveli, one can drive back to the turn-off at Asómatis and continue on westward for 7km to the next crossroads, where a road to the left leads down to Pláka Bay and the resort village of Plakiás. This is the most popular resort on the Libyan Sea south of Réthymnon, and there are a number of hotels and a holiday-village along the magnificent beach, which stretches between the two bold promontories that bound the bow-shaped bay, with Cape Kakomoúri on the east and Cape Stavrós on the west.

From Plakiás one can return to Réthymnon by one of two routes without retracing any of the previous itineraries. The most direct route (to be described now) takes one back across the waist of the island from Plakiás to Réthymnon, while the other way goes westward along the southern shore as far as Sfakiá, then crossing along the eastern side of the White Mountains. This latter route will be one of those followed in the next chapter.

Driving back from Plakiás, one returns to the crossroads passed earlier and goes on 2km farther to the next crossroads. There the road to the left goes off via Mírthios to the coastal road westward, while the road to the right heads northward toward Réthymnon. The latter route first passes through the wild Koutsifoú gorge, and after a drive of 6km brings one to Angouselianá. There the road turns eastward, and after 8km brings one to the crossroads at Áyios Vasílios, where one turns left onto the main highway that leads north to Réthymnon, a drive of 21km across the narrow waist that connects western Crete to the broader landmass at the centre of the Great Island.

The most interesting place to stop on the drive back to Réthymnon is Arméni, which is 11km beyond the Áyios Vasílios crossroads. The name of the village comes from the Armenians who were resettled here and elsewhere on the island by Nicephorus Phocas soon after his reconquest of Crete in 961, part of a Byzantine programme to re-establish Christian culture after the Saracen occupation. Two kilometres or so beyond the village a signpost indicates the way to an ancient site, a Minoan necropolis discovered in 1969 by the Greek archaeologist Tzedakis. During the course of several seasons of excavations Tzedakis uncovered numerous tombs from the Late Minoan period as well as one from the Mycenaean era. The funerary objects found in these tombs are now on exhibit in the Chaniá Archaeological Museum, along with some painted terracotta sarcophagi very similar to those from Clazomenae, an Ionian city on the Aegean coast of Asia Minor. The Arméni necropolis is one of the largest ever found on Crete, but as yet no trace has been found of the ancient city whose dead were buried here, though it must have been a very large settlement indeed to have had a cemetery of this extent.

After visiting the archaeological site at Arméni we returned to the highway and continued to drive north, soon reaching the outskirts of Réthymnon. The highway brought us into the main square of the town and we drove to our hotel down by the seafront, having completed our exploration of the country south of Réthymnon.

13

GGG

FROM RÉTHYMNON
TO CHANIÁ

The quickest and most direct way from Réthymnon to Chaniá is via the new superhighway, a distance of 72km that can be covered in little more than an hour, though those with more time to spare might want to stop off at some of the interesting places along the way. One can also take a more roundabout route via the south coast as far as Sfakiá, then cutting across the island to join the superhighway halfway between Réthymnon and Chaniá. Thus one sees the western side of Áyios Vasílios and Réthymnon provinces.

This longer route first takes one south of Réthymnon across the narrowest part of western Crete to the crossroads above Pláka Bay, where one then turns right onto the coastal highway, heading westwards for Sfakiá, a drive of 40km. Along this stretch the road winds along an elevated coastal strip between the mountains and the sea, passing a series of villages set a little distance up in the hills, beginning with Mírthios at the head of the river valley above Pláka Bay. Along this stretch the road comes down to the sea only at the turn-off to Frangokástello, 23km west of Mírthios, where after a drive of 3km one comes to the Venetian fortress from which the place takes its name, the Frankish Castle. Formerly Frangokástello stood alone on its sea-girt promontory, one of the most impressive sights on the south coast of Crete, but in recent years a little hamlet of summer houses has sprung up around it, with rooms to rent for the tourists who are attracted by the superb beach of pink-white sand that stretches along the shore below the walls of this very romantic-looking Venetian castle.

Frangokástello was erected by the Venetians in 1371, the only fortress other than Ierápetra that still stands on the southern coast of Crete. This fortress was the scene of an historic battle on 18 May 1828, when a besieged force of 1000 Greek rebels under General Hadjimichalis were annihilated by a Turkish army of 14,000 commanded by Mustafa Pasha. Hadjimichalis himself is said to have been beheaded by Mustafa Pasha, after which his corpse and those of his men were hacked to pieces by the Turks. After the Turks left Frangokástello the rebels were buried by the local villagers, with a nun gathering together the remains of Hadjimichalis and interring him in the crypt of the chapel of Áyios Harálambos. But on 18 May 1829, the first anniversary of the battle at Frangokástello, a strange phenomenon manifested itself to the few villagers who happened to be up and about a few minutes before dawn that morning, when they saw the *Drossoulítes*, the Dewy Shades (as they were later called) the ghosts of Hadjimichalis and his men moving across the battlefield as if to do battle with the Turks once again. This apparition has been seen again and again in the years since then, the *Drossoulítes* always appearing just before dawn moving across the same field where they had died in battle against the Turks on 18 May 1828, then disappearing with the morning mists as the sun rises above the surrounding crags, Hadjimichalis and his men vanishing once more.

After visiting Frangokástello, one drives back to the main road just beyond Patsianós, and from there one can continue westward along the coast road, crossing from Áyios Vasílios province into the province of Sfakiá, which forms the south-eastern part of the Prefecture of Chaniá. Nine kilometres farther along one comes to the crossroads at the main road that cut across the island via the Askífou Plain. Here one might take a 4-kilometre detour to the coast to visit Chóra Sfakión before going back across the island. On the way the road passes the village of Komitádes, where the people of Sfakiá held their provincial congresses before the Greek War of Independence, when for a time they maintained their independence from the Turks in their strongholds in the White Mountains. These popular assemblies of the Sfakians were held in the old church of Thymonianí Panayía, which one can still see on the way down to Chóra Sfakión, along with the old Church of the Twelve Apostles, one of several local churches with fragmentary frescoes from the Byzantine era.

Chóra Sfakión is the main port for the province of Sfakiá, the village comprising a picturesque cluster of white houses clustered around a cove under the south-eastern ramparts of the White Mountains, which from this point on slope down directly into the Libyan Sea, so that from here on the coast road degenerates into a dirt-track that winds its way along a narrow tier cut into the steeply sloping sides of the seaward hills, which farther west become even more and more precipitous.

The south coast westward from Chóra Sfakión will be explored in a later excursion south from Chaniá, and so for the time being one might just have a swim on the beach at Chóra Sfakión and then afterwards have lunch at one of the seaside tavernas there. One can also hire a boat for an excursion to the Cave of Daskaloyiannis, which is a short distance to the west of the port along the shore. This cave was the headquarters for the Sfakiote partisans in the revolt of 1770, the first Cretan rebellion against Ottoman rule, led by the local leader whose exploits now live on in the national epic poem of Crete, *The Song of Daskaloyiannis*.

Those who wish to spend a night or two in the village before going on to Chaniá might explore the south coast of western Crete by sea from here, for there is a regular round-trip ferry service between Chóra Sfakión, Loutró, Ayía Ruméli, Soúyia and Palaeochóra. This service is particularly convenient for those who want to hike through the Samariá Gorge, an expedition that will be described in a later chapter, for there is a ferry that makes the round-trip between Chora Sfakión and Ayía Ruméli, the little port at the end of the gorge.

Chóra Sfakión is also the main port of embarkation for the two little islands that lie 30–40km off the Cretan coast to the south, the larger one being Gávdos and the tiny one Gavdopoúla. Gávdos actually has half-a-dozen villages, the largest of which is Kastrí, while Gavdapoúla is uninhabited except for herdsmen who occasionally graze their flocks there. Gávdos, which in Roman times was knows as Clauda, is mentioned in *Acts* 27: 16, where the narrator tells of the storm at sea that struck Paul's boat after it left Kalí Liménes and headed attempted to cross to 'Pheonix . . . which is a haven of Crete, and lieth toward the south-west and north-west'. As one reads in *Acts* 27: 13–17:

> And when the south wind blew softly, supposing they had obtained their purpose, loosing thence, they sailed close by Crete. But not long after there rose against it a tempestuous wind, called Euroclydon. And when the ship was caught, and when we could not bear up into the wind, we let her drive. And running under a certain island which is called Clauda, we had much work to come by the boat . . .

Gávdos seems to have been inhabited as early as the Neolithic era, though the first permanent settlement there apparently dates from the post-Mycenaean era. The island seems to have been fairly populous during the early Byzantine era, when Clauda was the seat of a bishopric, though the see probably included the villages of Sfakiá as well. But the island seems to have been virtually abandoned during the later Byzantine period, when corsairs ravaged the Aegean, using this remote isle as one of their lairs. This pirates' nest would have been the open anchorage on the eastern side of the island known as Ship Bay, which in Boschini's seventeenth-century map of Il Regno di Candia is identified as Porto Sarachinico, the Port of the Saracens.

There is a local legend that Gávdos is the Homeric isle of Ogygia, where Odysseus stayed for seven years in the palace of the nymph Calypso. Most scholars disagree with this tradition, holding that Ogygia should be somewhere near Sicily or southern Italy, but ever since I first saw Gávdos, from the deck of an American troopship early one morning in October 1945, I was convinced that this lonely islet far south of Crete was Calypso's Isle. And now, 41 years later, I was looking at Gávdos once again, its silhouette barely visible far out on the Libyan Sea where my ship had passed on the homeward voyage after the end of World War II, and where the wanderings of Odysseus had brought him after the Trojan War.

We left Chóra Sfakión after lunch, driving back to the crossroads 4km to the east of the village, where we turned north and started driving across the waist of the island. As we drove up into the hills above the coast we looked up the coast and saw the Venetian castle at Frangokástello looking like a vision of medieval romance on its promontory far to the east, and then at a turn in the road we stopped to look out to the south toward Africa, where Gávdos floated serenely like a cloud far out on the shimmering blue of the Libyan Sea.

After the road has wound its way up from the coast at Sfakiá it passes through another one of the spectacular canyons that the cataclysmic forces of nature have produced here on the Great Island. This is the Nímbros Ravine, a gorge six to seven kilometres long, in some places only two or three metres wide when its opposing cliffs are as much as 300 metres high, the coloured veining and contours in the opposing precipices showing where they were torn apart in some prehistoric earthquake.

At the upper end of the gorge one comes to the village of Íbros, and a short way beyond this one passes a turn-off to the right that winds up into the mountains to the east, passing first through Ásfendos and then on into the heart of central Crete. Continuing along the main highway from Chóra Sfakión, one comes next to a road leading off to the right to Pétres, the southernmost of the villages of Askífou, the beautiful plateau that nestles in among the surrounding peaks and ridges that form part of the south-eastern ramparts of the White Mountains. The next two villages on the road through this lovely plateau are Ammoúdari and Karés, with a side-road leading off on the right to Goní, where the ruins of a Turkish fortress brood on a hilltop to the east. Then at the northern end of the plateau one comes to the Katré Ravine, the scene of several important battles during the Cretan revolutions against the Turks, figuring in the rebellions of 1770, 1821 and 1866. When Pashley paused through the Katré ravine in 1834 he found the roadside littered with the whitened bones of those who had died there thirteen years before, and thirty-two years later more fallen warriors were added to the grim piles of human remains in the gorge.

After going down the Katré Ravine, one passes from the province of Sfakiá to that of Apokóronas, the north-easternmost of the five regions of the Chaniá Prefecture. The road then descends into the vast coastal plain that projects out into the huge triangular peninsula of Vámos; this is bounded on the east by Kólpos Almiroú, the long gulf that stretches to the west of Réthymnon, and on the west by Kólpos Soúdas, the deep inlet of the sea that cuts in between the mainland and Akrotíri, the scrotum-like peninsula that projects north-eastward from its narrow neck just east of Chaniá. The most interesting place to stop on the last stretch of the road leading across the waist of the island is at Alíkampos, which is approached by a turn-off to the right 11km past the upper end of the Katré Ravine, continuing another 2km to the east. The village church of the Panayía in Alíkampos is adorned with frescoes done in 1315 by Ioánnis Pagomenos, one of the finest artists of the early Renaissance on the Great Island.

Returning to the main road across the island after visiting Alíkampos, 7km farther along one comes to Vríses, whose main square is shaded by giant *plátanos* trees. This is an ideal place to stop for lunch, in which case one should try the local yoghurt, said to be the best in Crete. Then afterwards one can continue on another kilometre or so to the main superhighway, where one turns and heads westward toward Chaniá.

Most travellers going west on the north coast from Réthymnon usually travel along the superhighway, which for the first 30km or so runs along the shore of the Aegean, passing a succession of excellent beaches. Otherwise, the first place of interest place that one passes is the Geráni bridge, 7km west of Réthymnon. During the construction of the new highway an ancient cave-sanctuary was discovered in a grotto below the bridge. Cult-objects found within the cave indicated that it had been used as a shrine in the Neolithic period, probably a sanctuary of the Great Earth Mother. The entrance to the cave is now locked to preserve it from vandals, but permission to visit it can be obtained from the Tourist Information Office in Réthymnon.

The other interesting sites on this first stretch of the north shore of Crete west of Réthymnon can best be approached by the old road, which curves well inland before it veers out to the coast again at Georgioúpoli, at the south-western end of the Gulf of Almiros. The old road branches off from the coastal highway 3km west of Réthymnon, heading south-west toward the White Mountains, which from this point on dominate the landscape to an increasing degree. The road passes first through the village of Atsipópoulo 6km out of Réthymnon, then Prinés (7km) and Goniá (10km). Then a short way beyond Goniá the road comes to the crossroads village of Áyios Andréas, where one turns left to approach the first of the ancient sites on this route; following the side road to the south for about 2.5km and passing the first turning on the left. This brings one to Monopári Kastélli, where one sees the fragmentary remains of an ancient fortress crowning a craggy acropolis hill. The site at Monopári Kastélli has never been excavated archaeologically, though John Pendlebury examined the site in 1935, finding a few pottery shards from the Hellenistic period and the remnants of the Venetian defence-walls. The fortress was one of the fourteen strongholds erected or rebuilt early in the thirteenth century by Enrico Pescatore, the Genoese warlord, who may have built here on the ruins of a Byzantine or Hellenistic castle. The Venetians took over the fortress after their conquest of Crete, but thereafter it seems to have been abandoned and allowed to fall into ruins. The present Greek name Monopári is a corruption of the Italian Bonriparo – 'The Good Fortress'.

Returning to the main road, one now drives on for another 4km, as far as another side-road leading south. Turning to the left there, one drives on for about 6km to Roústica, where one comes to the Monastery of Áyios Profítis Ilías, the Holy Prophet Elijah. This renowned monastery dates from the Venetian period, with an inscription on the belfry from 1637 and one on the lintel from 1641. The church has a wood-carved iconostasis with icons of the late Byzantine period, and within the monastery there are the remains of its original library, badly damaged during the Turkish sacks of the building in 1823 and 1866. Some of the old volumes from the collection here are now housed in the National Library in Paris, labelled 'Books from the St Elijah Roústica Monastery'. This was once a very prosperous monastery with widespread farmlands, but now its once numerous community has dwindled to just a handful of monks. Nevertheless, the *paniyíri* of St Prophet Elijah that is celebrated here every 20 July is a very popular one, attracting celebrants from all the surrounding villages.

Returning again to the main road, one now follows its winding route as it goes from the province of Réthymnon into Apokóronas province, passing the villages of Koúfi and Karotí. Then, as the road approaches the large village of Episkopí, one turns left onto another side-road leading south, the main branch leading to Asigoniá. Six kilometres along this road one passes the turn-off to Asigoniá, and another kilometre or so farther along one comes to Argiroúpoli, which is near the site of ancient Láppa, the second of the two archaeological sites along this route, the ruins having been discovered by Pashley in 1834. At that time the village was called Gaydaroúpolis, the Village of Asses, though the locals in self-defence themselves referred to it simply as Póli.

Topographical evidence and the testimony of ancient writers convinced Pashley that this was the site of ancient Láppa, which in its time was the most important city in this part of Crete, its domains extending right across the waist of the island from the Aegean to the Libyan Sea, where it had a port at Pheonix. A Byzantine source credited the founding of Láppa to Agamemnon, but this was not accepted by Pashley, and both he and Spratt believed that it had been first settled in Minoan times. The Lappaeans were renowned in ancient times for their valour, particularly when they held out against the Romans after the fall of Cydonía, Eleftherna, Knossós and Lýttos, their city finally stormed and destroyed by Quintus Caecilius Metellus in 67 BC. Láppa was rebuilt by Augustus following this victory at the Battle of Actium, and this was the town that survived on into modern times. The principal antiquity in the town is a miracle-working spring in the old church of Ayíi Parthenoë; this well is renowned throughout Greece and is probably a survival of an ancient shrine of Artemis.

Continuing on past Argiroúpoli, one comes to the end of the road about 5km farther along at Myriokéfala, a village perched at an altitude of 500m on the eastern spur of the White Mountains. Here one finds the Myriokéfala Monastery, one of the oldest in Crete, founded in the eleventh century and dedicated to the Nativity of the Virgin. The most treasured possession of the monastery is a sacred Byzantine icon of the Virgin's Birth said to have been painted by St Luke, the Divine Physician. This icon is carried around the monastery grounds in procession each year on 8 September, the feast day of the Virgin's Birth, when the people of the surrounding region gather here to celebrate a *paniyíri*.

Returning to the main road once again, a short way along one comes to Episkopí, a very old village that dates back to early Venetian times, its name recalling the fact that it was once the site of a bishopric. Four kilometres farther along the road passes the village of Drámia, identified by Pashley as the ancient Hydramion, of which some fragmentary ruins of the Hellenistic period can still be seen. Then 4km beyond Drámia the road comes to a turn-off to the left that leads to Limní Kourná, the only lake in Crete, which can be reached after a drive of just 3km to the south. The lake, which in antiquity was known as Coria, is quite an extraordinary sight, its uniqueness remarked upon by all travellers to Crete in times past. According to Pashley, there was a temple of Corian Athena on the shore of the lake, which is some two km in length, but this had disappeared already by the time of Spratt's visit.

A drive of 4km south from the lake brings one to the village of Kournás, which is first mentioned in a Venetian census of 1583. But the village must date back to Byzantine times, for the local church of Ayía Eiréne is adorned with fourteenth-century frescoes. There is also a Byzantine church of the fourteenth century in the village of Mathés, which is reached by a secondary road that leads off to the west and then the north from Lake Kourna.

Three kilometres beyond the turn-off to Lake Kourná the old road crosses the superhighway and leads out to the sea at Georgioúpoli, a coastal village that has now become a popular summer resort, with an excellent beach. The village is named for Prince George of the Hellenes, who served as High Commissioner of Crete in the years between the end of the Ottoman occupation and the final *énosis* of the Great Island with Greece in 1913. The village is situated in a very scenic location at the south-western corner of the Gulf of Almiros, where the coast veers sharply northward out to the great promontory of Drápano, which forms the apex of the triangular Vámos peninsula. Georgioúpoli is believed to occupy the site of Amphímalla, which Strabo in his *Geography* mentions as one of the prominent cities in ancient Crete. John Pendlebury in 1935 identified the ruins of a large ancient structure in the vicinity of Georgioúpoli that he believed to be part of Amphímalla, but this was torn down and there is now nothing to identify the site. However, the site of Amphímalla can be placed here with some certainty because of its proximity to the salt-stream known as Almyros, which flows into the sea at Georgioúpoli.

From Georgioúpoli onwards, one has the choice of driving on to Chaniá either by the superhighway or by one of several branches of the old road. The southern branch of the old road crosses the super-highway again a few kilometres along and brings one to Vríses, which is the terminal point for the road that crosses the waist of the island from Chorá Sfakión via Askífou. From Vríses the southernmost branch of the old road continues on towards Chaniá, with side roads on the left leading up to villages on the north-western slopes of the White Mountains. At Vríses itself one can drive south to Embrósneros, a distance of 4km to see the ruined *pýrgos* of Ibrahim Alidakis, which was besieged during one of the revolutions of the nineteenth century, a battle that is now immortalized in Cretan folksongs. In the vicinity of Embrósneros there is a cave-sanctuary of Áyios Antónios that is the subject of local legends, and nearby there is also the famous spring of 'Boutakás', whose flowing waters make a sound like the thunder of primeval forces. Farther along at the end of the road is the village of Vatoudiáris, which is renowned for a paradisical vale called 'The Garden of God'. Returning along this road to Vríses, one can make a short detour south-east to the village of Máza, where there is a very old Byzantine church dedicated to Áyios Nikólaos, with frescoes dated to 1325. A second road leads southwest from Vríses to Vafés, a distance of 4km, in the vicinity of which one finds the historic Cave of Kryonerída. Within the cave there are two old churches, one dedicated to Áyios Ioánnis Theologos and the other to Ayíi Asmatoi, the Incorporeal Saints, the latter with Byzantine frescoes. After making this detour then one can take the southern loop of the old road from Vríses toward Chaniá, which passes first through the villages of Nípos, Tzitzifés and Frés. At Nípos there are two Byzantine churches still standing, both of them with fragments of their original frescoes. Around Tzitzifés there are three large caves: 'Scotiní', 'Scolacás', and 'Marmaráspilio', besides the ruins of the palatial Venetian *pýrgos*, as well as a local beauty spot known as Vrísi, or the Fountain. At Frés there are two Byzantine churches, Áyios Yórgios and the Panayía, both of them decorated throughout with splendid paintings in fresco. Beyond Frés one comes to a crossroads, with the left branch going to Melidhóni and the right to Pemónia, in both of which there is an old Byzantine church with frescoes. The main branch of the road leads through a maze of crossroads to Néo

Chorió, which is set in a vast grove of olive trees with orchards of orange and tangerine trees in the background. Near the village there is a site known as Marmará where there are the ruins of an unidentified ancient city, and also nearby is a cave-sanctuary dedicated to Áyios Gerássimos. From Néo Chorió one can either drive north-west to Kalíves on Soúda Bay, or go north via Stýlos to the roads paralleling the bay. Those who take the latter route might want to pause in Stýlos, a lovely old village with springs shaded by venerable *plátanos* trees. There are two frescoed Byzantine churches in the village, one of them known as Monastíra and the other Áyios Ioánnis, the latter adorned with paintings dated 1280, the beginning of the Byzantine renaissance. There is also a necropolis in the vicinity of the village, at another site called Marmará, as well as some ancient storehouses at a place known as Scála, indicating that there must have been a town of some importance here in antiquity.

The seaward branch of the old road from Georgioúpoli takes one first to Vámos, capital of the Apokóronas province. This is a large village that dates back to Venetian times, first mentioned in the census of 1583. The village probably dates back to the late medieval era, though it is first mentioned in a Venetian census of 1583. The church of the Panayía at Katoméri is the oldest structure in the vicinity of the village, with frescoes of the late medieval period. Vámos is particularly lively in August, when young people from all over Crete congregate here for a festival of modern Greek music.

From Vámos one can choose between several routes to Chaniá. The more indirect of these, but also the most scenic, takes one first eastward to Kefalás, and then northward past Mount Drápano to Kokkino Khorió, where there is a good beach. From there one can take a detour of 2km out to Cape Drápano, from where there is a superb view of Soúda Bay, with the Akrotíri peninsula on the right and on the left the Maláxa ridge, the long rocky spur that extends from the northern tier of the White Mountains out to the inner end of the gulf. As Spratt describes this spendid scene, looking upon the White Mountains from this same vantage-point on Cape Drapano:

> Crete's second great mountain, and indeed it might almost be called the first, but for the celebrity of Ida, since it is within a few feet of the same height, and a larger mass, rises up in a bold, broad summit from the western side of the Apokorona district. It throws off from its northern root an oval iron-bound promontory or peninsula, measuring six and a half miles in diameter, which was

anciently named the Cyamon promontory; it is terminated by the sea-beat headland and bluff of Cape Malaxa. This peninsula forms one of the most important features in the contour of Crete; and under it is sheltered a deep gulf, the entrance to which is from the east, called the Gulf of Suda – a harbour which is one of the most capacious, safe, and easy of access in the Mediterranean. The shores confining the entrance are wild and picturesque in the extreme, especially the north-west shore of the Akrotiri, where bold cliffs overhang it. Cape Drepano terminates it on the east, in a narrow cliffy point, somewhat bent or curved like a reaping-hook (hence the name), alongside of which the largest ship could rub her sides without her keep touching the bottom.

From Cape Drápano one drives back to Kókkino Chorió, continuing from there along the coast road, passing Pláka, Almiría and Kalíves, a pretty seaside village whose excellent beach has made it a popular summer resort. At Kalíves the road begins to climb, and 4km farther along, at Kalámi, one commands a panoramic view of Soúda Bay and its enclosing shores, as the old road joins the superhighway to run along the southern shore of the gulf to its inner end. On the promontory at Kalámi stands the old fortress still known by its Turkish name of Itzeddin, now a prison. Across the bay, on a little islet called Soúda, just off the south-eastern extremity of Akrotíri, one sees another old fortress, even more medieval in its appearance than Itzeddin. These two fortresses were both built by the Venetians to guard the entrance to Soúda Bay. The fortress now known as Itzeddin fell to the Turks when they captured Chaniá in 1645, but the Venetians held the castle on Soúda island until 1715, one of the last two Cretan strongholds to be surrendered by the Serenissima to the Ottoman Empire at that time, the other being Graboúsa, an islet at the north-western tip of Crete.

Two kilometres beyond Kalámi there is a signposted turn-off to the site of ancient Áptera, which is approached by driving a kilometre or so to the village of Megála Khoráfia and then aother two kilometres to the archaeological site, known locally as Palaeócastro. Palaeócastro was identified as Áptera by Pashley, who also suggested that the site of the ancient town of Minoa was directly across the entrance to the gulf, on the shore of Akrotíri opposite Soúda Isle and its little archipelago, which together were known as Leucae, the White Isles. According to legend, this was where the Muses and Sirens contested for mastery in music and song. The Sirens, fabulous creatures who were half-bird and half-woman, threw themselves into the sea in despair, and the White Isles arose from the water as memorials to them. When the first town was founded on the southern shore of Soúda Bay it was called Áptera, or wingless, in commemoration to the fallen Sirens.

Áptera became one of the principal cities of Crete in the fifth century BC and maintained its eminence throughout the Hellenistic era, continuing to be a place of some importance in the medieval Byzantine period, until it was finally sacked by Saracen pirates, probably in the ninth century AD. The ruins of Áptera are scattered about on the top of the flat-topped acropolis hill, the structures ranging in date from the Greek, Roman and Byzantine periods, along with a monastery erected during the Ottoman period by the monks of St John of Pátmos. Among the ancient structures there is a small Doric temple of Apollo near the Roman theatre, a temple of Demeter from the Hellenistic era, a double structure that may be either a temple or a treasury, and the fine classical defence-walls that still partially enclose the site on its eastern and western sides. From the acropolis hill one has a superb view of Soúda Bay and its shores, with the fortress of Itzeddin just below on the Kalámi promontory and across the strait the ruined Venetian castle on Soúda isle.

After visiting Áptera, one returns to the main road, driving along the southern shore of Soúda Bay towards Chaniá. A short way along one passes the turn-off to Soúda, the port-town at the inner end of Soúda Bay, which has now become an important commercial harbour as well as being one of the principal bases of the Greek navy. There is absolutely nothing of interest to see in Soúda, which has never developed as a town despite the great importance of its port, for its growth has always been stunted by the close proximity of Chaniá. Nevertheless, the harbour at Soúda is a very impressive sight as one passes by on the superhighway, with an armada of shipping anchored at the inner end of the gulf.

Continuing past Soúda on the superhighway, one soon enters the outskirts of Chaniá, the principal city of western Crete. As we approached Chaniá ourselves, after our long drive around the eastern regions of Crete, we felt that we were coming home, for we had fallen in love with this fascinating old town, which is like no other city in the Greek world.

14

⊞⊞⊞

CHANIÁ

Chaniá is the second largest city on Crete, its population of about 40,000 exceeded only by Iráklion's 60,000. The city is capital of the Prefecture of Chaniá, which makes up the westernmost quarter of the island. Chaniá is also capital of Cydonía Province, which comprises the central region of the prefecture north of the White Mountains. This toponym comes from Cydonía, the ancient name of the city and of western Crete in general. Cydonía is also the Greek word for quince, a fact that R.F. Willetts comments upon in his *Cretan Cults and Festivals*, writing that 'The name of the people, rather than the name of the city, is likely to have been applied to the quince which has an early and continuous place in literature. The latter prominence of the people is indicated by the use of their name as an ethnic synonym for Cretan. Their earlier importance is emphasized by Strabo, and confirmed by Homer.' Homer writes of the Cydonians as one of the indigenous people of Crete, and the city of Cydonía is mentioned by Herodotus and Strabo, who considered it to be the third most powerful state on the Great Island, after Knossós and Górtyna. According to tradition, the Cydonians were descendants of King Cydon, a son of Apollo who became the first ruler of western Crete, a hero who was renowned for his hospitality. As the old Cretan saying goes, 'You are always welcome at Cydon's house!'

There has been speculation about the site of the ancient city of Cydonía, but it would appear to have been on the acropolis hill now known as Kastélli, the old Venetian quarter of Chaniá. Archaeological excavations have revealed evidence of human habitation on Kastélli from Noelithic times on through the Graeco-Roman period. The

Greek-Swedish excavation on Odós Kanaváro in Kastélli has unearthed a small part of the Late Minoan town, including four houses,
two streets and a small square, all of which appear to have been
destroyed in a great fire c. 1450 BC. Among the objects found on this
site are clay tablets with Linear A inscriptions, the earliest records ever
found in Cydonía, which is mentioned in records in the Knossós
archives. After the destruction the houses seem to have been
reinhabited for another seventy-five years or so, and then in c. 1375 the
whole settlement appears to have been rebuilt to a new plan, with the
town continuing in existence until c. 1100 BC. The Italian archaeologist Guarducci has also unearthed Mycenaean remains in Chaniá.
This would have been the town mentioned by Homer in Book III of
the *Odyssey*, where he writes of how part of the fleet of Menelaos was
wrecked on Crete on the homeward voyage from Troy, when the
wrath of Zeus 'cut the fleet in two parts, and drove some on Crete/
where the Cydonians lived around the streams of Ioardanus', the river
being identified with the Plátonas, which flows into the sea a few miles
west of Chaniá. In Book XIX of the *Odyssey* Homer indicates that the
Cydonians were an indigenous Cretan people, along with the
Eteocretans and the Pelasgians, although in his time the Great Ísland
was also inhabited by the warlike Dorians. Other archaeological finds
in Chaniá indicate that the city of Cydonía was inhabited throughout
the Dark Ages of the ancient world and on through the Archaic,
Classical and Hellenistic periods. The Archaic town of Cydonía is
mentioned in Book III of the *Histories* of Herodotus, where he writes
of a colony that Sámos founded there in 524 BC, and of how the local
Cretans rebelled with the help of Aegina six years later and enslaved
the Samian colonists. Cydonía appears to have been one of the most
powerful states in Crete, rivalling Knossós and Górtyna, and when the
Romans invaded the Great Island the Cydonians led the resistance to
their invasion.

Although Cydonía was conquered by the Romans, it remained a
considerable city throughout the imperial Roman era, and then
during the first Byzantine period in Crete it had the status of a
bishopric. But then Cydonía appears to have been destroyed during
the Saracen raids, and its name disappears from history in the late
medieval era, when another Dark Age descended upon the Great
Island.

A new age in the history of the town began early in the thirteenth
century, when the Italians took over Crete soon after the Latin knights
of the Fourth Crusade conquered Constantinople in 1204. The former

211

site of Cydonía was probably one of the fourteen strongholds erected or rebuilt on Crete by Enrico Pescatore, the Genoese Count of Malta, who controlled the Great Island until he signed an armistice with the Venetians in 1212. But the site of Cydonía was not occupied in force by the Venetians until 1252, when they founded there a new town that they called La Canae, of which the present Chaniá is a corruption. At that time the Serenissima granted ninety fiefs in the western half of the island, with half of them reserved for Venetians nobles dwelling in Chaniá, the other half for colonists who lived out on their lands. These Venetian grandees built mansions that one can still see today gracing the streets and squares of Kastélli, 'the Castle', the old quarter on the promontory between the two ports of Chaniá. As William Lithgow wrote of Kastélli, at the time of his visit to Chaniá in 1609, this elegant quarter

> contained 97 palaces, in which the Rector and the Venetian gentlemen dwell. There lie in continually seven companies of souldiers, who keepe centinelle on the walles, guarde the gates and marketplaces of the citie. Neither in the town nor Candia may any country peasant enter with weapons. Truly this citie may equal in strength either Tara in Dalmatia, or Luka or Lisorne, both in Tuscana, or matchless Palma or Friuly; for these five cities are so strong that in all my travels I never saw them matched.

Lithgow's visit to Chaniá took place just thirty-six years before it fell to the Turks. The Turkish invasion of Crete began in early summer of 1645, when a great Ottoman fleet arrived off the north-western coast of Crete under the command of Yussuf Pasha, landed an army just west of Chaniá that Turkish sources estimate to have been 40,000 strong, and put the town under siege and capturing it after 57 days.

During the first two centuries of Ottoman occupation their government was centred at Candia, the modern Iráklion, but then in 1850 the Turks transferred their capital to Chaniá. Spratt made his first visit to Chaniá just five years after it became the Ottoman capital of Crete, and he gives a fascinating description of the mixtures of people living there at the time, not only Cretans and Turks but also European merchants and officials and Arab refugees from North Africa; as he writes of the latter group:

> A large Arab village of between 2000 and 3000 souls has recently risen on the sandy shore just outside of the fortress on that side, the inhabitants of which, for the most part, come from Eygpt and the

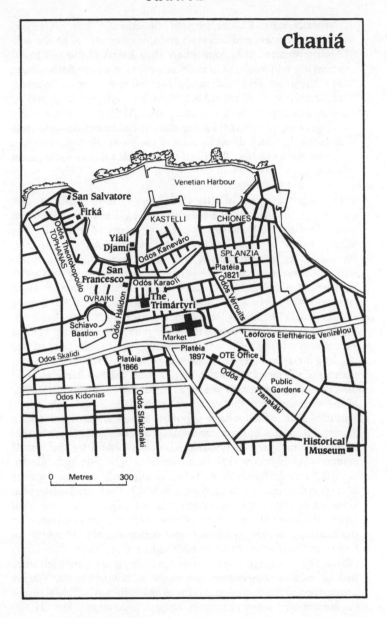

Chaniá

Cyrenaica since Khania became the capital. They are chiefly boatmen, porters and servants; and it may be said to be the only Arab settlement in Europe where their habits of life and habitations are fully retained in every respect as in a pure Arab village; and the most arid and sandy part of the shore is selected, apparently as most resembling their own African coast and its associated desert. It is a perfect little African community and village in all its features, having also a sprinkling of Bedouin tents adjacent, in which dwell families of the purest Bedouin race and colour, most of whom fled from the Cyrenaica during some recent famine.

The oldest quarters of Chaniá are down by the seafront, still partially surrounded by the massive defence-walls and wide moat constructed by the Venetians in the last century of their rule. The oldest quarter of all, Kastélli, is on an acropolis hill that was surrounded by its own defence-wall. Some noble fragments of this wall still remain, forming a bastion between the outer and inner harbours. One approaches old Chaniá along Odós Apokorónou, which takes one from the modern town down to the waterfront. The avenue ends in Plateía Elefthérios Venizélou, a picturesque square that opens up onto the south-east end of the outer port, whose *paralía* is lined with restaurants and cafés, with little fishing caiques and rowboats tied up along the quay. The lighthouse at the outer end of the port stands at the end of the long breakwater that encloses the two harbours, and directly opposite the tower known as Firká, the north-western anchor of the Venetian walls that enclosed the landward side of the town. Venizelos Square itself is more popularly known as Santriváni, taking its name from the Turkish *shadirvan*, the ornamental fountain that stands in a mosque courtyard, used by the faithful for their ritual ablutions before prayer. The *shadirvan* can still be seen in the garden of the Chaniá Archaeological Museum, which will be visited a little later on in this itinerary. The mosque to which it belonged can be seen along the *paralía* on the inner side of the port. This is known as Yiali Djami, the Shore Mosque. It dates from 1645, built immediately after the Turkish conquest of Chaniá, and is thus the oldest mosque on Crete – in fact the earliest Ottoman building of any kind on the Great Island. The mosque has been restored in recent years, a good job other than its eyesore of a concrete dome, and it now houses the Tourist Information Office as well as serving as an exhibition hall. Just before the mosque on that side of the port one sees the venerable Plaza Hotel, where we stayed during our first week in Chaniá, before we moved into Nikos' *pýrgos* (tower) on One Angel Street, which is just beside the Firka tower on the western side of the outer port. The Plaza Hotel is one of the oldest buildings along the port, and in early Ottoman times it is believed to have served as a *medrese*, or theological school, housing the Turkish students who pursued their Islamic studies at Yiali Djami. One very interesting architectural feature of the hotel is the old fountain that is built into the façade just below the stairway that leads to the little entrance lobby on the upper floor; this is apparently of Venetian construction, indicating that the building itself must predate the Turkish conquest of La Canae in 1645.

Our *pýrgos* stood just a few steps down Odós Angélou from the Firká tower. And so most of our walks through Chaniá began on the *paralía* below, sometimes strolling into town along the seafront, or, later in the afternoon, walking out around the point on our way to the beaches along the coast to the west. But, whichever way we came or went, we always stopped for a drink or a coffee at the Café Meltémi, which is on the *paralía* at the foot of Odós Angélou. And while there we would always have a few laughs with one of the owners of the Meltémi, Yani Papadoulakis, who would join us for a while at our table with his partners, the other Yáni and his wife Eleni, who together ran the café, the most delightful place on the Chaniá waterfront.

Our morning walk usually took us along the *paralía* as far as Santriváni, where Dolores would take a look around in the shops while I bought a newspaper and sat down at the coffeehouse on the square for a while. Then we would return along the shady back streets, first going along Odós Zambelíou and then on Odós Theotokopoúlou, then turning right onto Odós Angélou to come to the gateway of our old tower. Later in the morning we would walk out around the promontory to one of the beaches along the shore west of Chaniá, sometimes having lunch at one of the seaside tavernas there before returning to the *pýrgos* for the afternoon, when I would work on my guide to Crete and Dolores would enjoy her siesta. Then later in the afternoon, when the narrow streets of the old town were shaded from the merciless summer sun, I would explore the various quarters of Chaniá: Tophanás, Evraikí, Kastélli, Chiónes and Splánzia, all of which date back to Venetian times. Later I extended my strolls to see the more modern neighbourhoods farther out from the centre, most notably the garden suburb of Chalépa, which is on the higher ground to the south-east of the harbour. Then around sunset I walked down to the inner harbour, which is still called the Venetian Port, and there I would have my first drink of the evening in the taverna of Yorgo Drakakis. Yorgo would usually be sitting there by himself when I arrived, looking dreamily out over the Aegean from the door of his taverna, greeting me and then pouring me a beer or a *tsikoudiá*, depending on what kind of night it was going to be. Then he would take up his *lýra* and begin to play, singing softly to himself while now the two of us looked out dreamily over the Aegean at the splendours of the sunset. Dolores usually joined me there an hour or so after sunset, when we would take a walk through Kastélli or Splánzia or Chiónes, after which we would dine at one or another of our favourite restaurants. One of these was Michali's, a little taverna down at the far end of the Venetian port along the line of the medieval *arsenáli*, the great barrel-vaulted sheds that housed the enormous galleys of the Venetian fleet. Another favourite place was Fáka – the Mousetrap – a little hole-in-the-wall behind the *arsenáli*, where on certain unpredictable evenings the young bearded owner would take off his apron when he had served all of his customers and then play his *bouzoúki* while he and his friends sang *rebétika*, the sad and haunting and naughty music that came out of Smyrna after the diaspora from Asia Minor in 1923. Later in the summer, when the waterfront became very overcrowded with tourists, we walked out of Chaniá along the shore to the east where we found a wonderful little restaurant up on the edge of the cliff there, a garden-taverna run by a splendid character named Zafiri, a Greek version of Jackie Gleason. Our suppers in Zafiri's would usually last until midnight or so, later if the moon was full and shining on the Aegean below us. But no matter how late it was when we left Zafiri's we always looked into the taverna of Yorgo Drakakis before going home, having a nightcap there while we listened to the Cretan music that went on into the early hours of the morning, with a continual round of Cretan dances circling throughout the night.

The first part of Chaniá that I explored thoroughly was Kastélli, because this was where the ancient town of Cydonía was located, already centuries old when the fleet of Menelaos was wrecked off the shores of the Great Island. The main approach to Kastélli is via Odós Kaneváro, which begins on the eastern side of Santriváni square. This was the Corso of bygone La Canae, lined with the mansions of the Venetian nobility who lived there within the citadel. The landward walls of the citadel can be seen just to the right, a short way in from Odós Karaóli and Odós Sífaka, the two streets that form the southern boundary of Kastélli, while the sea-walls tower above the promontory between the outer and inner harbours. This citadel in its present form probably dates from the founding of the new town of La Canae in 1252, the Venetians perhaps building their inner defence-walls on the circuit of Byzantine or Roman walls that Enrico Pescatore had reconstructed for his stronghold here. About halfway up Odós Kaneváro on the left one sees the site excavated by the Greek-Swedish archaeological team who discovered the Minoan town of Cydoniá, destroyed c. 1450 BC and then rebuilt and continuing in existence until c. 1100 BC. These Minoan foundation walls make a remarkable sight against the background of the ruined Venetian citadel-walls just a short city-block away, ancient Cydoniá and medieval La Canae visible together on a street of modern Chaniá, making this town a veritable palimpsest of civilization, at least thirty-five centuries of continuous human existence on the same Cretan promontory.

The most beautiful street in Kastélli is Odós Líthinon, which leads off to the right from Odós Kaveváro just one short block in from Santriváni square. This venerable street leads up past a number of splendid mansions to a cul-de-sac at the top of the promontory, the heart of Venetian La Canae. The handsome old edifice at the top of the street was the Venetian Archives and Financial Exchange, with an inscription in Latin numerals giving the date 1623, just twenty-two years before the fall of La Canae to the Turks. But apparently the Venetian presence in Kastélli lingered on after the Turkish conquest, for in *Viaggio di Levante*, published at Bologna in 1688 by M. Benvegna, the author writes that during his stay in Chaniá, 'the beautiful places in which we lodged, on a site similar to that of Capua, reminded us of the architecture of Venice.'

Walking back down Odós Líthinon, one can then turn left at the first turning and wander back through the maze of Venetian alleyways into the north-east corner of Kastélli. There one finds the vast shell of an enormous Venetian building of palatial dimensions and elegance, with a loggia on its seaward side in which three columns support two ogive arches and a circular window, the balcony outside overlooking the Venetian port. This splendid edifice was known as the Arcade of San Marco, serving as the palace of the Venetian Rector of La Canae and the government centre for the administration of western Crete, its sheer size and splendour giving one some idea of the vast resources of the Serenissima's maritime empire.

A steep flight of steps beside the Arcade of San Marco leads down to the promontory between the outer and inner harbours, from where one can walk eastward along the cobbled quay of the Venetian port.

There along the landward side of the port one sees the majestic line of barrel-vaulted *arsenáli* that housed the great galleys of the Venetian navy, the ultimate source of the Serenissima's imperial power. On Coronelli's map of Chaniá, published in 1689, one can count about thirteen or fourteen of these *arsenáli*, of which nine still remain, most of them in fairly good repair considering their great age, some of them still being used for one commercial purpose of another, at least one of them still serving as a dry-dock for the vessels of Chaniá. The quay of the Venetian port is lined with caiques, yachts, motor- and rowing-boats, with an occasional sponge-boat from Kálymnos stopping off at the little pier to unload its cargo, the captain and his crew afterwards relaxing with a few swigs of *tsikoudiá* at the taverna of Yorgo Drakakis, looking like Jason and his Argonauts.

At the inner end of the Venetian port the quay leads around to the head of the breakwater, where a walkway leads out to the lighthouse at the entrance to the outer harbour. I walked out to the lighthouse once at dawn, where I had a stunning view of the town against the background of the White Mountains at the very moment when the sun rose, its first direct light glowing golden on the highest peaks of the range. Then I walked back to have a morning coffee at a little café tucked into a corner of one of the *arsenáli*, where I was soon joined by some of the local fishermen, who had just returned from a night's fishing on the Aegean. This is quite a different Chaniá from that of the outer port, where the waterfront in the morning is filled with tourists having European breakfasts. The quay of the Venetian port is serene and beautiful in the early sunlight, with just a few fishermen yawning contentedly as they sip their *tsikoudiá* before retiring for the day, leaving me alone with my notebook and my thoughts in the little café hidden away in the medieval boathouse.

One can continue past the inner end of the Venetian port, turning right on a road that passes the last of the *arsenáli*. This takes one across the base of the promontory that forms the inner end of the Venetian port, bringing one out to the broad bay still known by its Turkish name of Kumkapi, the Sand Gate. Here one can look back for a close view of the majestic bastion that formed the seaward anchor of the Venetian defence-walls on this side of La Canae, with the winged lion of San Marco looking down imperiously from a relief just beside the shore road.

The quarter just behind the *arsenáli* on the Venetian port is called Chiónes, and just to the south of that is another old neighbourhood, Splánzia. Both of these old quarters date back to Venetian times, when they were inhabited by the ordinary people of La Canae, the nobility dwelling exclusively in Kastélli. Both Chiónes and Splánzia are still distinctly working-class neighbourhoods, the streets and square alive with people throughout the day, mostly woman and children in the morning, joined by the local working men when their labours are finished in the evening, when everyone sits out in the cafés, particularly those in the Plateía 1821. The Plateía is named in commemoration of the year when the Greek War of Independence began, the year, too, when the Bishop of Chaniá was hung by the Turks in this square, where a memorial stands in his honour. At the east end of the square stands the large church of Áyios Nikólaos Splánzias, a fine minaret beside it remaining from the days when it served as a mosque. The building was originally part of a Dominican monastery founded in the Venetian period, converted into a mosque at the time of the Turkish conquest of La Canae in 1645, when it was named for the reigning Ottoman sultan, Ibrahim the Mad. The building continued to serve as the Mosque of Sultan Ibrahim until 1912, the year before *énosis*, when it was rededicated as the Church of Áyios Nikólaos. Walking around the church to its rear and then to the right, one finds an older and smaller church that is now virtually abandoned, used only for an annual service on the respective namedays of the saints to whom it is dedicated: Cosmás and Damianós, the sainted physicians who are known as the Penniless Saints, Anárgyri, because they never accepted payment from the poor patients whom they treated and cured of their illnesses. The church dates back to the sixteenth century and remained open through both the Venetian and Ottoman occupations, but has now been abandoned by its congregation in favour of the more commodious nearby church of Áyios Nikólaos.

There is still another old church at the north-west corner of Plateía 1821. This is a little Roman Catholic chapel dedicated to San Rocco, with a Latin inscription giving the date of foundation as 1630. This pretty little church has also been abandoned, for most of the Catholics in Chaniá now attend services in the Roman Catholic cathedral on Odós Hálidon, the main north-south street leading into Santriváni square.

After leaving Plateía 1821, one might turn left on Odós Vérovits and then go right at the second turning onto Odós Hadzimicháli Daliáni. A short way along this street, at number 23, one sees another fine old Ottoman minaret, although the mosque to which it was once attached has disappeared. Then continuing a little farther along the same street, one sees on the left a short street ending in a stairway, one of the approaches to the public market of Chaniá.

No stay in Chaniá is complete without spending a few hours in the public market, the most colourful and exciting place in town when it is open. This vast barn of a building is patterned on the public market in Marseilles, a cruciform edifice with entrances at the ends of each arm of the cross and a domed central area where they intersect. Everything that is produced or consumed in Crete is sold here, in shops or from stalls or barrows, and by itinerant peddlers, all of whom hawk their wares above the din of the passing throngs. Each kind of shop has its own special area in the market, with the fish and meat markets being the most colourful. There are also a number of little restaurants tucked away among the shops and stalls, my own favourite being a tiny taverna in the meat market, where I waited contentedly over a few beers while Dolores did our weekly shopping, feeling more a part of Chaniá when I did so than anywhere else in town.

The southern gateway of the public market leads out to Plateía 1897, which is crossed by the main east-west thoroughfare in modern Chaniá, here named Leofóros Hátzi Miháli Gianári. Across the street from the southern gate of the market Odós Tzanakáki leads off from the south-east corner of Plateía 1897, along the first block on the left passing the main office of OTE, the Telephone and Telegraph Company. Then some 300 metres farther along on the left one comes to the public gardens of Chaniá, a very pleasant park with a charming little zoo. There are several cafés in and around the park as well as an outdoor cinema, where we saw several excellent Greek films. We also spent several evenings at the sports grounds, which are just north of the public gardens, where frequent performances of Greek music and dance are held during the summer. On one weekend while we were in Chaniá we heard the two greatest composers of modern Greek music conducting their own works, with Manolis Hatzidakis on Saturday night and on Sunday night Mikis Theodorakis, both of them Cretans and performing before enthusiastic Cretan audiences. When the two of them sang together in the finale there was pandemonium, the most exciting moment of our whole summer on the Great Island.

Continuing along Odós Tzanakáki past the end of the public gardens, bear left onto Odós Sfakianáki, and across the street to the right on the second block one comes to an old mansion at number 20 that houses the Historical Museum of Crete. This museum is important particularly for its archives, which are classified into three periods: the Venetian occupation (1210–1669), the Turkish occupation (1669–1898), and the Cretan State under the Allied Powers (1898–1913). The museum also has a small but fascinating collection of memorabilia from these three periods, covering a span of more than seven centuries in the history of the Great Island, bringing one from the Middle Ages up to the beginning of modern times on Crete.

After visiting the Historical Museum, one can retrace the route to return to Plateía 1897, after which one can turn left to walk along Leofóros Hátzi Miháli Giánari, which takes one through the centre of downtown Chaniá. At the next intersection one comes to Plateía 1866, the main square of modern Chaniá, with the bus terminal off its south-east corner. Here one turns right on Odós Hálidon to head back towards Santriváni Square and the quarter of the old port. Along the first block of Hálidon the street passes through a breach in the outer defence-walls of Venetian La Canae, built in the mid-sixteenth century, and to the left one can see the enormous Schiavo Bastion, a circular fortress built to defend the south-western salient of the fortifications, which will be explored in more detail later on the present itinerary.

Continuing along Odós Hálidon, on the middle of the next block on the right one comes to the piazza on whose eastern end stands the Greek Orthodox cathedral of Chaniá, known as the Trimártyri, or the Three Martyrs, although it is dedicated to the Eisódeia Theotókou, the Annunciation of the Blessed Virgin. This edifice was erected in 1864, and its founder was actually a Moslem Turk, a wealthy Ottoman of Chaniá who believed that a sacred icon of the Virgin had saved the life of his son. This icon had originally been in a Byzantine church on the same site, a structure that later was converted into a soap-factory by the Venetians, and when the new cathedral was erected by its Turkish founder the sacred image was hung there in the nave, where it remains to the present day.

Continuing down Odós Hálidon past the piazza of the Trimártyri, one passes on the left the more modest edifice that serves as the Roman Catholic cathedral of Chaniá, dedicated to the Koimisis Theotókou, the Assumption of the Blessed Virgin. Directly across the street from this, on the corner of Hálidon and Hátzi Micháli Daliáni, there is a domed building that was originally a *hamam* or Turkish bath. Then a short way farther down Hálidon on the left one comes to the old Venetian church of San Francesco, which now serves as the Archaeological Museum of Chaniá.

San Francesco dates from the sixteenth century, the largest of the twenty-three churches that the Venetians erected in La Canae. It was originally built as the abbey-church for the Franciscan monks in La Canaea, dedicated to the founder of their order, St Francis of Assisi. The church originally had a campanile, first mentioned in a letter by Onorio Belli dated 1595, but this structure has long since vanished. The church was converted into a mosque by Yussuf Pasha shortly after his forces captured La Canae in 1645, at which time a minaret was erected at the north-west corner of the building, but that structure too has vanished except for its base, which can be seen in the garden beside the museum.

The entryway, which is on the eastern side of the building, leads into the narthex, or vestibule. This opens into the barrel-vaulted and ogive-arched nave, which is separated from the north and south aisles by six round arches on either side, with the wider north aisle being further divided along its length by a four-bayed portico with cross vaults on its right side. The lower area to the right, which is approached through a splendid Renaissance portal, shows the original level of the floor.

The museum houses antiquities from archaeological sites all over western Crete, including a number of interesting finds made in Chaniá itself, the site of the ancient town of Cydonía. The oldest objects in the museum are in one of the cases to the left of the entryway, which exhibits from the Platyvóla cave dating back to 3400 BC. The next group of cases on the left contain Minoan pottery, including finds made in Platyvóla, Perivólia, and in the Kastélli quarter of Chaniá. The beginning of the central aisle is flanked by a pair of painted terracotta sarcophagi from the necropolis; and to the right there is a Late Minoan bathtub that was later used as a sarcophagus, a find made in Chaniá. Other cases include: Cycladic vases from the Tsivourakis Collection; Neolithic pottery from the Kumaróspilio cave on Akrotíri; Minoan vases and imported Cypriot ware from the Kastélli quarter of Chaniá; two painted terracotta sarcophagi from the necropolis at Arméni; a late Minoan bathtub later used as a sarcophagus in Chaniá; Linear-A tablets from the archaeological site on Odós Kaneváro in the Kastélli quarter of Chaniá; two sarcophagi with skeletons still inside; a case of bronze objects, including a sword, a weapon which would have been in use when the ships of Menelaos were wrecked off the Cretan coast; a number of marble statuettes, including some charming figurines of children; several Graeco-Roman statues and busts, including a figure of Artemis and a colossal head of Hadrian, both from the Dhihtinaion; a number of funerary stele of the Classical period; cases of Graeco-Roman coins; four panels of a large Roman pavement, with scenes depicting Neptune and Amymone; a case of black-figure vases from Phalásarna, a site in western Crete; and, beside the door leading into the garden, two gigantic *pithoi*, similar to those seen in Knossós, Phaestós and Mállia.

The door on the right of the nave leads into the garden, where there are mostly ancient and medieval architectural fragments, as well as objects associated with the period when this was the mosque of Yussuf Pasha. On the far side of the garden to the right there is an exceedingly beautiful *shadirvan*, the ablution fountain that gave its name to Santriváni square. In Ottoman days the faithful would perform their ritual ablutions here before entering the mosque for the Friday noon prayers. The *shadirvan* is in the form of a miniature Seljuk *türbe*, or mausoleum, with a conical top and a decagonal façade, each of its sides framed by slim columns, with the side facing the front of the courtyard bearing a calligraphic dedicatory inscription in Osmanli, old Turkish written in Arabic script. In the centre of the courtyard there is the base of a Venetian fountain with spouts flanked by lion-heads. At the back end of the courtyard there is a monumental Venetian portal with a coat of arms above, along with the bust of a bearded man wearing a crested helmet, probably one of the Rectors of La Canae. The gate leads to what was once the *medrese*, the theological school attached to the Mosque of Yussuf Pasha. Elsewhere in the courtyard there are a few Turkish tombstones, which once marked the graves of the Islamic scholars who taught at the *medrese*, with one of the stones, representing the beautifully-folded turban of a dervish, now propped up on a drum of a Corinthian column.

There is a very pleasant café-bar, the Idhéoh Ántron, just beside the museum garden on Odós Zambelíou, the street that leads eastward from Santriváni square at the head of Odós Hálidon. Our favourite table at the Idhéon Ántron was just outside the garden wall from the *shadrivan* in the museum garden, the sight of which evokes memories of Chaniá in Ottoman times, particularly the old Turkish tombstones lying scattered around the Venetian fountain beside the church.

Odós Zambelíou leads westward from Santriváni square one block in from the *paralía*, a street lined with picturesque old Venetian houses, with one venerable mansion bearing a relief above its portal depicting the Lion of San Marco. Zambelíou is one of the two principal streets of Evraikí – the Jewish Quarter – which dates back to the early Venetian period, the other main street being Odós Kondyláki, the first turning to the left from Santriváni square. There is a splendid old Venetian palazzo at the upper end of Kondyláki on the left side. The building has recently been restored and now serves as a very luxurious restaurant and bar. Another picturesque street of Evraikí leads off to the left from Zambelíou a block beyond Kondiláki; this is Odós Theophánou, a dead-end lane that leads to the path around the great bastion of Schiavo. At the upper end of the street one comes to a splendid old portal, the only surviving gateway remaining from the walled Venetian town of La Canae. This was known to the Venetians as the Porto Retimiota, since one passed through it on the way to and from Réthymnon; in Turkish it was called Kale Kapi, the Tower Gate, since it lead to the Schiavo bastion, the principal fortress on the landward side of Chaniá. The gateway was once surmounted by a large framed panel with a relief of the winged Lion of San Marco, now in the Archaeological Museum.

Returning to Odós Zambelíou, one continues along to the end of the street, where a short alleyway named Odós Moskhón leads down to the *paralía*, leading one out of the Evraikí quarter. Halfway along Moskhon on the left a short step-street leads up to Odós Theo-tokopoúlou, which leads northwards midway between the Venetian land-walls and the *paralía*, to which it is connected by several short stepped-alleyways, taking one through the old quarter of Topanás. This was the Turkish quarter of the city, taking its name from Tophane, or Arsenal, an Ottoman armoury which was in this neighbourhood under the Venetian walls. This is the most picturesque section in the whole town, and one that we came to know and dearly love during our summer in Chaniá, walking through it on our way to and from our *pýrgos* on Odós Angélou, which turns off to the right near the end of Theotokopoúlos.

One can continue on to the end of Theotokopoúlou to the north-western end of the city, where the Venetian land-walls bend sharply in to block the end of the promontory that forms the western side of the outer port, curving back in along the harbour entrance as far as the Firká Tower. One can walk out around the end of the walls to see the best-preserved stretch of the outer defence-walls of Venetian La Canae. These walls were designed in 1536 by Michel Sammichele, the Venetian military engineer who also planned the fortifications of Iráklion. The walls of La Canae were completed in 1548, forming a circuit 3085 metres long around the three landward sides of the city, with a moat 10 metres deep and 50 metres wide around its periphery. The walls and the moat are very well preserved along this western side of the city, despite the fact that this was where the Ottoman army made its heaviest assaults during the siege of 1645, attacking from their beachhead west of the town. The massive redoubt that towers above the shore road at this point was known to the Venetians as San Demetrio. The western walls stretched from here in a mighty line to the powerful Schiavo Bastion, the fortifications bordered by the great moat, which is now a mosaic of vegetable gardens.

Walking back into the town along Odós Theotokopoúlou for a short way, one can turn right on a path a short way in to explore the interior of the San Demetrio Bastion, still in ruins from the Turkish siege of 1645. Across on the other side of Odós Theotokopoúlou one sees the picturesque ruins of the Venetian church of San Salvatore, converted into a mosque in 1645 by the commanding officer of the Ottoman artillery, Hassan Aga. San Salvatore was originally the chapel of a Venetian monastery, where the English tràveller William Lithgow stayed when he visited Chaniá in 1609, hiding there from the Venetians after having helped a prisoner escape from one of their galleys in the port.

Returning along Odós Theotokopoúlou, one can now turn left on Odós Angélou, the most picturesque street in all of old Chaniá, flanked by a number of splendid old Venetian mansions. Not the least splendid of these was our own cottage at One Angel Street, a *pýrgos*, or tower, which Nikos Stavroulakis believes to have been built early in the Venetian period, and which he purchased cheap after it had been reduced to a mere shell in a German air-raid. Nikos restored the tower beautifully, furnishing it with objects that would have been used there in Ottoman times, including splendid bronze *ojaks*, or conical hoods, over the great fireplaccs, where we sat around in oriental splendour with Nikos when he came out from Athens to visit the Cottage, usually spending our evenings talking about Ottoman days in old Chaniá.

While staying in the *pýrgos* that summer we also took an occasional stroll out to Chalépa, the beautiful garden suburb of Chaniá out along its eastern shore. There are buses to Chalépa from the centre of town, but we preferred to walk there, strolling along the shore road in Kumḱapi as far as the promontory at its eastern end, after which we followed Leofóros Elefthérios Venizélou, which first runs along the shore of the next bay to the east and then veers inland to bring one through the suburb of Chalépa. Chalépa first became popular in late Ottoman times, when its scenic location and healthier climate made it a favourite residence for the wealthier Chaniotes as well as foreign merchants and consuls. The heyday of Chalépa came during the Allied Occupation of Crete in 1898–1913, when Prince George of Crete lived in Chaniá as High Commissioner. The palatial 'mansion' in which Prince George lived during his tenure as High Commissioner can be seen on the left as one walks down the second block in from the sea along Leofóros Elefthérios Venizélou, standing at the near corner on Odós Frangokastéllou. Just across the street on the same side of the avenue is the house in which Eleftherios Venizelos lived when he was in Chaniá. The Venizelos House has now been converted into a museum, with memorabilia associated with the life and career of this great Cretan, twice prime minister of Greece, and the first Greek in modern times to emerge as a world-class political leader, his greatest achievement in the eyes of his countrymen being the achievement of the *énosis* of his native Crete with Greece. Directly across the street from the Venizelos House is the Roman Catholic church of St Joseph, while across from Prince George's house is the Greek Orthodox church of St Mary Magdalene. The latter church, which was endowed by Prince George's sister, the Grand Duchess Maria, is an amalgam of neo-Byzantine and neo-Gothic architectural style on the Russian model.

After our visit to Chalépa, we strolled back along the avenue to Zafiri's taverna on the cliff above the sea, and there as we had our first *tsikoudiá* at sunset we looked back across the bay towards Chaniá. As we did so I read Pashley's description of this view, written after he too had walked out from Chaniá to Chalépa, and once again I was struck by how little the scene had changed, though this passage had been written a century and a half before.

> About half an hour's walk from the gate of Chaniá is the village of Kalepa, situated on a rising ground not far from the shore. From above this village a beautiful view is obtained. On the spectator's left are seen the noble snow-clad Sfakian mountains, and part of the plain of Khania, which also lies extended before him. To his right is the fortified city, with its port and shipping; beyond which the eye, passing over the wide gulf of Khania, rests on the Dictynnaean promontory, and observes, still further in the distance, the Corycian cape, which terminates the view.

And so our days passed in Chaniá, as we strolled around the old town in the intervals between our exploration of the rest of the Great Island, thus enjoying one of the happiest summers of our lives.

15

EXCURSIONS FROM CHANIÁ

Virtually every day while we were staying in Chaniá we went for a swim at one of the beaches near the town, for during the summer it never rains on Crete and very rarely does a cloud appear in the clear blue sky, the brassy sun blazing down relentlessly, and so each noon we set off along the shore for a cooling dip in the Aegean. There are a succession of good beaches stretching for five km along the shore west of the town, the nearer ones approached by the *paralía* that leads on to the shore road at the Firká Tower, with the more distant beaches approached by side-roads leading off at several points along the highway leading westward from Chaniá.

Those who walk out to the nearer beaches might stop off once at the Firká Tower, whose entrance has now been converted into a Naval Museum, with some of the exhibits having to do with the recent maritime history of Chaniá, one photo showing Prince George arriving in the port to begin his tenure as High Commissioner of Crete. The grounds within the Firká Tower are used in summer for theatrical productions and for performances of Cretan music and dancing, several of which we attended during our holiday in Chaniá, adding much to our enjoyment of the town between our excursions around the Great Island.

When we first arrived in Crete in mid-June we had the beaches west of Chaniá to ourselves, walking out along the shore at midday until we found a deserted spot to swim, then strolling back to one of the seaside tavernas for lunch, usually being the only customers and being treated royally. But as the summer progressed the beaches outside of Chaniá became more and more crowded and at times we couldn't even find a free table at our favourite taverna, the last one along the shore beyond the town, and so we looked for a place farther afield where we could enjoy our midday swim. Our dear friend Yani Papadoulakis suggested that we drive out to the Akrotíri peninsula for a swim, and so we did, finding several places that were uncrowded even at the height of summer. And on our return from these outings we took the opportunity to explore the Akrotíri peninsula, where there are a number of interesting places to be seen.

Driving out along the shore eastward from Chaniá, the road veers inland slightly as it goes out on the neck of the Akrotíri peninsula, after which the main branch of the highway turns eastward to head out to the airport. Just at this point, 6km out of Chaniá, a signpost marked 'Venizelos Graves' indicates a turn-off to the left, which leads to the eminence known as Profítis Ilías, after a little chapel dedicated to that saint. Here one comes to a terrace high above the sea where two stone tablets bearing large crosses mark the graves of Eletherios Venizelos (1864–1936) and his son Sophocles, a splendid site with a magnificent view of Chaniá to the west and Akrotíri to the east. This is a fitting site for a memorial to Venizelos, the Father of modern Crete, for it was here that the Cretans first raised their national banner on 21 February 1897, and used their own bodies as a standard to hold the flag aloft again when the Allies shot down their flagpole, symbolizing the Cretan motto of 'Freedom or death'.

On our first excursions to the beaches of Akrotíri, we bypassed the turning to the airport and continued along the highway into the peninsula, 2km farther along coming to the crossroads village of Kounoupidianá, where branch roads lead off in several directions. The westernmost branch leads in 2km to a beautiful lagoon-like beach in a sandy cove on the western side of Órmos Kalávas, the large bay that indents the northern coast of the Akrotíri peninsula. There is another excellent beach at the southern end of Kalávas bay, reached by the road that runs from Kounoupidianá out to the north-western tip of the peninsula. This road ends at the village of Stavrós, where there is yet another good beach in the bay formed by Capes Tripití and Mavromoúri, the latter being one of the most familiar landmarks on the landscape viewed all summer from our balcony in Chaniá, this bold promontory forming the tip of Akrotíri as seen from the west.

Above the beach at Stavrós there is a remarkable grotto known as the Cave of Lera, with beautiful stalactites. The cave takes its name from Stephanos Lera, a Cretan rebel leader who hid there with his men at the beginning of the Greek War of Independence in 1821, only to be captured and hung two years later by Mustafa Pasha. Caverns like the Cave of Lera are known to the islanders as *Cresphýgeton*, a wonderful word aptly described by Pashley: '*Cresphygeton*, the Cretan's refuge, became the general name of grottos, thus supposed to be places of security from danger.' In 1959 a marble figurine of the Classical period was discovered in the Cave of Lera, an idol believed to be a representation of the nymph Acacallis, mother of King Kydon, the legendary ruler of Cydonía. This and other findings indicate that the grotto here was used as a cave-sanctuary as early as 1200 BC, continuing as a shrine up through the Hellenistic period.

Returning to the crossroads at Kounoupidianá, one can now take the branch of the road that leads eastward through the peninsula, turning left after 6km to take the road that leads north to Moní Ayía Triádha, the Monastery of the Holy Trinity, which is at the end of the route about 4km from the last crossroads. This is one of the most renowned monasteries in western Crete, founded 1631–34 by the Tzangarola, a Venetian family who became Hellenized after long residence on Crete and joined the Greek Orthodox Church.

From Ayía Triádha a rough road leads in the village of Koumarés and out toward the north-western corner of the peninsula to the Monastery of Áyios Ioánnis Gouvernétou. This monastery, which is dated by an inscription to 1537, is named for a local holy man named Áyios Ioánnis Ermítes, St John the Hermit, who is buried in a cave-sanctuary near Moní Katholikó, a ruined old monastery that can be reached by continuing on the same track beyond Gouvernéto out to the coast on the north-east corner of the peninsula.

As remote as this place is, a *paniyíri* is held out here each year on 7 October, the feast day of St John the Hermit. The prelude to the festival begins the previous day, when busloads of pilgrims came out from Chaniá to Ayía Triádha, then continuing on foot to Gouvernéto, where they spend the night at the monastery and attend nocturnal services. Then in the morning, after mass, the pilgrims continue on foot out to the deserted monastery of Katholikó, where they attend a memorial service in the cave-sanctuary where St John the Hermit lived and died, a very moving and evocative ceremony which must be many centuries old, perhaps going back to ancient times.

These caves out on the remote northern end of the Akrotíri peninsula must have been refuges for the first settlers on Crete in Neolithic times, and in the Koumaróspilia Cave the German archaeologist Jantzen has found human skulls dating back to at least 3400 BC. Dorothea M. A. Bate, who lived in Chaniá before World War

I, wrote an article on the caves of Crete that appears as an appendix in Trevor-Battye's *Camping on Crete*, and there she describes a number of caverns she explored on Akrotíri, including the ones mentioned by Pashley, but also finding others that have never been published, including a number with ancient remains, along with human bones and the fragmentary skeletons of a large elephant and a dwarf hippotamus!

Returning to Ayía Triádha and then back to the crossroads, one can now continue south for another 3km before turning left on the road that leads past Stérnes and the airport and goes on to the south-eastern tip of the peninsula. At Stérnes there are two old churches, one of them dedicated to Ayíi Pántes – All the Saints – and another to The Annunciation of the Virgin. Near the Church of the Annunciation a Late Minoan villa has recently been unearthed, along with houses and catacombs that appear to date from the very early Christian period on Crete.

Continuing past Stérnes to the south-eastern tip of Akrotíri, one finally comes to a fork at the end of the road, with both branches going down to beaches at the outer end of this side of Soúda Bay, just across from the Venetian fortress on Soúda Isle. This was the site of ancient Minóa, a town which seems to have been founded in the Classical era and to have continued in existence until Roman times, with some fragmentary remains noted at the tip of the peninsula by John Pendlebury in his archaeological survey of Crete just before World War II, though virtually nothing of interest is to be seen there today except the beautiful view of Soúda Bay and the picturesque Venetian castle on Soúda Islet.

During our summer in Chaniá we also explored the northern slopes of the White Mountains, whose majestic peaks and ramparts were always in view, particularly the harsh Maláxa Ridge, which extends right down to the base of the Akrotíri peninsula. Westward of the Maláxa Ridge there is a wide coastal plain between the White Mountains and the sea, the Chaniá Plain, one of the richest and most verdant regions in all of Crete, an abundance of olive groves and fruit orchards that has impressed travellers since Ottoman and even Venetian times. As William Lithgow describes this landscape:

> 'Trust me, I told along these rocks at one time, and within my sight, some sixty-seven villages; but when I entered the valley, I could not find a foote of ground unmanured, save for a narrow passing way wherein I was, the olives, pomegranates, dates, figges,

oranges, lemmons, and pomi del Adamo growing all through other, and at the rootes of which trees grow wheate, malvasie, muscadine, leaticke, wines, grenadiers, carnobiers, mellones, and all other sortes of fruites and hearbes the earth can yield to man, that for beauty, pleasure, and profit it may easily be surnamed the garden of the whole universe, being the goodliest plot, the diamond sparke, and the honny-spot of all Candy. There is no land more temperate for ayre, for it hath a double spring tyde; no soyle more fertile, and therefore it is called the combat of Bacchus and Ceres; nor region or valley more hospitable, in regard of the sea having such a noble haven cut through its bosome, being as it were the very resting-place of Neptune.'

During our summer on Crete we often drove or walked through the Chaniá plain on our way up to the villages on the northern slopes of the White Mountains. One drive that we took early on that summer was on the road that leads south from Chaniá across the plain and then up to the village of Maláxa, which is perched on the northern ledge of the Maláxa Ridge. From there one has a superb view of the coastal plain and the Akrotíri peninsula, with the centrepiece being Chaniá itself. We then returned to Chaniá by a more westerly road, which took us past the mountain hamlet of Panayiá and then in the plain below through the large village of Mourniés where the locals point with pride to an old stone mansion which they say was the birthplace of Venizelos.

Another local village that has historic associations with Venizelos is Thérisos, which is 17km south of Chaniá on the road that in the plain below passes through the village of Perivólia. Venizelos' mother came from Thérisos, and he established his headquarters there during the revolution he led in 1905. The house is now preserved as a national monument. The drive from Perivólia to Thérisos takes one through the dramatic Thérisos gorge, from which one emerges only at the outskirts of the village. The first time we went to Thérisos we actually walked there all the way from Chaniá, the only way one can fully appreciate the wild beauty of the Thérisos Gorge. But by the time we arrived in Thérisos we were exhausted and terribly parched after our walk through the dry gorge, and the only thing we looked for in the village was a café, which we found by the roadside with its chairs and table set out on its own little *plateía* shaded by a grape vine and giant platanos trees. After we had slaked our thirst we stayed on to have lunch at the café, and then we walked back to see the house that

Venizelos had used as his headquarters in 1905. We also visited two old churches in Thérisos, both of them apparently dating from the Venetian period and still serving the community. We went to a *paniyíri* at one of the churches in August, and later celebrated with the villagers in the *plateía* next to the café, eating, drinking and dancing through the afternoon and evening. When the church bell chimed at midnight an ancient *palikári* who had been dancing with his wife, daughters and granddaughters pulled a pistol from his belt and began firing it in the air in his wild and irrepressible joy, showering us with shattered grapes and leaves from the arbour above us, evoking visions of a Dionysian festival of old.

We walked up to Thérisos a number of times that summer, usually starting out in the cool of morning, spending the midday exploring the neighbouring slopes of the White Mountains, then enjoying a late-afternoon lunch at the café before starting back to Chaniá an hour or so before sunset, when the Thérisos gorge was full of deep purple shadows. We would emerge into the Chaniá plain in early twilight, when the surrounding countryside with its old villas and farm houses evokes visions of Venetian times.

One can use Thérisos as a base to explore the northern slopes of the White Mountains. One site of interest in its vicinity is the Sarakína Cave, where pottery finds indicate human habitation in ancient times. Like so many other caverns in the Cretan mountains, the Sarakína Cave has served as a refuge for the local people when their villages were attacked by enemies, as happened most recently during the German occupation in World War II.

Thérisos is also used as a base for climbing the White Mountains, another approach being from the village of Kámpi, which is at the end of the road that goes south from Chaniá via Mourniés; from there one can hike up to Vólikas, where there is a hostel maintained by the Mountaineering Club of Chaniá. The northernmost of the peaks of the White Mountains looms just above Thérisos to the south; this is Xeraokkefála, a mere 1238 metres high, while arrayed in successively higher tiers to the south and south-east are the peaks known as Kalóros (1925m); Maṽri (2069m); Melindáou (2133m); Griás Sorós (2331m) and Páhnes (2453m); the highest summit in the range. Then come the peaks on the southern tier: Trohári (2401m); Kástro (2218m) and Zaranakefála (2140m).

The closest approach one can make to the northern peaks of the White Mountains by road from Chaniá is via the dirt track that loops south between Thérisos and Mesklá, both of which are at the ends of asphalt roads leading south across the Chaniá plain and up into the foothills of Lefká Óri. There is a third main road going through the village of Lákki and on to the Omalós plateau and the famous Samariá Gorge. Thérisos, Mesklá and Lákki are at the heart of the Rhiza, the region on the northern slopes of the White Mountains that is celebrated in *ta rizítika tragoúdia*, the oldest and most beautiful songs in all of Cretan folklore. This wonderful region takes its name from the ancient city of Rhizenía, which was somewhere in the vicinity of the three villages of Thérisos, Mesklá and Lákki.

On one of our afternoon walks from Thérisos we headed southward on the dirt track that loops around the foothills of the White Mountains to Mesklá. But it was a terribly hot day and we stopped about halfway to Mesklá, across a valley from Zoúrva, the southern-most village of the Rhíza, just across the Potamós River from Lákki. Somewhere in there, we thought, was the ancient city of Rhizenía, for Yani Papadoulakis had told us that in the hills south of his village there were ruins on a site called Kastéllos, which some believed to be the Cydonian town from which the Rhíza took its name. But Rhizenía eluded us that day, and we resolved to search for it another time, perhaps using Mesklá as our base.

About a week later Yani Papadoulakis drove us up to Mesklá for a *paniyíri* there, but it was evening and there was no opportunity to go in search of Rhizenía. As events turned out we did not have time to visit the village and so the ruins of Kastéllo await us still, a hostage to Fortune for our return to Mesklá. But that evening Yani did take us to see the oldest church in Mesklá Sotíros Chrístou, Christ the Saviour, which has remnants of its original Byzantine frescoes, dated 1403. He also took us to the old chapel of Koímisis tis Panayías, which is next to the new church of the same name, where the *paniyíri* was being celebrated. The old chapel, which appears to date from the late Byzantine period, seems to have been built on the site of a Greek temple of Pandemiou Artemis, as evidenced by a mosaic pavement under the floor of the church.

The road to Mesklá and other villages in that part of the Rhíza takes one past a turn-off to Alikianóu, 13km from Chaniá to the south-west. Alikianóu and the other villages in this part of the Chaniá Plain are called Portokalachória, the Orange Villages, because they are situated in the midst of a vast orange grove, which has been called Crete's Garden of Eden. The village of Fournés alone possesses 120,000 orange trees, while Skinés has 90,000, its people celebrating an Orange Festival every Easter. There are a number of frescoed

Byzantine chapels in these villages and their surrounding orange groves, the oldest and most important being the church of Áyios Yórgios in Alikianóu, built in 1430, with beautiful frescoes remaining from 1430, just twenty-three years before the fall of Byzantium.

Alikianos was the scene of an extraordinary bloodbath during the Cretan revolt against the Venetians in the early sixteenth century, an uprising led by the Sfakian chieftain George Kandanoleon. Kandanoleon set up an independent government in Sfakiá and the Rhiza, with his capital at Mesklá, collecting taxes and administering laws in open defiance of the Venetian governor. But Kandanoleon eventually fell into a trap set by the governor and Francesco Molini, a Venetian noble who had an estate in Alikianóu. Molini offered his daughter as a bride for Kandanoleon's eldest son Petro, proposing that the two families thus establish an alliance. While Kandanoleon and his family were celebrating the wedding feast in Alikianóu, the governor and Molini brought in a force of Venetian soldiers and proceeded to slaughter them all, the beginning of a general massacre of rebellious Greeks throughout Crete.

And for those to whom this tale seems ancient history, there is a war memorial that should be noticed on the turn-off that leads to Alikianóu from the Chaniá-Mesklá road, commemorating those Cretans who were killed in these villages by the Germans during World War II. Such has life been here in the Rhíza, where the lush beauty of the surrounding orange groves makes one forget the long centuries of foreign oppression endured by these old villages below the White Mountains, now recalled only by the songs of *rizítika* such as *I Sklávi Ton Kourasón*, The Slaves of the Corsairs, which we heard an old Cretan sing one night in the taverna of Yorgo Drakakis in Chaniá, a threnody lamenting the raids of the *Barbaressi*, the Barbarians.

> Sun, when you come up tomorrow
> to give light to the whole world,
> Rise for all the world,
> for all the universe.
> But in the halls of the Barbaressi,
> Sun, don't rise.
> And if you do, set quickly.
> For they have many handsome slaves
> who suffer greatly,
> and your rays will be turned to water
> by their tears.

16

THE SAMARIÁ GORGE
AND SFAKIÁ

The most exciting of all the excursions one can make from Chaniá is to hike down the Samariá Gorge, the extraordinary canyon that begins at the Omalós Plateau and cuts through the western side of the White Mountains on its spectacular way down to the Libyan Sea, taking one into the heart of Sfakiá, the wild and remote region that has always been a centre of Cretan independence, the unconquerable core of the Great Island.

Since there is no road of any kind through the gorge, one must make the journey on foot from the Omalós Plateau down to the little port of Ayía Ruméli, a rough hike taking from four to six hours. Then from Ayía Ruméli one can take a ferry to Chóra Sfakión, from where there is a regular bus service to Chaniá. One can also take a ferry from Ayía Ruméli to either Soúyia or Paleochóra, both of which have bus-connections to Chaniá, though the route via Chóra Sfakión is the most popular and has the most frequent service. All of the travel agencies in Chaniá offer daily excursions to the Samariá Gorge during the summer, with the fare including the bus to Omalós, the ferry from Ayía Ruméli to Chóra Sfakión, and the bus from Chóra Sfakión back to Chaniá, a trip that begins at dawn and lasts till twilight even on the year's longest days in late June, which is when I took my homeric hike down the great gorge.

I began planning my excursion to the Samariá Gorge as soon as we were settled in our *pýrgos* in Chaniá, my main task being to walk myself into shape for this arduous trek. Dolores did not feel quite up to the hike at that time, and so I decided to make the trip with our son Brendan when he arrived to join us in Chaniá for a few weeks beginning in late June, and as soon as he was ready we bought our tickets for the following day, when we were to board our bus to Omalós at dawn in Santriváni Square.

Brendan and I made our way down along the quay in Chaniá just before dawn the next day, watching the sun rise over Akrotíri while we had our morning coffee at a café in Santriváni Square, waiting for our tour bus to appear. When the bus arrived we were the first to board, taking the seats just beside the driver so that we would have a full view of the scenery as we headed up to the Omalós Plateau. As soon as our tour group was complete the bus started off, driving out from the town along the main road to the south-west through the Chaniá Plain, the orange groves of the Portokalachoria glowing gloriously in the early morning sunlight. Our route turned south-eastward as we passed the turn-off to Alikianóu, taking us up the valley of the Pótamos River as far as Fournés, where we turned off the Mesklá road and headed up the side valley of a tributary stream, which we crossed as the road began winding up into the foothills of the White Mountains. Then 25km out of Chaniá we passed through Lákki, its tiered houses perched at an altitude of 500m, the last village on this route up to the Omalós Plateau.

Ten kilometres past Lákki the road finally crests the last ridge before the plateau and one suddenly has a view of the Omalós, an astonishing sight to see this absolutely flat plain far up here in the Sfakian highlands, an area of some 25 square km at an altitude of 1080m, surrounded by a mountain wall with peaks rising as high as 2000m. In winter the Omalós is deep in snow, as are its surrounding mountains, and when this melts the plain is a morass of overflowing streams and standing water, which by mid-April drains off through an enormous *katavóthron*, or cavern, whose upper end can be seen just beside the road on entering the plateau.

The road from Lákki enters the plateau at its north-eastern corner, coming to a fork there, with the route to the right going around the western side of the plain towards the western pass through the White Mountains at this point, while we followed the main road left from the fork as it headed around the eastern periphery of Omalós toward the head of the Samariá Gorge. This route linking Lákki and the Omalós plateau is known as 'the road of the Mousoúri', named for the Mousouros family, a local clan of mountaineers who led one of the Sfakian revolts against the Venetians in the sixteenth century. The Sfakian chieftain Daskaloyiannis also led his *palikária* along this road in 1770, beginning his abortive revolt against the Turks. Another rebel leader who took to this road in the cause of Cretan independence was Hatzimichalis Gianaris, who led the Sfakians in the 1866 revolt against the Turks. The house of Hatzimichalis still stands to the left of the road just beyond the fork, and beside it there is a little chapel dedicated to Áyios Panteleímon. Hatzimichalis built this chapel after he and his men escaped from a Turkish prison in Chaniá, crediting the saint with having interceded with God on their behalf, and when he died he was buried next to the church. As we passed the grave of Hatzimichalis Gianaris I was reminded of a drawing I had seen in Hilary Pym's *Songs of Greece*, showing a Cretan *palikári* standing beside a little chapel at the head of a rocky pass, illustrating the song called '*Póthos Polemistí*', *A Fighter's Longing*.

> When will the clear day dawn?
> When will February come
> for me to take my rifle,
> my lovely patroness,
> and go down to the Omalos,
> to the path of the Mousouri,
> to make mothers lose their sons,
> the women lose their husbands,
> the little children motherless,
> the babies crying in the night
>   and in the early dawn
> for milk and mother-love.

About 3km beyond the fork the road comes to an end at the little hamlet of Omalós, where there is a tourist pavilion with a restaurant and a few rooms for those who want to spend the night there, for it is forbidden to camp in the Samariá Gorge itself. After we got out of the bus Brendan and I headed off towards the entrance of the gorge, pausing for a moment to enjoy the view, for the sun had just risen above the mountains that rim the plateau to the east, flooding the plain with its golden light. I took out my map to identify the peaks that we could see around us on the ramparts of the Omalós. Off to the east we could see Kalóros, at an altitude of 1925m, and just to the south of that Melindáou (2133m); farther off to the south-west were Páhnes (2453m) and Psirístra (1766m); due south Psiláfi (1983m) and Volakias (2116m); and to the west Tourlí (1458m) and Kefála (1400m). I could see from my map that our hike would first take us south-east down from the plateau to the deserted village of Samariá, after which the gorge is named, and from there we would be going due

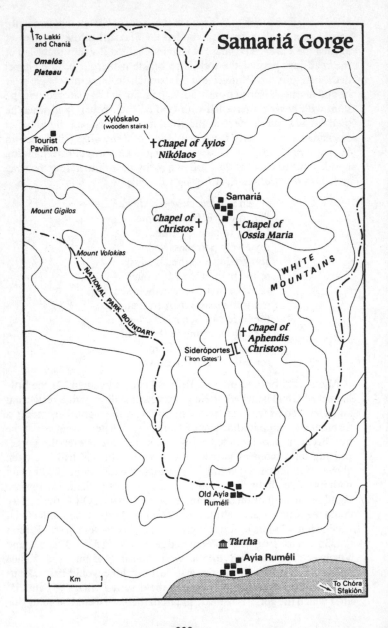

Samariá Gorge

To Lakki
and Chaniá

*Omalós
Plateau*

Xylóskalo
(wooden stairs)

Tourist
Pavilion

+ *Chapel of Áyios
Nikólaos*

Mount Gigilos

*Chapel of
Christos* +

Samariá

+ *Chapel of
Ossia Maria*

Mount Volokias

NATIONAL PARK BOUNDARY

WHITE
MOUNTAINS

+ *Chapel of
Aphendis
Christos*

Sideróportes
(ˈIron Gatesˈ)

Old Ayía
Ruméli

🏛 *Tárrha*

Ayía Ruméli

0   Km   1

To Chóra
Sfakión.

south, with Mount Psirístra on our left and Mount Volakiás on our right, except that by then we would be so deep within the canyon that we would not be able to see the peaks of the White Mountains on either side. The total length of our hike would be about 18km, taking us from an altitude of 1225m at the beginning of the path from the Omalós plateau into the gorge, the *Xylóskalo*, or Wooden Stairs, down to sea level at Ayía Ruméli, a homeric trek taking an average of six hours. Since we started out from Omalós at eight in the morning, we expected to have time for a swim and lunch at Ayía Ruméli, for the last ferry would not leave there until five in the afternoon.

The *Xylóskalo* is named for the logs with which the Sfakian mountaineers constructed the first path down from the Omalós plateau into the Samariá gorge. There is no record of when these 'wooden stairs' were first constructed, but the name Xylóskalo was already in use when Pashley passed this way in 1834, making his way up the gorge from Ayía Ruméli to the village of Samariá. Twenty-one years later Spratt set out from the Omalós plateau to make his way down the gorge, but his local guides persuaded him that it was too dangerous, and in any event he was seized with a sudden attack of illness and never made his way through the canyon.

It was just eight o'clock when we started down the *Xylóskalo*, the early morning sunlight just beginning to penetrate the profound purple shadows that began to open up below, the voices of the hikers ahead of us on the trail echoing back and forth between the converging walls of the abyss, the upper cliff faces giving off a roseate glow above us. The *Xylóskalo* is an easy walk today, a broad stepped path that even has a railing on the steepest part of its outward side, though as it descends deeper into the canyon it becomes more and more primitive, degenerating into a mere mule-path, disappearing altogether in many places as one crosses and recrosses the bed of the stream that pours down the canyon, the trail fording it on stepping-stones or barely flanking its rocky bank, the cliff walls getting closer and closer together, at one point, the Sideróportes, or Iron Gate, only four m. wide where the sheer walls are over 350m high. But these more difficult parts of the trail still lay ahead of us as we started off in high spirits down the first stretch of the *Xylóskalo*, the bracing and pellucid morning air making us feel like *palikária* as we marched down into the Samariá Gorge.

About 2km down the trail brought us to a clearing above the head of the stream that pours down through the gorge, and in the midst of the glade there we came to a little slate-roofed and whitewashed chapel shaded by a grove of pines and a stand of magnificent cypresses, said to be the tallest on Crete, their ancestors perhaps the source of the logs that, inverted, served as the pillars in the great palace at Knossós. The first foreign traveller to visit and describe this site was Pashley, who was led to explore the Samariá Gorge by tales that there were ancient ruins in the canyon; as he writes: 'From several Sphakians I learned that there were Hellenic remains near Haghia Rumeli, and the "ancient city of the Hellenes" is above Samariá. They add "it is said that a treasure is there concealed, but no one has yet discovered it." ' Pashley set out from the south coast on the morning of 7 May 1834, soon afterwards discovering the site of ancient Tarrha near the village of Ayía Ruméli, after which he made his way up the gorge as far as the chapel of Áyios Nikólaos. In the end Pashley failed to find 'the ancient city of the Hellenes' above Samariá, though he did discover some unidentifiable ruins in the canyon; nevertheless his expedition was a great advance in the exploration of the Great Island, since he gave a vivid description of the Samariá Gorge, the first in the travel literature of Crete.

After a brief rest at Áyios Nikólaos, we continued along the trail, heading south-west as the surrounding ridges and crags converged towards the head of the gorge. About an hour later we reached the deserted village of Samariá, crossing a bridge over the stream to visit the little ghost town. This hamlet dates back to at least Byzantine times. It survived the Saracen raids, Venetian and Turkish rule and German occupation in the Second World War, only to have its population evicted in 1962 when the Samariá Gorge was converted into a national park. And now the tourists who trek down the gorge in their many thousands every summer can look at the abandoned houses of Samariá, perhaps wondering, as we did, why the villagers could not have been allowed to stay here, for this was their gorge, where their ancestors had lived for many centuries, fighting off the foreign invaders who tried to enter Sfakiá. But now Sfakiá has fallen at last, succumbing to the invasion of modern tourism.

One can still see two of the village churches, with the chapel of Chrístos on the west side of the gorge and that of Ossía María on the east. The church of Ossía María is the older and more interesting of the two, built in 1379 and still retaining some of its original frescoes from the late Byzantine renaissance. The church was dedicated to the Holy Maria, an Egyptian courtesan who reformed and lived a saintly life here in the gorge as a nun after having had a vision of the Blessed Virgin. The Venetians referred to her church as San Maria, which was eventually corrupted to Samariá, from which the village and the gorge took their name. Up until 1962 the church had an interesting icon representing Ossía María painted in 1740 by a local Sfakian artist, but this is now kept in a monastery on Mount Áthos. In this icon the Holy Maria is shown wielding a claw-hammer to slay a horrible-looking monster in the Samariá Gorge, the craggy topography of the canyon clearly recognizable in the painting.

The lair of the dragon shown in the icon of Ossía María was probably on Gíngilos, the mountain just north of Mount Volokiás, the two peaks towering above the gorge just 3km due west of Samariá. Mount Gíngilos has a sinister reputation in Cretan folklore, said to be the abode of Satan and of various demons and evil spirits. Among the most dreaded of these were the vampires, or *vroukólakas*, also known on Crete as *katakhanás*. Pashley heard several frightening stories of vampires when he was in Sfakiá, and gives an account of the rite of exorcism which was used in the local churches then to deal with these dread creatures including the burning of the remains of departed Sfakiotes suspected of being *katakhanás*.

While in Sfakiá Pashley also heard tales of the Nereids, known in Greek as Neraídhes, the nymphs who were believed to inhabit springs, streams and caves. The principal haunt of the Nereids in the Samariá Gorge was at the foot of Mount Gíngilos in a cavern called Demonóspilos, the Cave of the Demons.

After leaving the village of Samariá we continued along the path, which heads due south at the beginning of the deepest part of the gorge, the cliff faces becoming inexorably higher and closer together, as we went back and forth across the stream, leaping like goats from one rock to another as we forded the rapidly flowing crossings, until at one point I slipped and fell in and was soaked up to my waist. So I sat on a huge rock in the sun to dry out while Brendan went on ahead, to wait for me at the next ford. As I sat there on the rock, soaked to the skin and feeling worn out and sorry for myself, a Greek gentleman about my own age, who had been sitting with his wife across the stream, crossed over and presented me with an orange. After thanking him, I peeled and ate the orange, and suddenly my day brightened up again, as shoes and clothes dried quickly in the blazing sun that was now, at noon, penetrating for the first time to the bottom of the gorge. My spirits not only revived but soared, and after I had put on my socks and shoes I started off down the trail, waving goodbye to my newfound Greek friends, wishing them *kaló drómo*, or good journey.

Brendan was waiting for me at the next ford, where he had just had a swim in the pool that had formed behind the rocks that had been piled up to make a crossing for the path. He was ready to go as soon as I arrived, and we headed off together, now having reached about the midway point in the gorge. A while later we passed on our left the little chapel of Aphéndis Chrístos, Christ the Lord, a little pathside shrine built during the Ottoman period by the local Sfakiote mountaineers at the upper end of the Sideróportes, the Iron Gates, the narrow pass that we were now approaching. During the rebellion against Ottoman rule in 1770 led by Daskaloyiannis, a force of 200 Sfakian *palikária* under Captain Yannis Bonatos held off a Turkish army at the Sideróportes, preventing them from making their way through the Samariá Gorge and up the *Xylóskalo* onto the Omalós plateau. In fact, the Sfakians could proudly claim that during the two and a half centuries of Ottoman rule in Crete the Turks never got past the Iron Gates into the Samariá Gorge.

Now finally we made our way into the Sideróportes, actually a series of 'gates', each one narrower and loftier than the one before, the last chasm only three to four m. wide at the river bed. We inched our way along from rock to rock, looking up occasionally with a sickening feeling of vertigo to see the two cliff faces extending up more than 600m, one precipice actually arching over in an almost complete vault at the top. We could see just a thin sliver of blue sky, the sunlight cutting into the abyss at noon to cast a dramatic roseate glow on the rock faces of the canyon, one of the most awesome sights I have ever seen on my travels.

After passing through the last and narrowest of the Iron Gates we emerged into a broadening valley and a gentler landscape, shaded from the blazing midday sun by an olive grove with stands of cypresses, pines, holm oaks and an occasional *plátanos*. Here after hours of climbing up and down rocky goat-paths and leaping from stone to stone across perilous fords we could finally stride out and stretch our legs, as we made our way down the valley toward the coast, finally coming to the lower entrance of the National Park of Samariá at the deserted village of Old Ayía Ruméli, abandoned since 1962, its people now living down in the new site at the port of Ayía Ruméli, about 2½km to the south. Here we stopped to look at the local church of Áyios Yórgios which dates back to Venetian times, once again saddened by the thought that this old sanctuary is now abandoned after having served as a sanctuary for the people of Ayía Ruméli for many centuries, the villagers having held off the Turks only to be forced out by the invasion of tourism.

Some of the local Sfakians are at least profiting from the hordes of tourists who pour through their old village, and one of them has opened an outdoor café just outside the lower gate of the national park of the Samariá Gorge. Brendan and I stopped there for half an hour before continuing along the last stretch of our walk, which brought us down along the river bank toward the sea and the port of Ayía Ruméli. On the way we passed an abandoned Venetian church and the ruins of a Turkish fortress. The church dates from the sixteenth century and was dedicated to the Madonna of Ayía Ruméli, with remains of a mosaic pavement around it apparently surviving from an earlier Graeco-Roman structure. Spratt was the first to report on these antiquities, suggesting that the church was built on the site of a temple to Apollo belonging to the ancient city of Tárrha, which Pashley thought he had identified some remnants of farther down the valley by the port.

Archaeological excavations have since revealed that Tárrha was first settled at least as early as the fifth century BC, continuing in existence until about the fifth century AD. During the early Hellenistic period, beginning in about 300 BC, Tárrha was one of a group of half a dozen cities on the south shore of western Crete that banded together in what was called the Confederation of Oreioi, which was later joined by Górtyna and Cyrenaica. By that time Tárrha was already noted for its temple of Tarrhanean Apollo, which was also associated with the cults of Artemis, Brytomartis and Acacallis, the mother of the legendary King Kydon, so this must have been one of the most important religious shrines of the ancient Cydonians, the ancestors of the Sfakians.

After looking at these few remnants of ancient Tárrha, we finally headed off on the last stretch of the path from the Samariá Gorge to the little port of Ayía Ruméli, where there are several tavernas on a beautiful beach of white pebbles. We walked to the far end of the beach and stripped down for a swim, an incredible pleasure after the gruelling hike down the Samariá Gorge, which had taken us exactly six hours, although Brendan afterwards claimed that he could have made it in four hours if he had been on his own, which is probably true. After our swim we dried off in the sun, and then we walked over to one of the tavernas, where we sat down to lunch at 2.30 pm, giving us exactly two and a half hours to relax and look around before the last ferry for Chóra Sfakión was due to leave at five o'clock.

We finished lunch at about 3.30 pm, after which Brendan went down to the beach to sun himself for a while before taking a last swim, while I stayed in the taverna, looking at the magnificent shoreline that stretched off for miles on both sides of the Ayía Ruméli bay, studying my map and notes to identify the various sites described by Pashley and Spratt, the first modern travellers to explore the south coast of Crete.

The most inaccessible part of the south coast of western Crete is the stretch between Ayía Ruméli and Soúyia, the next port to the west, for there are no roads at all in this region, the mountains plunging directly down into the Libyan Sea. As Pashley writes:

> The wildest and most picturesque part of the coast of Crete commences to the eastward of Suia; for the roots of the Omalo Mountains, and also those of the higher group of the Madara Vouna or White Mountains, following them to the eastward, press upon the shore here in remarkably bold and precipitous ridges, which are separated or cleft by deep valleys and steep gorges that are almost inaccessible except for the sea. The first of these is about six miles east of Suia, called Tripiti . . . this part of the coast is remarkably picturesque. Two peaked crags almost touch at the entrance of the gorge, as two portals to its entrance; but the valley expands immediately within them . . . About a mile up it I found some ancient terraces on the side of the hill to the left, with vestiges of habitation upon them; and upon a rude slab of limestone built into one of these was an inscription referring to a temple of Serapis, which must have stood somewhere on this site.

Spratt identified Cape Tripití as the site of ancient Poikilassós, one of the cities in the Confederation of Oreioi. Poikilassós seems to have continued in existence until the medieval Byzantine period, but since then the site has been completely abandoned, and no modern settlement was ever made along that coast around Cape Tripití. The entrance to the gorge at Cape Tripití is one of the most remote anchorages on the Great Island, which is why it was used as a secret harbour by the British Mission to Crete during World War II.

The ferry for Chóra Sfakión began loading up at 4.30 pm, so Brendan and I went aboard then, finding a seat out on the fantail where we would have a clear view of the coast. The ferry left promptly at 5 pm, and as we left the port I looked back at the Samariá Gorge, which was clearly visible as a great cleft cutting through the White Mountains. This view of the gorge from the sea made me a little nostalgic, though we had only walked through it just a few hours before, because for that short time we had been in the heart of old Sfakiá, and I wondered if I would ever see it again.

I had brought along a pair of binoculars, and as we steamed along just a few hundred metres offshore I scanned the coast, checking my map and notes to find the places of interest described by Pashley and Spratt. But I was soon mesmerized by the sheer magnificence of the coast itself, for in the entire stretch from Ayía Ruméli to Chóra Sfakión the White Mountains plunge directly into the sea without an intervening coastal plain, with the great range mirrored in the most beautifully blue water I have ever seen. Through my binoculars I could see the dirt-track that leads along the coast from the Samariá Gorge as far as Loutró, the only village on the sea between Ayía Ruméli and Chóra Sfakión. About 3km to the east of Ayía Ruméli this track passes the shrine of Áyios Pávlos, which I could now see clearly through my binoculars, a little chapel standing just above the shore below the colossal background of Mount Páhnes, the highest peak in the White Mountains. The present chapel dates to the twelfth century, but it is probably built on the site of a much earlier Byzantine shrine dedicated to St Paul, who, tradition holds, made his first converts to Christianity on Crete at a spring here after landing at Phoenice, the haven mentioned in Acts 27: 12.

After rounding the broad headland that forms the eastern side of Ayía Ruméli bay, the ferry suddenly headed in to a beautiful cove almost hidden away between promontories on either side, and there we came into a landing at the very pretty hamlet of Loutró. This is the site identified as Phoenice, and while we docked briefly here to pick up a few passengers I read Spratt's description of the site:

> The wild and open bay of Roumeli is succeeded, at six miles to the eastward, by a small but high promontory, upon the east side of which is a narrow inlet turned towards the west, which forms the winter port of the Sfakians, and is called Lutro; and it is the only port on the south coast of Crete in which a vessel could find security for the whole season. This fact will identify it as the ancient port Phoenice mentioned by St Luke in his account of the voyage of St Paul (Acts, xxviii. 12), as 'an haven of Crete, that lieth towards the south-west and north-west', and in which it was desired to winter with the Alexandrian ship after quitting the less secure Kaloi Limnes or Fair Havens, – an identification which is further confirmed by the ruins of the city Phoenice which at present exist upon it, and from its name being still applied to the wide bay on the western side of the promontory.

Loutró seemed a perfect place for a certain type of vacation, a completely out-of-the-way spot on the remote south coast of Crete, with a pretty village on the sea and a beach just beside it, with a number of interesting places to see in the vicinity. The site of ancient Phoenice is on the near side of the promontory that encloses the cove to the east, with the ruins mostly dating from the late Roman and early Byzantine periods, along with some vaulted Venetian *arsenáli*. The chapels on the promontory is dedicated to Sotíros Chrísto, Christ the Saviour; this was founded in the late Byzantine period and is still adorned with some of its original frescoes. There is also an interesting old building in the port known as the Cangelariá Kyverníou, or Chancellery; in 1821 the central government of the Cretan revolutionary movement convened here, holding their first meeting on 20 May of that year.

The coastal track from Ayía Ruméli ends at Loutró, but other tracks lead up from there to the mountain village of Anópoli. Anópoli, the prinicpal village of Sfakiá, is connected by a good road with Chóra Sfakión, and as our ferry headed around the coast after leaving Loutró we could see a lone car driving up in that direction.

Anópoli is one of the oldest and most historic villages in Sfakiá. This was the centre of many of the revolts that started in Sfakiá, most notably the one led in 1770 by Daskaloyiannis, whose house can still be seen in Anópoli, with the cave in which he and his men met down on the shore near Chóra Sfakión. Another monument to be seen in Anópoli is the Church of the Metamorphosis, which still has fragmentary remains of its Byzantine frescoes. Outside the village there are also traces of the ancient city of Anópoli, first identified by Pashley.

From Anópoli there is a rough dirt tract that leads westward along this highland plain to the villages of Arádhena and Áyios Ioánnis, then cutting down precipitously to the coast at Áyios Pávlos. Pashley found ruins around the village of Arádhena that led him to identify here the ancient city of the same name, noted in Hellenistic history as having been an ally of King Eumenes of Pergamum. Among these ruins there is a spot known to the locals as 'The Dancing-Place of the Hellenes', the origins of the name probably being fanciful. The principal monument in Arádhena itself is the church of Áyios Michális Archistratighós, the Archangel Michael; this dates from the Byzantine period, apparently constructed on the site of a more ancient structure, and it is still decorated with some of its original frescoes.

The road continues on to Áyios Ioánnis, which is the back-of-the-beyond in Sfakiá, standing high above the Libyan Sea under the massed peaks of Mounts Páhnes, Troháris and Zaranokefála. There is also a frescoed Byzantine church in Áyios Ioánnis, dedicated to the Panayía, indicating that these remote Sfakian mountain villages have been inhabited since the medieval era, and in some cases back into antiquity. There are also a number of caves in the vicinity of the village, known as Paterorypais, Kormokópos and Drakoláki. The largest of these is Drakoláki, the Cave of the Dragon, which is the subject of local legend, said to be inhabited by Nereids, 'the beautiful ladies' who led men to their doom.

As our ferry steamed along the coast past Loutró I watched the mountain road from Anópoli as it wound down toward the coast, and then as we rounded the next promontory I saw it lead into the village of Chóra Sfakión, where we now headed into the port. We anchored at the pier there and disembarked, following the crowds as they walked through the village to the buses waiting in the open area outside. There we boarded a bus for Chaniá, and within ten minutes we were off, heading back across the width of Crete for the second time that day, going up the Nimbros Ravine to the Askífou Plateau, then down the Katré Ravine to the Apokóronas Plain. Then at Vríses we turned left onto the superhighway, and within the hour we were back in Chaniá, having made a complete circuit of the White Mountains, a homeric trip that for a few hours had taken us into the heart of old Sfakiá.

17

WESTERNMOST CRETE

During our summer in Chaniá we made several trips through and around the westernmost part of Crete, the region that lies beyond the main massif of the White Mountains. On these trips we usually travelled by public bus, going out to our destination in the morning, exploring the surroundings at the end of the line during the midday hours, and then returning on the last bus to Chaniá in the early evening. Chaniá is particularly well placed for seeing this part of the island, for the main highway goes westward from there along the north coast to Kastélli, the main town at the north-western corner of Crete, with transverse roads cutting across to Soúyia and Paleochóra, the two ports on the south-west coast. In this way we came to know a part of Crete that is less visited by foreigners than other regions of the Great Island, the area that in antiquity had been the Kingdom of Cydonía.

On one of our trips Dolores and I took the bus down to Soúyia, an excursion that took us diagonally across the width of the island just westward of the main massif of the White Mountains. The first part of the route is the same as the one that Brendan and I had taken to the Samariá Gorge, with the Soúyia road turning off at Alikianóu. From there the route leads through the paradisical orange groves of Skinés, the first village along the Soúyia road after the turn-off. Beyond Skinés the road leads up a river valley as it passes through Lagós, then crossing to another valley as it goes through Néa Roúmata and near Prasés. Here one passes from the province of Cydonía to that of Sélinou, which occupies the south-western quarter of the Chaniá Prefecture. From Prasés the road winds through the highlands that form the western extension of the White Mountains, as the route takes one between the peaks that rim the Omalós plateau to the west and the isolated western peak known as Apopigádi, at an altitude of 1331m.

Just opposite Mount Apopigádi a turn-off to the left leads into the valley of Ayía Eiréne, through which a road leads to the western side of the Omalós plateau. This was the route that Spratt took after he left the Omalós plateau, coming out to the main route to the south here opposite Mount Apopigádi, and following it down to the coast at Soúyia, taking the same course as the modern highway. As he did so he paused at two ancient sites, Élyros and Hyrtakína, both of which had been discovered by Pashley. Élyros and Hyrtakína were two cities in the Confederation of Oreioi, the league that was formed in south-west Crete c. 300 BC, other charter members being Tárrha, Poikilassós, Lissós and Sýia. The latter four cities were all on the south-western coast of Crete, Tárrha the most easterly, with Sýia on the site of modern Soúyia, while Élyros and Hyrtakína were a short distance inland on the southern slope of the mountains to the south-west of the Omalós plateau. Élyros was renowned in antiquity as the birthplace of the poet Thaletas, a predecessor of Homer, who, according to Strabo, was the inventor of the *cretic* rhythm used in the songs and paeans of the Great Island.

After the turn-off to Rodováni, the road to Soúyia runs eastward for about 4km before making a hairpin turn above Moní, where the local church of Áyios Nikólaos has frescoes dating to 1315. Then after Moní the road runs straight down toward the coast, passing on the left a turn-off to Koustoyérako 3km above Soúyia. Koustoyérako is renowned as the birthplace of George Kandanoleon, leader of the great Cretan revolt against Venetian rule in the sixteenth century, who was buried here in his native village after he had been executed by the Venetians. The grave of Kandanoleon can still be seen beside a church outside the village, which has been destroyed several times since his death; first by the Venetians after the sixteenth-century revolt; then by the Turks in both the eighteenth and nineteenth centuries; and most recently by the Germans during World War II.

The bus finally brought us down to the south coast at Soúyia, a little coastal hamlet that in recent years has become popular as an out-of-the-way summer resort. We took a brief swim at the beach there and then had lunch at a seaside taverna, after which we set out to explore the local antiquities, once again using Pashley and Spratt as our guides.

Pashley identified Soúyia as ancient Sýia, one of the cities of the Confederation of Oerioi, concluding that it had served as the port of

Élyros, with most of the ruins dating from the late Roman and early Byzantine periods. Spratt examined the site more thoroughly, discovering the ancient port, now filled in by an upheaval of the earth. The most important structure remaining from ancient Sýia is an early Byzantine basilica, probably dating from the sixth century AD. The basilica still has much of its original mosaic pavement, most of it decorated in a geometric design, but with one splendid panel depicting a deer and peacocks embowered in vines. The splendour of this mosaic decoration is a testimony to the cultural sophistication of Sýia at the very end of antiquity in Crete, just a century or so before the Saracen corsairs destroyed this and all other cities on the coasts of the Great Island.

West of Soúyia the serrated shore of Órmos Soúyias curves outward in a series of three promontories, the westernmost of which is Cape Flomés, and beyond that is the broad bow-shaped bay known as Órmos Selínou Kastélli, with Paleochóra standing on its westernmost headland. There is a rough dirt-track along the coast from Soúyia to Paleochóra, but the only practicable route between those two coastal hamlets is the inland road via Rodováni, which we decided we would take on a later excursion to the south coast.

The only place of interest on the coast between Soúyia and Paleochóva is the ancient city of Lissós, which is just 2 or 3km west of Soúyia, approached either on the coastal track or by boat from the port. Lissós was the westernmost of the four coastal cities in the Confederation of Oreioi, with its port in a cove about midway between Sýia and Cape Flomés, the site now known as Áyios Kýrko, from a church of that name that now stands there on the shore, along with a chapel of the Panayía. Other than these chapels and a few scattered ruins, there is virtually nothing to be seen of this ancient city today.

A few days after our trip to Soúyia we took the bus down to Paleochóra, a route that brought us down to the south coast farther to the west of our previous excursion. The first 20km of this route took us along the coast west of Chaniá, a stretch that we knew very well from our long walks along the beaches there, strolling as far as Ayía Marína, about 6km beyond the town. Just beyond Ayía Marína one sees the islet of Ayíi Theódori, the ancient Akytos, its craggy form looking like the hideous head of some prehistoric monster, which in legend was thought to have been petrified by the gods when it tried to devour the Great Island. Archaeologists have discovered a cavern on the islet that seems to have been used as a shrine c. 2000 BC, with another cave-sanctuary of slightly later date also found across the way at Ayía Marína, among the very few Minoan sites yet unearthed in westernmost Crete. Ayíi Theódori was fortified early on by the Venetians, but it was the first stronghold on Crete to fall to the Turks when they invaded the Great Island in 1645, just before the siege of Chaniá, its gallant garrison fighting to the last man. Today Ayíi Theódori is used as a game preserve for *agrími*, the wild goats of Crete, and excursion boats from Ayía Marína take one around the islet for a possible glimpse of these marvellous beasts.

Eleven kilometres out of Chaniá the highway passes the village of Plataniás on the left and then crosses the Platanás River. Both the village and the river take their name from the lofty platanos trees that grow here in such dappled splendour, adding much to the beauty of the Chaniá Plain. Pashley identified Plataniás with the ancient Iordanus, the river mentioned by Homer in Book III of the *Odyssey*. Pashley also believed that somewhere nearby was the site of Pergamum, a Cretan city mentioned by a number of ancient writers, with Virgil representing Aeneas as its founder, leading the Trojan survivors here after their city had been conquered by Agamemnon's army. But the Trojan colony on Crete was short-lived, for soon after they landed they were struck by a terrible plague, and so Aeneas and his people were forced to move on, eventually carving out a new kingdom for themselves in Italy, where in Virgil's epic they became the founders of what would become the Roman civilization. And so, as we passed Plataniás, I recalled the lines from the *Aenead* where Aeneas tells of their departure from Crete, as they sail off from the Great Island into the unknown.

> We soon abandoned the new colony
> Leaving few souls behind, and making sail
> In the decked ships we took to the waste sea.

The shore beyond Plataniás is a succession of beautiful sand-beaches that stretch on for miles to the west, interrupted only by the Greek military airport at Máleme. This is where the German invasion of Crete began on 20 May 1941, when the Luftwaffe landed a division of airborne troops at Máleme, opposed by British and Commonwealth forces along with a hastily-organized contingent of Greek soldiers and the local villagers, who fought with typical Cretan heroism. According to an eyewitness account by a New Zealand officer, quoted by Alan Clark in *The Fall of Crete*, when the German paratroopers landed they were harried 'by the entire population of the district, including woman, children, and even dogs; those Cretans would use any weapon, flintlock rifles captured from the Turks a hundred years ago, axes, and even spades.' But despite this spirited resistance Máleme airport fell to the paratroopers within two days, and by 10 May 1941 the Battle of Crete was over, with the Germans in control of the Great Island, though the Cretan partisans and the commandos of the British Mission to Occupied Crete would oppose them with increasing effectiveness through the four years of enemy occupation.

After passing Máleme one soon comes to Tavronítis, 20km from Chaniá, where there is a turn-off that leads left to the Paleochóra road. The first stretch of the Paleochóra road heads south along the left bank of the Tavronítis River, a wide stream that waters the broadest and most fertile part of the coastal plain that stretches westward from Chaniá, here crossing the border between the provinces of Cydoniá and Kísamos, the latter comprising the north-westernmost corner of Crete. The first village of any size that one comes to along the Paleochóra road is Voukoliés, which has two frescoed Byzantine churches; one of them is dedicated to the Archangel Michael, erected in 1392; the second is St Constantine in Nembros, dated 1452, just a year before the fall of Byzantium. There is also an old *pýrgos* in the village that has a miraculous well with curative waters. Besides these monuments, Voukoliés is also renowned for its great market fair, a bazaar that dates back at least to Ottoman times.

Once past Voukoliés the road heads south-westward along the eastern border of Kísamos province; then at Kakópetro, where the route makes a huge S-bend, one crosses over into Sélinos province. Fifty kilometres from Chaniá the road comes to the mountain village of Flória, perched at an altitude of 580m midway between the Aegean and the Libyan Sea. This is actually two villages, the upper one called Apáno Flório and the lower Káto Flório, both of them with Byzantine churches. The most important of these is the church of Áyios Yórgios in Káto Flórino, dating from 1497 and with frescoes by the painter G. Provatopoulo, with thirteen panels of wall-paintings surviving. Apáno Flório has the church of Áyion Patéron, the Holy Fathers, dating from 1462, which was originally decorated with frescoes by the celebrated artist Zeno Digeni, but these have now been destroyed.

Fifty-eight kilometres out of Chaniá the road comes to Kándanos, the capital of Sélinos province, set at an altitude of 420m in a green valley that is one vast olive grove. The village perpetuates the name of ancient Kándanos, whose ruins Pashley discovered on the hill of Áyia Eiréne, south of modern Kándanos and in the general vicinity of its satellite villages, Kádros, Spaniáko and Kálamo. One inscription since recovered from these ruins contains a dedication to Zeus Agoraios, in which Zeus is worshipped as the god of the marketplace. This is an epithet not found elsewhere in Crete, perhaps indicating the Doric origin of those who founded Kándanos, which appears to have been the name of the surrounding district as much as it was that of the central city, much as is the case of the present village.

Its medieval status as both a Greek Orthodox and Roman Catholic bishopric have left Kándanos a rich heritage of medieval art and architecture, for in the village there are fifteen Byzantine churches still standing, many of them adorned with their original frescoes, with another five in ruins, as well as many other Byzantine chapels surviving in nearby villages. The churches in Kándanos and its satellite hamlets are, together with their dates, when known: in Kándanos itself: the Archangel Michael (1328), and Áyios Ioánnis (1329); in Anisaráki: Ayía Ánna (1457), Panayía (17 panels of frescoes), and Ayía Paraskeví; in Plemenianá: Sotíros Christos; in Tzevremianá: Panayía (fourteenth century); in Lambrianá: Ayía Kyriakí (1405); in Venoudianá: Áyios Yórgios; in Tsaghareliana (Chrispilí): Panayía; in Koufalotó (Áyios Apóstolos): Áyii Apóstoli; in Kavalarianiá: Archangel Michael; in Trachiniáko: Áyios Profítis Iliás, and Áyios Ioánnis (1328-9); Skoudiana: Panayía (an early Byzantine structure, probably of the fifth/sixth century). In the village of Kádros, which is on the site of ancient Kátri, there are the church of Ioánnis Chrysóstomos, and the church of the Nativity of the Virgin, the latter adorned with paintings done in 1331-2 by the celebrated Cretan artist Ioánnis Pagoménos. In the village of Kakodíki there are four churches among its satellite hamlets: in Veidika: the Panayía (frescoes done in 1331-2 by Ioánnis Pagoménos), and the Meta-morphosis; in Astrátigo: the Archangel Michael (1387); and in Tzinalianá: Áyios Isídorus (1421).

As we passed through Kándanos on our bus ride to Paleochóra, we resolved that we would come back there again to explore the village and its surrounding countryside to find the many Byzantine churches hidden away there in the vast olive grove that covers the slopes of these westernmost Cretan mountains as they descend in massed tiers to the sea. There are also a number of ancient sites to be seen in this region as well; with Hyrtakína and Élyros just to the south and south-east, respectively, approached by the secondary road that leads down from the main highway at Plemenianá; and with ancient Kándanos just to the south-west, approached from the main road via the turn-off to Kádros and Spaniákos. But unfortunately our time on Crete was now running down to its last two weeks and there were still places that we had to see out on the westernmost parts of the Great Island, and so the countryside around Kándanos awaits us still.

The last stretch of the road from Kándanos down to the south coast follows the left bank of the Kakodikianós River, crossing over to the right bank just before the stream reaches the Libyan Sea. Then one finally comes in sight of Paleochóra, the Bride of the Libyan Sea, a sea-girt promontory crowned with the ruins of a medieval Venetian fortress, with the modern village clustering on the east side of the isthmus leading out to the peninsula, a long sandy beach stretching off on the western arc of the bay known in Greek as Órmos Selínou Kastélli.

The bay takes its name from that of the old Venetian fortress that surmounts the acropolis – Sélinos Kastélli – the Castle of Selino. The fortress was erected in 1282 by the Venetian governor of Crete at the time, Marino Gradinico, who built it after putting down a serious revolt in western Crete by the brothers Hortatzis. But the castle did not prevent future insurrections for another rebellion broke out in 1283 under the leadership of Alexis Kallergis, who had been an ally of the Venetians in putting down the revolt by the Hortatzis brothers. Kallergis eventually came to terms with the Venetians, but then in 1332 his grandson Vardas Kallergis led another rebellion, seizing Sélinos Kastélli and holding it for a time until he was put down by the forces of the Serenissima. In 1539 the fortress was taken and sacked by the Ottoman pirate-admiral Barbarossa, after which it remained in ruins until it was restored in 1595 by Benetto Dolfin, the Venetian Rector in Chaniá. Then in 1653 the Turks attacked the fortress by land and sea and captured it after a short siege. The fortress was then garrisoned by the Turks, but in late Ottoman times it was abandoned and began to fall into ruins. When Pashley visited Sélinos Kastélli in 1834 he found that the fortress and the little village beneath it were abandoned and in ruins, but since then Paleochóra has revived, inhabited largely by Sfakians who moved here from their ruined mountain villages after World War II, some of them now prospering because of the popularity of the summer resort that has developed here in recent years.

Paleochóra stands on the easternmost of three promontories that jut out into the Libyan Sea at the south-western corner of Crete, the next cape being Trahíli, 4km to the west, and Ákti Kríos 4km west of that is the Cold Cape, known in times past as Kriumetopon, the Ram's Head. Then 7km to the north-west of Cape Kríos is the tiny islet of

Elafonísi, a spit of sand almost connected to the shore at the westernmost point in Crete. Elafonísi was once one of three islets called the Musagorae, the other two having since disappeared, but Spratt believed that these two lost isles are still present in the form of Capes Kríos and Sélino, the Paleochóra promontory, having been joined to the mainland in the great subsidence that has tilted the whole island of Crete since antiquity and changed the topography of the coastline.

There is a good road leading westward along the coast for 7km from Paleochóra as far as Koundoúra, a village just inland from Cape Trahíli. From there a dirt-track leads around the south-west corner of Crete, passing Cape Kríos and going up the coast almost as far as Elafonísi, where there is one of the most beautiful beaches on all of Crete. We thought of going there by taxi from Paleochóra, but the road is completely impossible for a car beyond Koundoúra, and so we decided that we would see Elafonísi on a later excursion, approaching it by the road from Kastélli.

A dirt-road leads inland from Koundoúra to Sklavopoúla, a village set at an altitude of 640m in the mountains at the south-western corner of Crete, one of the most remote communities in this part of the Great Island. Pashley tentatively identified Sklavopoúla as the site of Doulópolis, a Dorian city known to have been located in south-western Crete, and which in its prime could field an army of a thousand warriors. But no remains of ancient Doulópolis have as yet been identified on the site by archaeological findings, and so its location remains undetermined. The present name of the village, Sklavopoúla, or the Village of the Slavs, is believed to stem from a resettlement there by Nicephorus Phocas after his reconquest of Crete from the Saracens in AD 961, the settlers being Armenians from Bulgaria. In any event, the new settlers seem to have become thoroughly Hellenized before long, for there are seven Byzantine churches still standing in the village and its vicinity, with two of them retaining nearly all of their original wall-paintings. These are the churches of the Panayía and of the Sotíros Christos, both of which are adorned with thirteen paintings from their original decoration of the late Byzantine period. A third church in Sklavopoúla, Áyios Yórgios, has fragmentary frescoes dating from 1290.

One can return from Sklavopoúla via Kalamiós and Voutás, from where there is a good road back to Paleochóra. There is a Byzantine church still standing in Kalamiós, and in Voutás the church of Ayía Paraskeví in Kityron has frescoes dating from 1372. Four kilometres farther along the road back to Paleochóra the road passes Kondo-kinígi, where there is still another Byzantine church, and from there one can take a secondary road north to Sarakína, where there are four more frescoed chapels of the late Byzantine period, evidence of how densely settled this remote region was in late Byzantium.

A few days after our trip to Paleochóra, we rented a car in Chaniá to explore the westernmost region of Crete, going off in search of places that were out of reach of the bus lines to the south coast. We began by driving from Chaniá westward along the coast to explore the Rhodopoú peninsula, the easternmost and largest of the two great capes that project out from the north-western end of Crete, looking as if they were talismanic 'horns of consecration'.

The first part of our drive took us along the same route that we had followed a few days before on our bus-ride to the south coast, covering new ground after we passed the turn-off to the Paleochóra road at Tavronítis. There we also crossed the Tavronítis River, the boundary between Cydonía and Kísamos provinces. Then 3km farther along we turned right off the main highway onto a road that goes down the eastern shore of the Rhodopoú peninsula for a short way. A short way down this road we stopped for a drink at Kolimvári, a coastal hamlet that has now become a summer resort, with two hotels along with seaside tavernas, a pleasant place to pause when setting out to explore the Rhodopoú peninsula.

The Rhodopoú peninsula is really quite an amazing sight, an emormous appendage sticking straight out from the coast of western Crete at a sharp right angle, 18km long and only 5km wide at its broadest part, with a mountainous spine whose ridge is nearly 750 metres high at its two peaks, plummeting into the sea from a promontory 370 metres high at Zovígli, above Cape Spánda. In times past the whole peninsula was called Cape Spánda, which in antiquity was known as Tityros. The only villages on the peninsula are on the isthmus that connects the mountainous spine of Rhodopoú to the mainland. Otherwise Rhodopoú is completely uninhabited except for its two famous monasteries, the Hodeghétrias and Áyios Ioánnis Gióna. But in antiquity there was a city out near the tip of the peninsula, named for its renowned shrine of Brytomartis, the Dhiktýnaion. As Spratt wrote of his site, discovered by Pococke in 1745:

The promontory of Spada is mountainous and picturesquely wild, especially towards its extremity, from its elevation there, and from the several cliffy gorges and ravines descending to the coast from its summit, which is 2500 feet above the sea, although the average breadth of the promontory is only two miles and a half. The most northern and most picturesque of these gorges is near its north-east extreme, where the valley opens to the sea at a small cove well sheltered from the north. It is on the little plain at the mouth of this cove, and of the two deep valleys or gorges that open into it, that the ancient town of Dictynna was situated . . . The temple of Britomartis at Dictynna, for which it was celebrated, stood, however, upon the level plateau over the south point of the bay . . . where there are still several square blocks of marble lying on the platform that supported it . . . Pococke also mentions that a statue of the goddess in Parian marble had been discovered previously to his visit, and destroyed, but that he had obtained the sandaled foot, which was exquisitely wrought.

One can hire a boar at Kolimvári to go out to the site of the Dhiktýnaion, which is on the north-eastern tip of the peninsula, just inside Cape Skála. The principal remnant here is the platform of the temple of Brytomartis, which is, as Spratt describes it, about 110m long and 70m broad, with a large cistern adjacent to it, its huge volume testimony to the large number of people who flocked to the shrine. Then, as Spratt described the ruins of the city of Dhiktínna:

> The remains of the city lie for the most part in the bed of the gorge below the temple, and seem to be nearly all of late Roman date, and in some places supported with brick arches: many were habitations. Some are large and circular, as if they had been churches and baths, others appear to have been monasteries during a still later period, and, from their state of preservation, appear as if the place has been suddenly abandoned, for the walls of many of them are several feet high. It thus seems to have preserved its sanctity after the introduction of Christianity, and the devotion to Dictynna to have been transferred, at the conversion of the priesthood, to St George, who is now the local titulary saint.

The precipitous promontory above Cape Skála is renowned in legend as the place from which the nymph Dhiktínna threw herself into the sea to escape the embraces of King Minos, an ancient myth that was evoked when I saw the great headland at the end of the Rhodopoú peninsula. As Spratt relates this deeply-layered legend:

> Dictynna, Brytomartis, Diana and Artemis are sometimes used

synonymously for the goddess of hunting by the ancients of different localities, whilst according to some authors Brytomartis and Dictynna were considered to be only companions for *protégées* of Artemis or Diana. An ancient Cretan tradition, noted by several authors, states that Dictynna was a surname applied to Brytomartis in the island because, it is said, when she threw herself into the sea here, to escape the pursuit of its deified king Minos, she was rescued by the net of a fisherman (the name signifying 'of the net'); and the bold cliffy coast enclosing the cove, and the blue depth of the deep sea close off it, doubtless favoured the invention of the legend of her leap and the mode of her escape from drowning.

On the way back from Dhiktínna by boat, one might stop to see the great cave at Ellinóspilos, which is about 5km north of Kolimvári along the coast. Archaeological exploration of the cave indicates that it was inhabited in the Neolithic period, as early as c. 3000 BC, and that a cave-sanctuary existed there in pre-Minoan times. This was one of the oldest evidences of human habitation on Crete up until recent years, but then in 1968 a chance discovery made while blasting for a new road beyond Afráta unearthed evidence for far earlier human existence on the peninsula, discovering human bones, including fragments of skulls, dating back to the Mesolithic era, some 20,000 to 25,000 years old. This find far outdates in antiquity any other human remains ever found on Crete or the Aegean islands, indicating that the Great Island was inhabited in the Stone Age, its first inhabitants probably dwelling in Ellinóspilios and other caverns on the island, where their descendants were still returning to find refuge from their enemies as recently as the end of the last century.

The monastery of the Hodeghétria is just a short way down the road from Kolimvári, its church and monastic buildings overlooking the western end of the Gulf of Chaniá. The monastery is also called Goniá, which in Greek means 'corner', because it is quite literally on the corner where the shore of the Rhodopoú peninsula turns off rectilinearly from the north shore of Crete. The other name of the monastery, Hodeghétria, comes from the famous icon of the Panayía Hodeghétria, the 'Conductress', to whom the institution is dedicated. The Hodeghétria was venerated as the Protectress of Constantinople, carried in procession along the walls of the city when it was under siege, and after the fall of Constantinople copies of the icon were taken off to other parts of the Greek world, where they are the objects of veneration to the present day. The monastery of the Hodeghétria here was founded in 1618 and was sacked by the Turks in 1645, at the time of the Ottoman capture of Chaniá. The monastery was rebuilt in 1662, restored in 1798, and another floor added to it in the nineteenth century. When Pashley visited the Hodeghétria in 1834 he noted that 'the church of this monastery contains a greater number of those paintings with which the Greeks love to adorn the interior of their places of religious worship than is usually met with in Crete . . . One of them bears the date 1642.' These icons still adorn the monastic church of the Hodeghétria, including one dated 1637 and signed by the Cretan painter Konstantinos Palaiokapas. The monastery of the Hodeghétria played an important role in all of the many Cretan revolutions against Ottoman rule, serving as a refuge for the women and children of the *palikária* who were fighting against the Turks. The monastery today houses the Greek Orthodox Academy of Crete, where international congresses on theology are held periodically. The feast day of the Panayía Hodeghétria is celebrated here annually on 15 August, a *paniyíri* that attacts people from all over the surrounding area.

Driving back to the main road from Kolimvári, we turned right 2km farther along and then drove 5km back along the isthmus of the peninsula to the village of Rhodopós. From Rhodopós a rough track leads back along the spine of the peninsula to the monastery of Áyios Ioánnis Gíona, a hike of about two and a half hours. (Another path branches off from this about halfway along on the right and goes all the way out to the site of the Dhiktynaion, a full day's walk round-trip from Rhodopós.) Very little is known about the history of the monastery of Áyios Ioánnis Gíona, but it was probably founded late in the Venetian period. The monastery celebrates the feast day of St John on 28–9 August, the most popular *paniyíri* in all of western Crete, with people flocking here from all over the region to participate in the festivities. It is a very stirring site to see these crowds of Cretans congregated here out on the remote Rhodopoú peninsula for this *paniyíri*, which is probably a survival of the ancient festival held at the shrine of Dhiktinna, another example of the continuity of culture on the Great Island.

There are some interesting old villages on the Chaniá plain just inland from the Rhodopoú peninsula, with one possible excursion through some of these looping south from the main road at the same crossroads as the Kolimvári turn-off. Three kilometres south of the turn-off the road comes to the village of Spiliá, named after its cave, which is on a hilltop nearby. Within the cavern there is a shrine dedicated to Áyios Ioánnis Ermítis, St John the Hermit, whose monastery is out on the Akrotíri peninsula. Services are held at both the monastery and here in the Spiliá cavern every 7 October, the saint's feast day. On these *paniyíria* as many as 1500 people crowd into the shrine of St John here in the Spiliá cavern, an absolutely haunting experience that evokes visions of ancient cave-sanctuaries on the Great Island in pre-Minoan times.

The village church of the Koímisis tis Theotókou in Spiliá dates from the fourteenth century, and recently some of its original fresco decoration was uncovered from beneath the plaster that had hidden it for centuries, revealing beautiful religious paintings from the height of the Byzantine renaissance. There is another old church in Spiliá dedicated to the Archangel Michael, and this is adorned with a beautiful iconostasis of carved wood, probably dating from the late Venetian period.

Four kilometres south of Spiliá the road comes to the village of Drakóna, the birthplace of Yorgo Drakonianos, a hero of the Greek War of Independence in 1821. The village church of Áyios Stéphanos is one of the oldest on Crete, thought to date from c. 900, with its vaulted ceiling still covered with its original decoration in fresco, eight paintings in all. Another interesting old building in the village is the '*Konáki*', once the residence of the bishops of Kísamos.

Some 3 to 4km farther along the road comes to Episkopí, whose name stems from the fact that it was once an episcopal seat, the residence of the bishops of Kísamos, who at times also resided in nearby Drakóna. The village church of the Archangel Michael was the cathedral of this bishopric, an edifice dating from the tenth century and enlarged in the eleventh century. This is a unique structure with a rotunda forming the central part of its nave, the only church of its type on Crete.

After passing through Episkopí the road loops back north and passes through the village of Nochiá just before returning to the main highway to Kastélli. Nochiá has two frescoed Byzantine churches, one of them dedicated to St John and the other to Constantine the Great, the sainted founder of Constantinople. John Pendlebury found some Minoan shards around the church in 1935, indicating that the site had been inhabited in the period 1700–1100 BC. Pendlebury also found shards in Nochiá dating to the Hellenistic and Roman periods, leading him to suggest that this was the site of ancient Pergamos, or Pergamum, the city founded by Aeneas, but no definite evidence has been unearthed to support this identification.

After passing through Nochiá the diversionary route leads back to the main highway, where one turns left to head for Kastélli. This brings one to the eastern end of the plain of Kastélli-Kisámou, which extends along the southern shore of the Gulf of Kisamos. One can drive down to the south-eastern corner of the gulf at Nopígia, taking a turn-off to the right 4km after regaining the main highway to Kastélli, and on the beach there one can take in the extraordinary view, with the Rhodopoú peninsula bounding this great U-shaped bight on the east, and on the west the almost equally long and even narrower peninsula that ends in Ákri Voúxa, or Cape Bousa, which is thus described by Spratt:

> The wild and preciptious promontory of Busa stretches out from the west side of Kisamo Bay toward the isle of Cerigo and the Morea, as an arm parallel to its opposite headland of Spanda, which, with the gradually retiring ridges that ascend from the coast, and encircle the head of the deep gulf or bay of Kisamo, give rise to the idea, on entering it from the sea, of sailing up a gigantic stadium. Upon the theatre-like semicircle of hills rising from its extremity stood the four cities I have noticed, Mithymna, Rhokka, Polyrrhenia and Kissamon.

Pashley found vestiges of the ancient city of Míthymna at Nopígia, near the local church of Áyios Yórgios. These ruins now seem to have vanished, but Pashley's identification of the site still makes interesting reading, for he mentions that there was a nearby temple of Artemis Rhokkaea, a cult that was also popular in ancient Réthymnos:

> The remains existing at the chapel of Haghios Gheroghios, though slight, are yet sufficient to indicate the existence of an ancient city on the spot. Now we shall see by and by that there was a city Rhokka, where Artemis Rhokkaea was worshipped, a little inland, to the south of this place; and a curious story told by Aelian, respecting a remedy for hydrophobia discovered by a Cretan fisherman, shews plainly that there was a village named Methymna on the shore, and near the temple of Artemis Rhokkaea. I think that there is no doubt of this being the site of Methymna.

But the site of Rhókka eluded Pashley, though he refers to Pococke's identification of the ancient city near the present village of Rhókka, which is 6km to the south of the main highway, approached by a turn-off just opposite to the one to Nopígia. Spratt visited Rhókka and identified the ancient city there, though he was disappointed in his search for the temple of Artemis Rhokkaea, which he thought he might have found at a site farther south near the village of Trialónia, the 'Three Threshing Floors'. But most travellers like ourselves will probably be content with a view of the site of ancient Rhókka, named for the huge conical rock that rise above the surrounding plateau to a height of 80 to 100m, crowned by the ruins of ancient structures, though not of the temple of Artemis Rhokkaea.

Returning to the main road, one turns left once again to head for Kastélli, then 7km farther along at Drapaniás passing the turn-off to the main road south through the Ayía Sofiá gorge to the south coast. Then 5km farther along the road finally comes to Kastélli, or to give the town its full name, Kastélli Kisámou. Kastélli is the largest town in westernmost Crete, capital of the province of Kísamos, the seat of the metropolitan of this district, and the general centre of life in this otherwise remote north-western corner of the Great Island. There were at last count four hotels and a number of pensions in Kastélli, as well as several tavernas, making the town a convenient base for exploring the north-western corner of Crete, and so after our arrival we booked into a little motel along the shore and then went for lunch at a marvellously situated taverna on a promontory overlooking the sea, with a magnificent view of the gulf and the great peninsulas that bound it on either side out as far as the northern horizon, with Cape Spánda far off to the north-east and the north-west Cape Voúxa and the islet of Ágria Graboúsa, the north-westernmost points in Crete.

The present town of Kastélli stands on the site of ancient Kísamos, which served as the port for the inland city of Polyrhenia. Kísamos was an autonomous post-Minoan settlement, and John Pendlebury in his 1935 survey found antiquities there dating from the Orientalizing, Archaic, Classical, Hellenistic and Roman eras, indicating that it was continuously inhabited from the Dark Ages of the ancient world up until the beginning of the Christian era.

After lunch we set off to see the site of ancient Polyrhénia, which is approached by a road leading south from the main highway just east of Kastélli. The drive is 8km from the centre of Kastélli, and on the way one passes the convent of Parthenónas, whose nuns help support themselves by selling the products of their weaving. The road finally winds up to the ruins of Polyrhénia, known locally as Áno Palaeócastro, which is set at an altitude of 275m above sea level, with a splendid view of the Gulf of Kísamos. This is a perfect setting for Polyrhénia, whose name means 'Of the Many Flocks', a city that in its time ruled all of the land that one can see from this hilltop site.

Polyrhénia was founded by the Dorians in the eighth century BC, and during the Dorian period it was one of the most important cities in all of Crete. The city survived throughout antiquity, the Byzantine and Venetian periods, and on into the early Ottoman era, but when Pashley visited the site in 1834 it had been long abandoned.

Another interesting archaeological site in the vicinity of Kastélli is Phalásarna, which is on the western side of the base of the narrowing peninsula that ends in Cape Vouxa. One sets out for Phalásarna by driving along the coast beyond Kastélli as far as Cape Kavonísi, where the road cuts inland and brings one to Plátanos. At the crossroads there the main road leads down along the western coast of Crete toward the south-west corner of the Great Island, which we explored on a later excursion, but on the present trip we turned right at Plátanos on the road that leads down to Órmos Livádi, a wide bay at the base of the peninsula that forms the north-western extremity of Crete. Three kilometres along the road comes to a fork. We took the right branch to drive down to the northern side of the bay, where there is a long sandy beach, one of the most beautiful on Crete. We stopped there for a swim and then drove on past the headland to the north of the bay, Cape Koutrí, where we came to the site of ancient Phalásarna.

Phalásarna was one of the cities founded by the Dorians during the Dark Ages of the ancient Greek world; according to Strabo it was the port of Polyrhénia, and the geographer Scylax of Caryanda writes that it had an artificial harbour and a temple sacred to Artemis Dhiktinna, whose main sanctuary was the Dhiktýnaion on the Rhodopoú peninsula. When Spratt first came upon Phalásarna he was puzzled by the fact that he could not find any evidence of an ancient mole that might have enclosed the ancient harbour, for the rocky shore here is open to the western sea, without even a beach to draw up ships. But then on a subsequent visit his observations led him to conclude that the shore here had risen some seven metres vertically since the founding of the city, thus leaving the harbour of Phalásarna high and dry, part of a general tilting of the whole island that had taken place since antiquity. This change in sea level would have ruined Phalásarna, for without its port there was no reason for a city here in this remote corner of Crete, and so its populace must have abandoned it after this great elevation of the shore, which was probably part of an enormous seismic disturbance which would have wrecked this and other communities in the region. And so what is left here on this rocky promontory is a veritable ghost-town, still ringled by remnants of its ancient defence-walls and honeycombed with tombs, with a rock-hewn throne that particularly fascinated Pashley.

The rock-hewn seat can still be seen at Phalásarna, perhaps the throne of the high priestess of Artemis Dhiktinnaion, whose temple would have been close by. This is one of the most romantic sights in all of Crete, the empty throne standing there among the tomb-haunted ruins above the beautiful coast of westernmost Crete, a ghost town abandoned now for more than a thousand years.

We spent the night in Kastélli after our visit to Phalásarna, and then the next day we set out to explore the peninsula that forms the western shore of the Gulf of Kísamos, hiring a boat to take us around Akri Voúxa. As Spratt writes of this unique peninsula and its offshore islets, after describing the Gulf of Kísamos:

> Its western arm, Cape Busa, was the ancient Corycus, upon the summit of which it would seem, from his work, that Buondelmonte, the Florentine traveller, saw some remains of a city . . . The 'Stadiasmus' places a port called Agneion five miles from the cape, where there was also a temple to Apollo. This port I recognize to be the little sheltered bay of Agios Sostis, where coasters come and secure to the shore when seeking refuge against the strong meltems and westerly gales, and where there is a chapel to the saint of this name in place of the temple, but no other habitation or remains of any significance. The Tritus promontory, of the same author, or the perforated cape must be Cape Busa itself. Two bold rocky islands and a peninsula lie off its extremity; these are the ancient Corycae, then three islands and a peninsula as now, the latter having been joined to the promontory by a recent upheaval of the coast. The two islands are now known as the Agria Grabusa, lying direct off the cape, and to the south-west, the famed stronghold of Grabusa, or Karabusa, with an indifferent harbour, of the same name, within the ledge of rock extending from it. This celebrated fortress was one of the last strongholds retained by the Venetians in the East, who built it upon the rock soon after they became possessed of Crete, to prevent its port continuing to be made, as it then was, the resort and retreat of Moorish corsairs at the very threshold of the archipelago. It is said to have been finally bartered by them to a vizier of the Sultan's for a barrel of sequins. But they retained Suda and Spinalonga some time after their surrender of Grabusa.

On our boat-ride around Voúxa we had a clear view of the two islands off the cape. The largest of these, just off the cape to the north, forming the north-westernmost point of Crete, is Ágria, or Wild Graboúsa, while 3km to the south-west is Ímeri, or Tame Graboúsa, a sea-girt crag on which the Venetians built their fortress of Graboúsa. Graboúsa was one of the last three Venetian strongholds on Crete, in fact in all of the East, the other two being Soúda and Spinalónga. The Venetian fortress here at Graboúsa was surrendered to the Turks in 1691 by its two venal commanders, Neapolitan officers in the service of the Serenissima, who sold the islet to the local pasha and absconded with the money. After looking at the romantic ruins of the Venetian fortress, we sailed into a cove just to the south of the islet, where there is a beautiful beach of red coral protected from the westerly seas by Cape Tigáni. We swam there and then hiked across the tip of the peninsula to look for the site of ancient Agneion, a Doric city that had a renowned temple of Apollo, mentioned by Spratt and other travellers. We found the little chapel of Áyios Sostis that Stratt mentions as being on the site of Agneion, giving its name to the cove there on the north-western side of the Gulf of Kísamos, but we found no traces of the ancient city. Nevertheless, the hike was worth the effort, for there we had a magnificent view of the Gulf of Kísamos and its surrounding shores, with the Rhodopoú peninsula to the east, and to the south the mountains of Kísamos province, the westernmost extension of Leuká Óri, the White Mountains. This remote promontory, with its lost temple of Apollo, seems to me to have been the landmark mentioned by Virgil in Book III of the *Aeneid*, where he describes the first landing that Aeneas and his people made on the Great Island, just before they founded their ill-fated city of Pergamum. As Aeneas tells the tale:

> Before long
> The cloudy peaks of the Leucatan mountain
> Came in view – Apollo's promontory,
> Seamen are wary of. Here we put in
> And hauled up, tired, near the little town,
> Our anchors out, our sterns high on the shingle.

After our boat ride around Cape Voúxa we spent another night in Kastélli. Then the next morning we were off, driving back eastward along the main highway as far as Drapaniás, where we turned right to head out towards the south-western corner of Crete, on what would be our last exploration of the Great Island that summer.

The road from Drapaniás goes south and then south-west along the left bank of the Tyflós River, which rises on the slopes of Mount Ayios

Dikéos Iov, the westernmost peak on Crete, with an altitude of 1182m. Five kilometres south of Drapaniás the road comes to the village of Voulgháro, which is at the confluence of the Tyflós and Analios Rivers. The name of the village leads one to suspect that this was one of the places where the Emperor Nicephorus Phocas resettled Christians from Bulgaria after the reconquest of Crete from the Saracens in 961. There are three frescoed Byzantine churches in and around Volgháro: Áyios Nikólaos in Mourí; Áyios Yórgios in Mákrona; and Ayía Varvára in Latzianá, with the latter building constructed with architectural members taken from an ancient temple that once stood on the same site.

Four kilometres south of Voulgháro the road passes through Topólia, where the village church of Ayía Paraskeví is still adorned with its original frescoes of the late Byzantine period. Two neighbouring hamlets also have frescoed Byzantine churches; Áyios Panteleímon in Aligitziana, and Áyios Yórgios in Tsourouniana, the latter dating from 1330–9.

Beyond Topólina the road passes through a tunnel as it approaches the Koutsomatádos Ravine, one of the most beautiful canyons on Crete. Within the ravine the road passes close to the mouth of the great Ayia Sofia Cave, one of the largest and most spectacular caverns on Crete.

Six kilometres beyond Topólia the road comes to Mýloi, where a side road to the left heads south to Paleochóra, while the main route continues on towards the south-west, 5km farther along coming to Élos, a pretty mountain village set at an altitude of 560m. We stopped for a drink here at a roadside café, for this is one of the most beautiful landscapes in all of Crete, the mountains and valleys covered with a superb forest of chestnut trees. Élos is one of the Enneachória, the 'Nine Villages', actually a group of about fifteen hamlets set here in this remote highland region in westernmost Crete. Élos is mentioned in a Venetian census of 1583, but the village is undoubtedly much older than that, for it has two frescoed Byzantine churches. This and the other villages of the Enneachória were probably in ancient times part of the domain of Inachorium, a town known to have been situated here in the westernmost corner of Crete, with the modern name of this region undoubtedly being a corruption of the ancient toponym. As Spratt writes in describing this lovely countryside that we looked out on from our roadside café in Élos:

The extreme western part of Crete, although very mountainous and barren in its aspect from seaward, contains several very fertile valleys, the finest of which is that of Enneakhoria, which doubtless takes its name from a small town that formerly stood near it, named Inachorium, and mentioned by Ptolemy only.

While in Élos we stopped in the village *bakáliko*, or grocery, to buy some food and wine for a picnic lunch, for there would be no cafés or restaurants at the remote beach where we were going to spend the afternoon, on the promontory just opposite the islet of Elafonísi, the westernmost point in Crete. Then after shopping at the *bakáliko* we drove on, as the road now headed due west on the northern flank of Mount Áyios Díkeos Ióv, named for Job the Just, who is venerated in a chapel atop this remote peak.

Four kilometres farther along the asphalt road comes to an end at Kefáli, another village of the Enneachória, set at an altitude of 440m. The local church of the Metamórphosis tou Sotíros, the Transfiguration of Christ, dates from 1320, and it still retains all of its original fresco decoration, a dozen paintings from the height of the Byzantine renaissance, preserved here in this remote village in the far western corner of Crete.

From Kefáli we took a secondary road that leads down to the village of Váthi, formerly known as Kouneni, another one of the Enneachória, at an altitude of 320m. This distinguished old village has four frescoed Byzantine churches; the oldest of these is Áyios Yórgios, dated 1284; the others, of uncertain date, are the Archangel Michael, the Panayía, the Áyios Ioánnis Chrysóstomos. It is thought that somewhere close by was the site of Inachorium, the ancient city whose name is perpetuated by the Enneachória, but its remains still await discovery.

Beyond Váthi the road degenerates into a rough dirt track that leads down from the mountains to Órmos Stómio, the bay just above the south-western promontory of Crete. There the road passes the tiny hamlet of Stómio at the inner end of the bay, after which it goes out on the promontory a short way to the Monastery of the Chrysoskalítissa, the penultimate stop on our last excursion of the summer. This is one of the most picturesque sights in all of Crete, the whitewashed monastic buildings perched like a medieval citadel on a pinnacle of rock above the sea at the south-western extremity of the Great Island. The monastery is approached by a flight of ninety steps, and tradition holds that one of these is made of gold, but only the pure of heart can see this golden step, and then only through the intercession of the

Blessed Virgin. And so the shrine is called the Chrysoskalítissa, Our Lady of the Golden Step, a name as romantic as the picture-postcard setting of this lovely old monastery, which we visited on the penultimate stop of our last journey on the Great Island that summer.

The last stage of that drive from Kastélli took us from the Chrysoskalítissa due south along a rough dirt-track to the very end of the line, leaving us at road's end on the beach opposite the little islet of Elafonísi, the westernmost point in Crete. This is the most beautiful beach on all of Crete, a long lagoon-like scimitar of pink-white sand where the waves of the Aegean merge with those of the Libyan Sea, the isle of Elafonísi looking like a South Sea coral reef shimmering in the shallows just offshore, so close that we swam out to it and sat there for an hour, looking back on the Great Island that we had explored through the whole of that long and wonderful summer, now coming to a close. Then we swam back to shore and set up our picnic in the shade of a tamarisk tree, its branches twisted into a Medusa's head of tortured limbs bent back by the terrible Livas – the Libyan Wind – the furnace-blast that blows straight across from the sands of Libya over 230 miles of open sea a few days each summer, striking the Great Island here at its most exposed promontory. The Livas was blowing that day, and we took shelter from it and the blazing sun under our tamarisk tree, where we spun out our picnic through the whole of that afternoon, emptying our cooler-full of cold retsina that we had bought at the *bakáliko* in Élos that morning. And so we spent our last day on Crete that summer, regretting that we would have to fly back from Chaniá to Athens the following day, leaving our beloved Cottage on One Angel Street. But we tried not to think of that as we sat under our tamarisk tree on the beach at Elafonísi, gazing out across the sea as we sipped our *retsína*, thinking of all the wonderful times we had enjoyed on the Great Island that summer. Then Dolores took a brief nap in the deepest dappled shade of the tamarisk, resting for the long drive back to Chaniá, while I walked down to the shore, for the *lívas* had abated and was now just a warm breeze blowing plumes of spray my way from the turquoise sea that seemed to shimmer clear across the sea to Africa. Then I thought back to when I had first seen this wind-plumed sea, early one morning in October 1945, when our troopship passed this way on our homeward voyage after the end of World War II, catching a glimpse of the White Mountains as we headed westward into the Mediterranean. And now I looked back from the beach at Elafonísi to see the White Mountains again, the same majestic peaks that I had first looked upon from the flying bridge of the troopship 41 years before, now as then wondering when I would look upon the shores of Crete once again. And I think of that again as I write these lines, five thousand miles away from my beloved Crete, wondering when I will return to the Great Island.

GLOSSARY

acropolis: the upper city.

agora: market-place; the civic centre of an ancient Greek city.

amphora: a Greek vase.

anionic: non-representational.

ano: upper.

arsenali: Venetian arsenals, or dry-docks.

Ayios (m.), **Ayia** (f.), **Ayii** (pl.): Saint(s).

basilica: the Roman exchange and court of law; an oblong rectangular building usually with an aisle around and an apse at one end, an architectural type used in early Byzantine churches.

bucrania: the horns and frontal bones of a bull.

castro: castle or fortress.

enosis: union; in this case union between Crete and Greece.

epano: upper.

horns of consecration: stylised bull's horns, associated with Minoan shrines.

icon: religious picture in a Byzantine church.

iconostasis: wooden screen on which icons are placed in a Greek church, separating the chancel from the nave.

idole: idol; representation of a deity.

kastelli: castle.

kato: below or lower.

kernos: cult vessel with a number of small receptacles for offerings.

kouloura: Greek word meaning round or hollow; Minoan storage pits.

krater: large, open two-handled bowl used for mixing wine.

larnaca, larnakes (pl.): terracotta coffin.

lyra: the Cretan lyre.

mantinades: extemporaneous Cretan poems.

medrese: Moslem theological school.

megaron: the principal hall of a Mycenaean palace.

moni: monastery.

narthex: the inner vestibule of a Byzantine church.

nymphaion: an ornamental fountain; so called because it was sacred to the nymphs.

odeion: a small theatre, often roofed, in which rehearsals and musical performances were held.

odos: street.

ouzo: an anise-flavoured Greek aperitif.

palaeo: ancient.

palikari, palikaria (pl.): a heroic Greek man.

Panayia: the All-Holy Virgin.

paralia: seaside promenade.

peristyle: a covered colonnade which surrounds a temple.

pithos, pithoi (pl.): huge jar(s) used for the storage of grain or oil.

platanos: plane tree.

plateia: central square in a Greek town or village.

porta: gate or door.

propylaeum: the entrance gate-building of the temenos or sacred enclosure of a temple.

propylon: a very simple building of the propylaeum type.

prytaneion: the state dining-room of a senate committee building in an ancient Greek city.

pyrgos, pyrgioi (pl.): watchtower.

ryton: vessel designed for the pouring of libations; often a tapering shape with a hole at the tip, sometimes in animal form.

shadirvan: ablution fountain in a Turkish mosque.

tholos: circular vaulted building used as a tomb in the Mycenaean era.

tsikoudia: powerful Cretan alcoholic drink.

vrisi: fountain.

CHRONOLOGY

Neolithic Period, *c.* 6000–3000 BC.
Bronze Age, 3000–1100.
Prepalatial Period, 2600–2000.
Protopalatial Period, 2000–1700.
Neopalatial Period, 1700–1400.
Postpalatial Period, 1400–1100.
Dark Ages of the Ancient World, 1100–700.
Archaic Period, 700–490.
Classical Period, 490–323.
Hellenistic Period, 323–67.
Roman Period, 67 BC – AD 330.
First Byzantine Period, 330–824.
Saracan Occupation of Crete, 824–961.
Second Byzantine Period, 961–1212.
Venetian Period, 1212–1669.
Turkish Occupation of Crete, 1669–1898.
Allied Control in Crete, 1898–1913.
Unification of Crete with Greece (Enosis), 1913.
German Occupation of Crete, 1941–45.

BIBLIOGRAPHY

Albaugh, Leland, *Crete, A Case Study of an Underdeveloped Area* (Rockefeller Report on Post-War Crete, Princeton, 1953)

Altherr, Franz, and Guanella, Hanni, *Crete as Seen Today* (Zurich, 1971)

Alexiou, Stylianos, *Minoan Civilization* (Heraklion, 1973)

Alexiou, Platon, Guanella, and Von Matt, *Ancient Crete* (London, 1967)

Bowman, John, *The Travellers' Guide to Crete* (sixth edition, London, 1985)

Branigan, Keith, *The Tombs of Mesará; a Study of Funerary Architecture and Ritual in Southern Crete, 2800–1700 BC* (London, 1970)

Bryan, Robin, *Crete* (London, 1969)

Cadogan, Gerald, *Palaces of Minoan Crete* (London, 1980)

Cameron, Pat, *Blue Guide Crete* (fourth edition, London, 1985)

Chadwick, John, *The Decipherment of Linear B* (Cambridge, 1958); *The Mycenaean World* (Cambridge, 1976)

Cheetham, Nicolas, *Medieval Greece* (New Haven and London, 1981)

Clark, Alan, *The Fall of Crete* (London, 1962)

Cottrell, Leonard, *The Bull of Minos* (London, 1953)

Davaras, Costa, *Guide to Cretan Antiquities* (Athens, undated); *Hagios Nikolaos Museum* (Athens, undated); *Phaistos, Haghia Triada, Gortyn* (Athens, undated)

Dawkins, R. M., 'Folk Memory on Crete', *Folklore* (1942)

Doren, David MacNeil, *The Winds of Crete* (London, 1971)

Elliadi, M. N., *Crete, Past and Present* (London 1933)

Evans, Sir Arthur, *The Palace of Minos: An Account of the Early Cretan Civilization as Illustrated by the Discoveries at Knossos* (London, 1921–35)

Efendi, Evliya, *Narrative of Travels* (Istanbul, c1670; English translation by J. von Hammer, London, 1834)

Fielding, Xan, *The Stronghold; an Account of the Four Seasons in the White Mountains* (London, 1953)

Gerola, Giuseppe, *Monumenti Veneti nell 'isola di Creta* (London, 1905–32)

Godfrey, Jonnie, and Karslake, Elizabeth, *Landscapes of Eastern Crete*

273

(London, 1986); *Landscapes of Western Crete* (London, 1987)

Graham, James W., *The Palaces of Crete* (Princeton, 1962); *Minoan Crete* (Athens, undated)

Hall, Edith H., *Excavations in Eastern Crete* (Philadelphia, 1914)

Hawkes, Jacquetta, *Dawn of the Gods* (New York, 1968)

Higgins, Ronald A., *Minoan and Mycenaean Art* (London, 1967)

Hood, Sinclair, *The Minoans: Crete in the Bronze Age* (London, 1971); *The Bronze Age Palace at Knossos: Plan and Section* (Athens, 1981)

Hood, Sinclair, and Smyth, David, *Archaeological Survey of the Knossos Area* (second edition, Athens, 1981)

Hopkins, Adam, *Crete – Its Past, Present, and People* (London, 1977)

Hutchinson, R. W., *Prehistoric Crete* (London, 1962)

Huxley and Taylor, *Flowers of Greece and the Aegean* (London, 1976)

Italian Archaeological School of Athens, *Ancient Crete: A Hundred Years of Italian Archaeology* (1884–1984) (Rome, 1985)

Jeffrey, L. H., *Archaic Greece: The City-States* c. 700–500 BC (London, 1976)

Kazantzakis, Niko, *Freedom and Death* (Oxford, 1956); *The Odyssey: A Modern Sequel* (translated by Kimon Friar, London, 1958); *Zorba the Greek* (Oxford, 1959)

Kalokyris, Konstantin, *The Byzantine Wall Paintings of Crete* (New York, 1973)

Lawson, J. C., *Modern Greek Folklore and Ancient Greek Religion* (Cambridge, 1916)

Lithgow, William, *Rare Adventures and Painful Peregrinations* (London, 1632)

Luce, J. V., *The End of Atlantis*, (London, 1969)

Maniadakis, Kostas, *Crete: Knossos-Phaestos* (Athens, 1961)

Manoussakas, M. J., 'La Littérature crétois à l'époque vénitienne', in *Hellénisme contemporain* (mars–juin 1955)

Marinatos, Spyridon, *Crete and Mycenae* (New York, 1966)

Marshall, F. H., and Mavrogordato, J., *Three Cretan Plays* (Oxford, 1929)

Matton, Raymond, *La Crète au cours des siècles* (Athens, 1957)

Matz, Friedrich, *The Art of Crete and Early Greece; the Prelude of Greek Art* (New York, 1962)

Morgan, Gareth, *Cretan Poetry: Sources and Inspiration* (Heraklion, 1960) (offprint from *Kritika Chronica*, vol. XIV)

Mellersh, Harold E. L., *The Destruction of Knossos; the Rise and Fall of Minoan Crete* (New York, 1976)

Miller, William, *Essays on the Latin Orient* (Cambridge, 1921)

Nenedakis, A., *Guide to Réthymnon* (Athens, undated)

Nilsson, Martin, *The Minoan-Mycenaean Religion and its Survival in Greek Religion* (Gleerup, 1950); *Greek Folk Religion* (New York, 1961)

Notopoulos, James A., 'Homer and Cretan Homeric Poetry', *American Journal of Philology*, vol. LXXIII, 3

Page, Denys L., *The Santorini Volcano and the Desolation of Minoan Crete* (London, 1976)

Palmer, Leonard R., *Mycenaean and Minoan; Aegean Pre-History in the Light of the Linear B Tablets* (New York, 1965)

Pashley, Robert, *Travels in Crete* (2 vols., (London, 1837; reprinted 1976)

Pendlebury, J. D. S., *The Archaeology of Crete* (London, 1939)

Platon, Nicolas, *Crete* (London, 1966)

Pococke, Richard, *A Description of the East* (London, 1745)

Powell, Dilys, *The Villa Ariadne* (London, 1973)

Prevelakis, Pandelis, *The Tale of a Town* (English translation by Kenneth Johnstone) (Athens, 1977)

Psychoundakis, George, *The Cretan Runner* (English translation and Introduction by Patrick Leigh Fermor) (London, 1965)

Pym, Hilary, *The Songs of Greece* (London, undated)

Renault, Mary, *The King Must Die* (London, 1971); *The Bull From the Sea* (London, 1976)

Sakellarakis, E., *Eastern Crete* (Athens, undated)

Sakellarakis, J. A., *Illustrated Guide to the Herakleion Museum* (Athens, 1982)

Skinner, J. E. Hilary, *Roughing It in Crete*, 1967 (London, 1968)

Spanakis, Stergios G., *Crete: A Guide* (2 vols) (Heraklion, 1968)

Spratt, Captain T. A. B., *Travels and Researches in Crete* (2 vols.) (London, 1865; reprinted 1965)

de Tournefort, Joseph, *A Voyage into the Levant* (Paris, 1717; English translation, London, 1718)

Trevor-Battye, Aubuyn, *Camping in Crete* (London, 1913)

Willetts, R. F. *Aristocratic Society in Ancient Crete* (London, 1955); *Cretan Cults and Festivals* (London, 1962); *Ancient Crete, A Social History* (London, 1965)

INDEX

Also available from Tauris Parke Paperbacks

Evia
Travels on an Undiscovered Greek Island

Sarah Wheeler

The seahorse-shaped island of Evia – Euboia in classical history and Negroponte for many centuries – is the second largest in Greece, yet it is almost completely undiscovered by tourists. Separated from the mainland by only a sliver of sea, Evia has had a turbulent history. Today it encapsulates the Greece of decades ago – unspoilt and pristine, a haven for the more discerning traveller. *Evia*, Sara Wheeler's first book, is the story of a five-month journey she made from the southern tip to the north of the island. Instantly enchanted by the landscape and languid pace of Evia, Wheeler immersed herself in the local way of life, where she witnessed centuries-old traditions, attended a goatherd's wedding and Bronze Age excavations, was harassed by Orthodox nuns, and spent nights in monasteries and village homes. Her story is a beautifully rendered account of a way of life that in the rest of Greece has all but disappeared and of an island on the cusp of change.

Paperback, 312pp, 1 map, 19 black & white photographs
ISBN 978 1 84511 340 7

> *'A fascinating journey in a very undiscovered part of Greece. It is entertainment for the connoisseur of journeys.'*   Peter Levi

www.taurisparkepaperbacks.com

Strolling Through Athens
Fourteen Unforgettable Walks Through Europe's Oldest City

John Freely

Athens, city of the gods, birthplace of democracy, artistic and cultural centre of the ancient world, is one of Europe's most fascinating and complex cities, steeped in myth and legend. In this indispensable guide John Freely leads the reader on an ingenious and enlightening series of walks to the city's most vibrant and historic areas, from the magnificent Parthenon, centre of Athens for four thousand years, to the winding streets of Plaka, the crumbling ruins of the Agora and the colour and bustle of Monastiraki. This guide, more than any other, reveals how the heart of ancient Athens still beats beneath the living, modern city.

Paperback, 288pp, 14 plans, 16 maps
ISBN 978 1 86064 595 2

*'There is no end to it in this city – wherever we walk we
set foot upon history.'* Lucius Cicero

Also available from Tauris Parke Paperbacks

A Byzantine Journey

John Ash

A high point of civilization and artistic accomplishment, the Byzantine Empire has also been the object of great misunderstanding and prejudice. This is a portrayal of its cultural history focusing on its surreal landscapes and fantastic monuments. The book starts in Istanbul and crosses the Sea of Marmara to travel through Anatolia, the region of Asiatic Turkey which was the source of the Empire's wealth and manpower. John Ash finds his way through a country of anachronisms and contrasts, of bloody feuds and frescoed cave-churches, of saints and sinners, of emperors and sultans. The book introduces the reader to an exotic cast of characters, including the impassioned aesthete Theophilus, the great mystical poet Rumi, the bishop and necromancer Theodore Santabarenos and the Empress Theophano.

Paperback, 352pp, 19 black & white photographs
ISBN 9781 84511 307 0

> *'And therefore I have sailed the seas and come
> To the holy city of Byzantium.'*
> Yeats, *Sailing to Byzantium*

www.taurisparkepaperbacks.com

Also available from Tauris Parke Paperbacks

The Western Shores of Turkey
Discovering the Aegean and Mediterranean Coasts

John Freely

The Western coast of Turkey has captivated travellers for centuries. With its dramatic mountains and idyllic bays and promontories scattered with ancient ruins, it is not only one of the most beautiful parts of the country, but is also of great historical interest. *The Western Shores of Turkey* is the distillation of a succession of journeys that John Freely made along this coast – an odyssey spanning a quarter of a century. From Istanbul to Antakya (Antioch) on the Syrian border, he discovered both the charm of modern Turkey and the wonders of its past. The result is an informative guide and a remarkable travelogue for all who follow in his footsteps.

Paperback, 424pp, 12 black & white photographs

ISBN 978 1 85043 618 8

> '*John Freely's enchanting guide to the western shores of Turkey ... is a work of genuine scholarship ... charmingly conveyed ... I fell in love with the book and stayed enamoured until the final page.* The Western Shores of Turkey *will accompany me when I revisit Anatolia ... The book exhibits a profound affection for the Turks and their language and culture.*'
>   *The Sunday Times*

www.taurisparkepaperbacks.com